KNIGHTS OF THE AIR

Dedicated to the
1388 Canadian airmen
who did not return
from the
"War to End All Wars"

KNIGHTS
OF THE
AIR

Canadian Fighter Pilots in the First World War

David L. Bashow

Paintings and Illustrations by
Stephen P. Quick

McArthur & Company

Toronto

2000

First published in Canada by McArthur & Company, 2000

Canadian Cataloguing in Publication Data

Bashow, David L., 1946-
    Knights of the air

  ISBN 1-55278-162-3

  1. World War, 1914-1918 – Biography. 2. World War, 1914-1918 – Aerial operations. 3. Fighter pilots – Biography. I. Quick, Stephen P. II. Title.

  D507.B370 2000   940.4'4'0922   C00-931474-1

Composition and Design by *Michael P. Callaghan*
Cover by *Mad Dog Design Connection Inc.*
Typesetting and Electronic Imaging by *Moons of Jupiter Inc.* (Toronto)
Printed in Canada by *Friesens*

McArthur & Company
322 King Street West, Suite 402
Toronto, ON, M5V 1J2

10 9 8 7 6 5 4 3 2 1

The publisher would like to acknowledge the financial support of the Government of Canada through the Book Publishing Industry Development Program (BPIDP) for our publishing activities. The publisher further wishes to acknowledge the financial support of the Ontario Arts Council for our publishing program.

Andy McKeever (right), "king of the two-seaters", in the cockpit of his Bristol fighter

*"Only the spirit of attack born
in a brave heart will bring success
to any fighter aircraft,
no matter how highly developed
it may be."*

— GENERALLEUTNANT ADOLF GALLAND

ACKNOWLEDGEMENTS

Knights of the Air was a team effort from the outset. With respect to the manuscript, I am very grateful to the following organizations and individuals for granting me permission to quote from their works: James Lorimer and Company, Harbour Publishing Company, McGill-Queen's University Press, Allan English, Arthur Bishop, Alan Bennett, Norman Franks, Ross McKenzie, and Dan McCaffrey. Beyond the formal granting of permissions, these individuals were universally supportive and encouraging of this venture.

Warm thanks to Rosemary Shipton, editor *extraodinaire*, who also saved me from myself on more than one occasion. From Air Force Heritage and History, Captain Mat Joost was extremely helpful in the acquisition of photographs, as were the irrepressible, always cheerful Fiona Smith Hale and Ian Leslie at the National Aviation Museum. Marc Ducharme of the museum's archives assisted enormously by providing unlimited access to the Creagen Collection. At DND's Directorate of History and Heritage, Lieutenant-Colonel Dan Mackay was a great help, as was his father, William. Thanks also to Tim Dube at the National Archives, to Major Lowell Butters at the National Defence Headquarters, to Brian Costello of Carleton Place, to Ron MacDonald of the Canadian Air Force Memorial Museum at Trenton, Dale Cline of Moose Jaw, Saskatchewan, to Colin Pomfret of Millgrove, Ontario, to Gerry Locklin of the Royal Military College graphic arts department, and to the many others who gave so unselfishly of their time and thoughts.

Lastly, but most significantly, a very special thanks to my dear wife Heather, for not only her cheerful support in typing the entire manuscript, but for her endless patience with my obsession herein.

Dave Bashow
Kingston, Ontario
September, 2000

As with any work of import in one's life there are those who make the task one of enrichment. I would echo the thanks already expressed by Dave and would like to thank a few of the other players who have brought this work to fruition. To Don Sedgewick who has been both a mentor and a tireless team mate, to the gang at Aviation World, Andy Cline, Bill Lane and the resident WWI expert Marc Pijanka, and to all of the friends who have pushed a brush into my hand over the years, most notably Robert St. Pierre, Marilyn Booth, Angel Guerra, Ginette Petit and Robert Roch, I owe a debt that cannot be expressed in words. I would like to thank Kim McArthur for her belief in this project and especially Michael Callaghan for his blood, sweat and tears. To those not mentioned I say thank-you. Most importantly, I would like to thank my partner Catherine for her patience, her vision and the gift that she brings to our life.

Stephen Quick
Montreal, Quebec

CONTENTS

FOREWORD

Canada's self image of "peaceable kingdom" and "unmilitary people" is carved deeply in the nation's psyche, but vanishes, author David L. Bashow reminds us, when the kingdom is too far provoked. Then appears a fighting spirit — an uncommon aggressiveness and untested valour — not to extract a spoil from battle, but restore the peace disturbed.

Too often the twentieth century summoned that spirit, and at too high a cost — on the ground, at sea, and in the air. Early in the century, for the first time ever, men in arms "slipped the surly bonds of earth" and waged a new kind of warfare by air. The Great War began but eleven years after the Wright brothers, Kitty Hawk and mankind's first tentative steps into the era of powered and sustained flight. Over four years, above the most awful carnage below, the airplane ascended from being an obscurity of limited value, to absolute necessity as a weapon of war. Pioneers of that transition rode a steep and unforgiving learning curve.

Initially the airplane was deemed to be nothing but an observation and spotting platform, to assist land or sea engagements. Gradually its additional value in attack became evident to participants, and the notion of airpower was born. The airplane's ability to deliver weapons directly against enemy forces contributed to the tactical objective. Both sides saw the potential and so the race was on — to win aerial advantage for friend and denial for foe.

Inevitably the contest pitched airplane against airplane, man against man, skill against skill. The War to End All Wars spawned multinational masters of this new aeronautical art. Airborne and armed, they merged in the skies over Europe. The heated competition that ensued, like the joust of old, was chivalrous, intense, and deadly. Peace-loving Canucks found their own "knights of the air" to be particularly bold and adept aviators. They were also fierce warriors. Among 171 Canadian aces with at least five air-to-air victories, ten of them had more than thirty victories. This book describes the significance of this new air power while highlighting, in particular, the legend of the top ten aces.

Canada produced more than her share of empire aces, even as she produced disproportionate numbers of aircrew. They came from city or farm, in duty or adventure, for country or glory. No matter; they excelled. They learned of safety in numbers, advantage in technology, strength in tactics, success in attack. They died, even as they savaged, in appalling numbers and in horrible ways. In the end, most were content to do their duty; but some were fiercely competitive — for the most kills and the top honours.

David Bashow relates these things with a clear, engaging writing style. He brings to his task an historian's passion for the event, a researcher's thirst for evidence, and a fighter pilot's empathy. He has been there, done that! How else could one produce such drama with words, save of course by focusing them with exquisite original paintings by Stephen P. Quick, and maps of the battles to finesse the mental picture desired. Among a wider readership, Bashow will appeal most with his text to the technologist, historian, flying enthusiast, military tactician and strategist. But all will be engaged by the skills of a masterful storyteller.

And what of Canada's ace of aces — William Avery "Billy" Bishop and his 72 confirmed victories? Through exhaustive research, prolific endnotes, and sound reasoning, Bashow moves the veracity yardstick for this brilliant and courageous warrior to quite credible new heights. By this he raises the bar for the anti-hero crowd who may now simply retire their king, for they are in precarious state of "check".

Lieutenant-General (Retired) Robert W. Morton, CMM, CD, Canadian Forces
Stittsville, Ontario
August, 2000

Bob Morton, a Canadian fighter pilot, is a former deputy commander-in-chief of NORAD, and the past honorary national president of the Air Force Association of Canada.

PROLOGUE

"Thus the August madness descended."
— THOMAS MANN

The First World War, known euphemistically as the Great War and naïvely as the War To End All Wars, was a truly global conflagration. Roughly nine million combatants forfeited their lives in this democracy of suffering. The Western Front was the most lethal theatre of battle: there, French and German fatalities numbered one for each six men who served, while British losses averaged one in eight. Three men were wounded or seriously injured for every individual who perished.[1] The war would span 1500 days, commencing for Britain and its empire on August 4, 1914, and ending in armistice on November 11, 1918. But for the physically and spiritually mutilated survivors, and for the loved ones of the fallen, the war would last forever.

Canada, with an estimated population of just under eight million in 1914,[2] fielded a fighting land force of four full divisions in a complete Canadian Corps, which eventually boasted 619,636 men on the Western Front. Of this Canadian Expeditionary Force, 59,544 members were killed overseas, while a further 172,950 were wounded, often cruelly maimed.[3] These casualty figures do not include Canadians from the air and naval services, the Canadian Cavalry Brigade, and combat and support troops directly attached to the British Expeditionary Force. Nor do they include the substantial number of casualties among men from Newfoundland.[4]

The First World War was remarkable in its time for its technological innovations – particularly for the introduction of the airplane as a viable weapon of war. In all, 22,812 Canadians are known to have served with the British flying services during the war, of which 13,160 served as aircrew. Of these, 1388, or roughly 11 percent, were killed, out of a British Empire air service total of 6166 fatalities. An additional 1130 were wounded or injured, and 377 were interred or became prisoners of war.[5] Canadian casualties relative to total British air losses during the Great War reflect the increasing degree of Canadianization of the Allied air effort as the conflict progressed. Canadians were not actively recruited for the air services until the British were faced with potentially crippling manpower shortages following the disastrous Somme offensive of 1916. In 1915 the Canadian percentage of empire aircrew was 6.0 percent; in 1916, 9.7 percent; in 1917, 11.6 percent; and in 1918, 16.8 percent.[6] At least 495 British decorations for gallantry, as well as 170 Mentioned in Dispatches and a large number of foreign awards, were presented to this courageous band of aerial warriors from the young Dominion of Canada.

The scout or fighter pilots who became "aces," those involved alone or with others in the destruction of five or more enemy aircraft, have attracted the most attention. Of the 863 known British Empire aces, at least 171 were Canadian, a disproportionate number from a nation with such a small population at the time. Perhaps more to the point, of the twenty-six empire aces with thirty or more victory claims, ten were Canadian, including the highest (William A. Bishop, 72), the second highest (Raymond Collishaw, tied with Edward "Mick" Mannock, 61), and two more among the top seven, all of whom had fifty or more victories.[7] To paraphrase Shakespeare, this book will explore in depth the Great War combat careers of "this few, this happy few, this band of brothers."

CHAPTER ONE

GENESIS

1914-1915

*"The aircraft is all very well for sport –
for the army it is useless."*

– Marshal Ferdinand Foch

When Archduke Franz Ferdinand, heir apparent to the Austro-Hungarian throne, was felled by a nationalist assassin's bullet in the sleepy Serbian town of Sarajevo on June 28, 1914, few Canadians took much notice. The murder of prominent people in the Balkans had long been considered a legitimate tool for the disenchanted to express their grievances and draw attention to their cause. The domino effect of this particular event could not be broadly foreseen. However, it became the tinder that rapidly set Europe and much of the globe ablaze.

On the Continent, the Great Powers had squared off against each other in two antagonistic camps. On one side stood Germany, Austria-Hungary, and, to a lesser extent, Italy, forming the Triple Alliance, or Central Powers.[1] Opposing them were France, Britain, and Russia (the Triple Entente). "Heightened by imperialist rivalries, national pride, fanatical nationalism, ambitious statesmen, and the constant talk of war," historian Patricia Giesler commented, "all were ready for the inevitable slide."[2] Austria became convinced that the Serbian government was directly involved in the assassination and, backed by Germany, sent a harsh ultimatum to the Serbs. Eventually, Serbia met virtually all the Austrian demands, but to no avail. Austria-Hungary, intent on conquest, declared war on Serbia on July 28 and was bombarding Belgrade from ships in its Danube flotilla the following day. Russia, long the self-proclaimed protector of all Slav nations, was quick to mobilize in response. Germany in turn demanded assurances of non-involvement via ultimatums to both Russia and France. When these demands went unanswered, Germany declared war on Russia on August 1, and on France two days later. France promptly turned to Britain for support. After Germany invaded neutral Belgium on August 4, the British sent their own ultimatum to Berlin for an immediate German withdrawal, but it, too, was ignored. By midnight on August 4, Britain was officially at war with the Triple Alliance. Under the statecraft arrangements of the day, so, automatically, were all the nations of the British Empire, including Canada.

Canada, in mental lockstep with the rest of the empire, viewed the upcoming campaign with a light-hearted enthusiasm. Support for the war was strong in urban centres, especially those of predominantly British settlement and heritage. Roused by the charismatic Sam Hughes, Prime Minister Robert Borden's Minister of Militia, Canada had the first of four Canadian divisions in England by October. By year's end, over 56,000 men had been recruited for the Canadian Expeditionary Force, though, compared with the splendid British regular army of the day, the Canadian volunteers were woefully ill-equipped and unprepared for combat. Many long months of training in England were required before they took their place as the 1st Division in the lines the following February.[3] These early volunteers viewed the war as a great moral crusade and an opportunity for adventure. It would provide excitement for those stuck in humdrum lives, it would be good for the economy, and, moreover, the boys would trounce the forces of the Kaiser and be home by Christmas. But the boys were not home for Christmas 1914, or for several Christmases thereafter. Far too many never returned at all. Nevertheless, in the summer of 1914 a naïve Canada, eager to broaden its acceptance on the international stage, had no idea of the sacrifices that would be required to win a measure of national autonomy and global recognition.

Generals on both sides of the conflict predicted quick victories, won by fluid, rapid advances of infantry, light artillery, and cavalry. They thought that victory lay only in attack, and the concept of compromise, let alone defeat, was unthinkable. In the prevailing atmosphere of national crusades, a long and bloody war was inevitable, since heavy artillery, the machine gun, and the raising of huge conscript armies favoured defensive rather than offensive action.

All the Great Powers had war plans, and all of them failed early. Germany's Schlieffen Plan called for a quick routing of the French, followed by an onslaught against the less rapidly mobilizing Russians. In spite of early victories, the German advance lost its momentum and, after British and French counter-attacks, German soldiers were driven back to the Aisne River in the First Battle of the Marne. The French in turn launched Plan XVII, which also failed when concerted drives against Germany in Alsace and Lorraine were defeated. In the east, the Russians initially repulsed the Austrians and moved into East Prussia. However, the

Opposite: A Nieuport 12, similar to the Nieuport 10 in which A. Strachan Ince of Toronto became the first Canadian to decisively shoot down a German aircraft, December 14, 1915.

Germans under General Paul von Hindenburg quickly rebounded, handing the Russian armies serious defeats first at the Masurian Lakes and then at Tannenberg. In the west, after the Miracle of the Marne, the Allies and the Germans tried to outflank each other as the Germans made a desperate bid to seize the Channel ports. At the end of October the British Expeditionary Force stopped the numerically superior Germans at Ypres in Flanders, but lost more than half of its regular army. Amid total military deadlock, an elaborate and unbroken system of trenches on both sides of the lines extended by Christmas 1914 all the way from the Channel coast south to the Swiss frontier. The slaughter along the 600-mile front was about to begin. Glory-obsessed generals, with no comprehension of the revolutionary changes that were occurring on the battlefield, repeatedly called on their men to exercise raw courage and to break through the near-impregnable defences. In most cases, before the final year of the war, these desperate offensives were so hopelessly inept that they made the Crimean War's Charge of the Light Brigade in 1854 or Custer's Last Stand at Little Bighorn in 1879 seem sensible in comparison.

Technological advances profoundly influenced the conduct of the Great War, but none was more dramatic than the aircraft. At the outset, all the major participants had rudimentary air services, but the military élite considered them of limited use. From this near-total obscurity, however, the airplane emerged over the next four years as an absolute military necessity.

By the end of 1911 the British Army and the Royal Navy could collectively field three airships and four to six heavier-than-air aircraft, manned by roughly twenty aviators. In comparison, the French and Germans had much larger military aviation organizations. The British, therefore, formed the Royal Flying Corps (RFC) as a unified service in 1912. It would possess a central flying school, a military wing to work with the army, a naval wing to provide parallel support for the navy, a reserve, and the Royal Aircraft Factory, located at Farnborough, to design and build military aircraft for the fledgling service.

Parent service parochialisms soon strained relations in the new corps, and the Admiralty, in particular, was loath to allow its air affairs to escape its direct control. A new branch, the Royal Naval Air Service (RNAS), had received official sanction by the outbreak of the war. With few exceptions, the Admiralty carried out its own flight training and ordered its own aircraft direct from manufacturers, avoiding the products of the Royal Aircraft Factory. Consequently, the factory produced aircraft restricted to the army's needs.

By the commencement of hostilities the RFC had effectively become a component of the army, and the RNAS a component of the Royal Navy, and both reflected their parent services' philosophies and preoccupations. By way of example, in preparation for war the RFC stressed mobility, the ability to move with the army. It concentrated on acquiring airplanes and gathered up several different types: some French, including sizable numbers of Blériot Type XI monoplanes; some limited purchases direct from British manufacturers; and a growing number of variants acquired from the Royal Aircraft Factory. The first enduring product from Farnborough was the BE2, designed by Geoffrey de Havilland, a two-seat biplane with tractor, or frontally mounted, engine construction and considerable aerodynamic stability. This design emanated from the RFC's initial concept that aircraft would be used primarily for reconnaissance, and, as such, they required a stable observation platform. This philosophy reflected what Canadian historian Sydney F. Wise has called the three major factors that governed the development and use of the RFC during the war: "the nature of the land battle, the structure of the British Army, and the principle … that the air arm existed solely to serve the ground forces." The RFC was therefore characterized by "symmetrical order and subordination of role."[4]

The RNAS, in contrast, pursued different applications. Given its primary duty to contain the German High Seas Fleet through control of the seas, oceans, and coastal regions essential to the prosecution of the land campaign, it also protected Allied shipping and the vital shipping lanes. Because the RNAS reflected the mobility and flexibility of response that marked all naval operations, it was quite individualistic, free-spirited, and considerably less rigid than the RFC in both outlook and organization. In September 1914 Lord Kitchener made the RNAS responsible for the aerial defence of the United Kingdom despite its being ill-equipped for this task. It retained this responsibility until January 1916, even though the RFC, through the War Office, was technically responsible for "aerial supremacy in the British Isles."[5] A chain of coastal naval air stations developed rapidly, and, by late summer in 1914, the RNAS establishment had grown to 128 officers, 700 ratings, 7 airships, and 71 aircraft. Its first presence in France to support the British Expeditionary Force (BEF) was 2 Wing, which from August 27, 1914, patrolled the English Channel in the Dunkirk region with nine aircraft of five different types.

The Admiralty considered defensive patrolling to be a waste of time and resources. Instead, it favoured as many offensive engagements as possible. The exploits of the gallant little band in the Flanders lodgment at Dunkirk were of a particularly offensive nature; they bombed enemy naval installations in the hope of destroying the German airship fleet on the ground before it could be used against England. One noteworthy incident in early August involved Flight Lieutenant R.L.G. Marix, who, in a Sopwith Tabloid, bombed airship sheds in Düsseldorf and destroyed the roof of one with two 20-lb. bombs, causing a brand new Zeppelin, the LZ 9, to burst into flames. The RNAS establishment at Dunkirk remained the service's largest operational base for much of the war, owing to its strategic location on both the left flank of the Allied armies and the vital English Channel. Because of this potential for operational versatility, Dunkirk's activities "often reflected the most advanced and innovative thinking of the Admiralty Air Department."[6]

By contrast, the RFC was less cavalier and flamboyant, but also more practical and enduring. Shaped in every important aspect by its relationship to the ground forces, its organization and size reflected those of the British Expeditionary Force. The RFC's basic units, the squadrons, each served a specific army corps, and, as the BEF grew, so did the RFC in numbers of squadrons. Expansion also brought specialization, though it took time:

The first RFC squadrons in France performed the whole range of tasks then demanded of them, but from an early stage distinct duties, and therefore specialized aircraft, equipment, and training, were imposed on each squadron. At the corps level, the prime requirements to be met were cooperation with the artillery and the provision of tactical and photographic reconnaissance. At

the "army" level were squadrons whose duties were also connected with ground operations, but in a less direct way: their tasks were bombing and air fighting. The prime duty of the fighter squadron was to provide protection so that all other formations could carry out their work. As the RFC reached operational maturity by 1916, corps and army wings were grouped together, so that each of the British armies on the Western Front was served by an RFC Brigade.[7]

RFC pilot in the cockpit of a Morane Bullet

Four of the RFC's seven squadrons, consisting of 105 officers, 755 other ranks, and 63 aircraft, went to France with the BEF. By August 19, 1914, the corps had flown its first reconnaissance missions, the value of which was quickly made clear. Given the rapidity of the German advance, but allowing for the constant updating of enemy

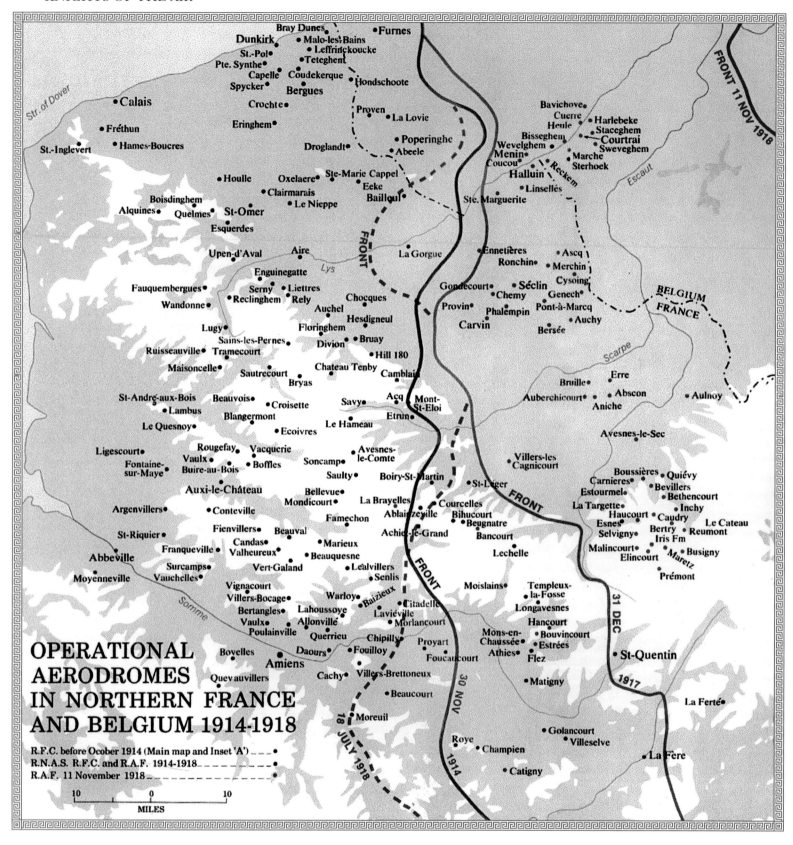

OPERATIONAL AERODROMES IN NORTHERN FRANCE AND BELGIUM 1914-1918

R.F.C. before Ocober 1914 (Main map and Inset 'A')
R.N.A.S. R.F.C. and R.A.F. 1914-1918
R.A.F. 11 November 1918

10   0   10
|———|———|———|
MILES

strengths, locations, and movements as provided by the RFC, Allied ground losses were significantly less than was otherwise likely. The emphasis that had earlier been placed on RFC mobility had quickly paid off, for the initially dynamic German advances would otherwise have engulfed the corps. Within a month, the RFC was also using wireless telegraphy successfully, and this skill proved to be useful, as the corps frequently spotted for the

guns of the Royal Artillery. By November 1914 the RFC had reorganized on the basis of wings instead of squadrons as the primary formations, and, by the spring of 1915, RFC France comprised three wings with eight squadrons and an operational strength of eighty to ninety aircraft, with a further eighteen in ready reserve.

In terms of air combat, aircrew from both sides were initially content to leave each other in relative peace, and for good reason. At first, none of the aircraft in service were designed specifically for combat, and since aircraft were rare across wide fronts, encounters were few and far between. The earliest aircraft were frail, slow-moving machines that were frequently difficult to handle. Many of them lacked ailerons, and the pilots controlled them about their roll axis only by differential wing warping, pulling on flying wires through a control column to change the shape of an airfoil. It was difficult to keep these vulnerable machines under control in relatively static conditions, let alone during dynamic manoeuvring. Aircrew were also preoccupied with avoiding enemy ground fire and mobile German anti-aircraft guns.

At the outset of hostilities, an unspoken code among the warring aviators held that it was ungentlemanly to employ aggressive tactics against their opposite numbers. It was also not easy, given the plethora of different aircraft types in service, for untrained observers to distinguish between friend and foe. While some form of identification marking was an obvious necessity, they were not in universal use during the early months of the war. The French had adopted a tricolour roundel in 1912 with a red circle outermost, and the Germans marked their airframes with the black Maltese Crosses of the old Teutonic Knights. Initially, the British entered the war with no national markings whatsoever, and RFC pilots themselves painted Union Jacks in prominent positions on their aircraft. By December 1914 the British flying services had adopted the French roundel pattern in the colours of the Jack, but with blue as the outside circle.[8]

Along with airframe structural frailties, the first aircraft engines were also rudimentary. Again, the British did not initially possess many indigenously designed powerplants, but generally copied or imported successful French air-cooled radial engine types, notably the LeRhône and the Gnôme. These engines possessed seven or nine radially disposed cylinders revolving around a stationary crankshaft. They were relatively compact and light, which gave them an excellent power-to-weight ratio, allowing the French to concentrate on building aircraft that were both light and fast. The rotary engine had some vagaries, however. Gyroscopic effect and the torque generated by the engine meant that the novice airman found these craft difficult to control. Skilled pilots, however, could

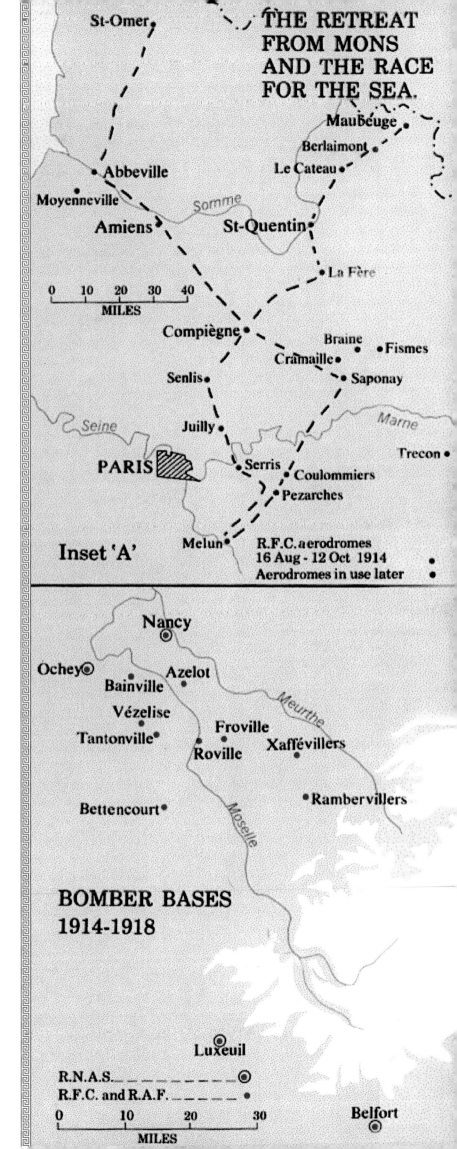

exploit these characteristics in combat, particularly by forcing turning engagements in the direction that followed the natural torque of the engine.

The Germans tended to favour heavier, high-performance, water-cooled stationary engines with in-line cylinders, particularly powerplants produced by Mercedes Benz and Austro-Daimler, and based on their firms' experiences with automobile racing. These engines were more robust than the frail rotaries, but also required heavier and stronger airframes to carry them. An interesting and disconcerting side effect of the rotary engines concerned their method of lubrication. They used cas-

as the Oberursel rotary, and was successfully used in several of their own scout types.[9]

Although the early airmen were generally content to leave their opposite numbers alone, the more aggressive members of the fraternity soon began to take a revolver, a carbine, and occasionally even grenades aloft with them on reconnaissance or spotting missions. One RFC pilot had a Lewis machine gun mounted on his aircraft, to be fired by his observer. As more powerful aircraft arrived at the front, this armament became a standard practice, although it was initially intended for defensive rather than offensive action.

The ubiquitous and long-suffering Royal Aircraft Factory's BE2 observation aircraft

tor oil to avoid lubricant dilution in the vapour-filled crankcase, but the noxious spray and fumes created as it heated caused widespread nausea among the aircrew. Still, the advantages offered by the early radials more than offset their deficiencies. The LeRhône, which was the better of the two French types, was actually copied by the Germans

One innovative way of disrupting the early operations of hostile aircraft was recalled by an anonymous British aviator. The object, he was told, was to overtake the enemy, then perform a turning dive in front of him. The intrepid aviator remarked that he had been assured this action would create air pockets sufficient to send the enemy crashing to the ground.[10] Considering the fragility of aircraft at this early stage of the war, he may well have been correct.

Innovation in aerial combat was not restricted to the lower echelons. When it appeared that Paris would be overrun in 1914, several of the French aircraft dedicated for defence of the city were experimentally armed with 37 mm cannons that had been removed from the Eiffel Tower. These aircraft flew what was probably the first fighter-type mission of the war on August 30, 1914. Although the threat rapidly receded, the concept of using aircraft as attackers of enemy aircraft did not. A plan for the expansion of the French Air Service, submitted to the minister of war in early October, proposed that sixteen of the projected sixty-five escadrilles (squadrons) would specialize in reconnaissance and *chasse* (air fighting).[11] General Joseph Joffre was an early proponent of fighter-type aircraft, to be used to pursue and destroy enemy aircraft. As early as February 1915 reference is recorded to the *barrage*, a form of aerial blockade from fighter-type aircraft used to deny access to hostile aircraft.

The French seem to have led the other belligerents in the employment of aircraft in specified hunting roles. The first known victory in air-to-air combat was recorded by a Frenchman. In the autumn of 1914 Sergeant Joseph Franz had armed his Voisin 3 pusher biplane with an 8 mm Hotchkiss machine gun, to be fired by his gunner, Corporal Lewis Quenault. On October 5, 1914, this pair downed a German two-seater reconnaissance Aviatik in which the observer in the front seat had been armed with only an automatic rifle. After a series of turns over the French lines near Fort Brimont at 7000 feet, during which each pilot jockeyed for the best firing position for his observer, Quenault got in a series of single shots,[12] the last of which killed the German pilot. The Aviatik flipped and spun out of control, smoke gushing from its 100 horsepower Mercedes D1 engine, and crashed with a loud explosion at the edge of a wooded area. The pilot and the observer, Wilhelm Schlichting and Fritz von Zangen, respectively, became the first in a long list of airmen from both sides to die in air-to-air combat.[13]

From the beginning of the war, Britain produced a few fast, light, single-seat aircraft. Unlike the French, who used fighters *en masse* in specialized units, the British supplied these aircraft in small numbers to their general-purpose two-seater squadrons for high-speed scouting duties behind enemy lines. These aircraft were at least marginally faster and more manoeuvrable than the BE2s, Farmans, and Blériots being used for reconnaissance and artillery observation. By early 1915 every RFC general-duties squadron was so equipped.

Since the Royal Aircraft Factory was not yet producing scout aircraft, except for the SE2a, which served briefly with 3 Squadron, the RFC followed the RNAS in purchases from independent manufacturers. Initially the ubiquitous BE2 units had the scouting/escort role foisted on them, but Sopwith, Vickers, Bristol, and Martinsyde scouts soon took their place in limited numbers alongside several French types, all serving as escorts to the slower reconnaissance aircraft. Throughout the entire war period, the British and the other Allies used French aircraft types extensively in combat.

Early aerial engagements determined some of the essential requirements for specialized fighter aircraft. Along with manoeuvrability and structural robustness, the scouts needed speed to be fast enough to run down their prey. And since these aircraft did not carry observers, they needed an offensive weapons capability. One highly useful French-type scout used extensively by the British during the early months of the war was the Morane-Saulnier series of monoplanes. The first of this variant was the two-seat Type L Parasol model, which featured a single high wing mounted above the fuselage. It was much faster than contemporary German aircraft, and lateral control was exercised primitively through the wing warping method pioneered by the Wright Brothers in the previous decade. Captain Cecil Lewis, a well-known Parasol pilot, suggested that, aerodynamically, the only known position to which it automatically reverted was the vertical nose dive! It was felt to be dangerous and even treacherous to fly, permitted no liberties by the pilot, and demanded his full attention during every second of flight. Initially, the Parasol's pilots were armed only with pistols and cavalry carbines, but pilot innovation knew no bounds. On June 6, 1915, Flight Sub-Lieutenant R.A.J. Warneford of the RNAS became the first pilot to destroy a Zeppelin, LZ 37, in the air by raining incendiary bombs on it from his Parasol scout.

Machine guns were variously mounted on the fuselage immediately ahead of the pilot and aimed

The Morane Type L
Parasol Scout

to fire over the propeller arc, or attached to the fuselage at an angle, again to clear the propeller. These arrangements were far from ideal, as the weapons were difficult to aim and fire in flight. A derivative of the Parasol was the mid-wing N

though it performed many other roles, including bombing and reconnaissance. Again, it was frequently armed with a Lewis gun offset to miss the propeller, and saw service in small numbers in both the RNAS and the RFC. An early favourite of

model, known in the RFC as the Bullet because of its massive propeller spinner and streamlined fuselage. It reached the Western Front during the summer of 1914 and saw a lot of action with the British, though only in small numbers.

From Britain, the Sopwith Tabloid was the first purposefully employed single-seat biplane scout,

the RFC was the Bristol Scout, which was widely available by early 1915. A single-seat biplane, the Bristol was soundly built and fast. In 1915 it often carried a SMLE rifle, with the stock sawed off and the gun obliquely mounted on the fuselage, along with a Mauser pistol and a number of rifle grenades. Some Bristols also had one or two Lewis guns mounted to fire clear of the propeller. Major Lanoe G. Hawker of 6 Squadron RFC won the first Victoria Cross to be awarded for aerial combat in such a machine. On July 25, 1915, in the Passchendaele area, he attacked three enemy two-seaters, all equipped with machine guns. He drove the first down, severely damaged the second, and felled the third in flames. Hawker would eventually fall to the guns of German ace Manfred von Richthofen on November 23, 1916, after one of the classic prolonged duels in the history of air combat.

By January 1915 the French had also fielded an excellent tractor-engined biplane scout, the Nieuport XI "Bébé," the progenitor of a long series of fine scouting aircraft from this company. Of sesquiplane wing design, the Bébé's lower planes had only half the total wing area of the upper planes. In lifting capacity, the Nieuport was more aerodynamically similar to a high parasol monoplane than to a biplane, since its lower planes were designed primarily to bolster the structural integrity of the aircraft. Again, a Lewis gun was mounted on the top wing, firing above the propeller and activated by a trip wire from the cockpit. Like the British, the French tended to spread their Nieuports among the two-seater squadrons. The sole exception in the early months of the war was Escadrille N.65 based at Malzéville, near Nancy, which bore responsibility for both bomber escort and regional air defence.

On all the fighting single-seaters of the period, the weapons mountings were far from ideal, particularly the upper-wing Lewis gun mountings. Gun jams were frequent and, to replace an empty ammunition drum, the pilot had to stand up in the aircraft, hold the control column between his knees, and use both hands on the drum. All the while, he hoped he would not lose control of his inherently unstable aircraft or be attacked while he was in this vulnerable position. In May 1915 Lieutenant Louis Strange of 6 Squadron experienced the hazards of this arrangement. Flying the squadron's single scout and armed with a wing-mounted Lewis gun, he attacked a two-seat Aviatik over Menin, well inside the German lines. After inconclusively exhausting his first drum of forty-seven rounds, Strange released his safety belt and stood up to change drums. The scout stalled, flipped over on its back, and tossed the hapless pilot over the side at 8000 feet. Hanging onto the Lewis gun in a spinning, upside-down aircraft, Strange finally managed to grasp one of the centre-section struts and haul himself back aboard. Still inverted and spinning, he skilfully brought the scout back under control — only to drop with such force into his wicker seat as he righted the aircraft that he went right through the bottom of it, and seat pieces jammed the flight controls. By the time Strange managed to clear enough of the debris to regain control, he was dangerously close to the ground. Still, he limped back to his airfield at tree-top height, armed with an amazing tale to tell. Strange survived the war, a highly decorated lieutenant-colonel.[14]

By the spring of 1915 the aircraft was coming into its own as a weapon of war. In March the assault on Neuve Chappelle was significantly assisted by the availability of maps fashioned solely by aerial photography. Bombing and interdiction missions behind enemy lines became more routine, and the leisurely pace of the war in the air disappeared. The scout/fighter role was treated seriously, and fertile imaginations were hard at work to improve their lethality. If a machine gun could be installed to fire along the line of flight of the aircraft, for example, the pilot's problems with respect to deflection shooting would be greatly simplified. To solve this issue, a system had to be devised to fire the weapon through the aircraft's propeller arc.

French Lieutenant Roland Garros, a celebrated pre-war aviator, barnstormer, and inventor serving in Escadrille MS.23, devised a forward firing mounting for the Hotchkiss machine gun on his Morane Type L Parasol. To enable it to fire in the line of flight of the aircraft and through the propeller arc, he attached wedges of armoured steel to the back of his propeller blades to deflect any rounds that hit the propeller — calculated to be about one in ten. The modification was crude and dangerous, for the deflection direction could not be predicted with any accuracy, nor could the possible ricochet damage to both aircraft and pilot. This innovation still damaged the propeller blades and was prone to throwing the engine out of balance, but, on the whole, it worked reasonably well. Certainly it confounded the enemy, who thought they were still safe from the frontal fire of a tractor-engined aircraft. On April 1, 1915, Garros shot down an incredulous German pilot, Hugo Ackner, and his observer, Fritz Dietrichs, in a two-seat Albatros at 10,000 feet over the French lines. Next he shot down two more German aircraft and damaged others, to the chagrin of the Imperial German Air Service, which was in a state of near-panic over this innovation. However, on April 19, Garros' engine failed and he was forced down and captured behind enemy lines near Courtai.

Although the Germans initially felt disadvantaged by the Morane Parasol and its bullet deflection system, their despondency did not last long. Dutch aircraft designer Anthony Fokker was just completing military trials of a mid-wing monoplane specifically designed for scouting purposes — his famous Eindekker series. Fokker had based

his design extensively on the mid-wing Morane-Saulnier N model and powered it with an 80 horse-power Oberusel rotary engine. While later models of this aircraft would have an uprated 100 horse-

power engine, the Eindekkers were none too robust and possessed a propensity for both wing flutter and structural failures during violent manoeuvring. Most important were Fokker's armament innovations for this aircraft. After studying the Garros modification, Fokker was quick to grasp its limitations. He also knew that a mechanical interrupter gear,[15] which could link a gun to the aircraft engine, had already been invented and patented. While Fokker did not invent the interrupter gear, he improved on the initiatives of others. By mating a machine gun to an interrupter gear

Hauptmann Oswald Boelcke, an exceptional air warrior

mounted on his new scout, he was able to field a formidable weapon of war, one in which a machine gun could at last be fired with impunity through the propeller arc.

Allied losses rose sharply from the late summer onwards, and this era, known as the "Fokker Scourge," prevailed until the spring of 1916. "Fokker Fodder" became an unwelcome sobriquet for

A captured Fokker Eindekker

Initially, the Germans used their scouts in much the same way as did the RFC: they dispersed them among the Feldfliegerabteilungen (general purpose squadrons). At FlAbt 62, they were flown by Leutnant Oswald Boelcke and his star pupil, Fähnrich Max Immelmann. On July 6, 1915, however, Boelcke distinguished himself by shooting down a French Morane, in conjunction with his observer-gunner, Leutnant von Wuehlisch, from a new C-class biplane. This achievement was publicly touted as Germany's first victory in aerial combat. Thus, the impact of the new German single-seat fighter was only gradually felt, and a mere sixteen aerial combats would be recorded for the entire month of August. The Eindekkers saw only limited use, for they were forbidden to cross the Allied lines in case they were captured and their interrupter gear mechanism was copied.[16]

most of the plodding reconnaissance aircraft in the Entente inventory. The only bright spot for the RFC occurred on July 25, when 11 Squadron arrived in France as the first scout-designated unit of the corps. Ironically, it was equipped with a two-seat pusher-engined biplane, the Vickers FB5 Gun Bus, which was heavy and not much faster than the aircraft it was charged with escorting. Although the gunner commanded an unrestricted field of fire from the extreme nose of the aircraft, the Vickers were certainly no match for the nimble little Fokkers.

On the German side, Leutnant Kurt Wintgens would record the first score for an Eindekker on July 1. Later that month, eleven front-line pilots were flying the EII variant of the aircraft with an uprated engine. Immelmann, now a Leutnant, actually beat Boelcke to the scoring punch with the new machines on August 1, 1915, when they both attacked a force of British BE2cs, or "Quirks," as they were referred to in the corps. BE2s would become the chief victims of the Eindekkers during the coming months, for they were slow and unmanoeuvrable, with a limited defensive capability. On this occasion, Boelcke's gun jammed, but Immelmann was successful in bringing one of the BE2cs down. He subsequently fêted the wounded pilot, a Lieutenant Reid, in the gentlemanly manner characteristic of the period until Reid was turned over for processing as a prisoner of war (POW). Immelmann became the fair-haired boy of the German press corps, which found in the young *Adler von Lille*, the Eagle from Lille, a highly marketable public relations asset.

Both Immelmann and Boelcke were innovative warriors, and Immelmann was credited by name with an enduring air combat manoeuvre that became part of the repertoire of all German scout pilots. In attacks from behind, the Immelmann Turn allowed for a defensive escape by pulling up in a half-loop, followed by a half-roll and dive to right the aircraft. The Eindekker pilot could then escape in the opposite direction or half-roll again and dive onto the tail of his opponent, energized by his advantage of height. Looping

manoeuvres had long been performed in the air, but Immelmann was largely responsible for their application to aerial combat. Boelcke, in contrast, excelled in the broader evolution of air combat tactics and recommended thorough comparative tactical appraisals of both friendly and enemy aircraft. He emphasized the advantage of height and the use of the sun to confuse and surprise the enemy, as well as the supreme importance of aerial marksmanship and a diverse repertoire of aerobatic abilities. As an early pioneer of the concept of massing forces in intelligent groupings according to function, Boelcke taught that, in combat, one aircraft should be the primary attacker, while others were made responsible for guarding the attacker's vulnerable tail area while he was engaged with the enemy.

Immelmann and Boelcke initially flew as a combat team, but once they were fighting over different areas of the front they became friendly rivals as their scores continued to mount. When they had eight confirmed victories each in January 1916, they were both awarded the Fatherland's highest decoration — the blue-enameled Maltese Cross known as the Ordre pour le Mérite, or the Blue Max. Their victory scores officially instituted the ace acknowledgment system in Germany:[17] the score of eight victories was used as a yardstick for this award, though the qualification criteria was later doubled to sixteen in the face of mounting successes by significant numbers of airmen.

During the autumn of 1915 aerial activity intensified and, with it, came an alarming overall increase in Allied losses. The imperative of finding a match

Vickers FB5 Gun Bus

for the new German scouts had been clearly defined; otherwise, Entente loss rates would continue to skyrocket. On August 19, 1915, Colonel Hugh Trenchard was given command of all RFC units in France. It had readily become apparent to him that the aircraft types equipping the RFC in France were totally unsuitable to counter the quality of the German opposition. What was urgently needed was a potent scout aircraft, designed specifically for the extreme flight dynamics of air combat. Ironically, such designs were readily available among several of the independent manufacturers, but government policy did not allow their purchase. Instead, corps policy continued to equip for the most part from the Royal Aircraft Factory at Farnborough, which by and large still produced updated variants of the already outmoded BE2. Meanwhile, the BE2s were hacked down in droves by the Germans, and frequently took two men to their deaths when they fell.

Although this policy was myopic, it had little impact on the British public, since the air losses were eclipsed by the horrendous casualties of the ground war. However, the Germans did not have things all their own way even during the Fokker Scourge, for it was only a temporary period of ascendancy. Throughout the war, air supremacy, which generally fell to the side having the best aircraft, was in a state of periodic flux between the Allied and the Alliance air services, and this see-saw struggle continued until the closing months of the war.

As for Canadian governmental policy towards military aviation in general, and the formation of an indigenous Canadian airforce in particular, Sydney F. Wise contends it was "variously negative, indifferent, inconsistent and puzzling. It was almost always ill-informed. Yet the behaviour of the government was undoubtedly a faithful reflection of the public mind."[18] In essence, the war brought forward so many concerns associated with fielding an enormous deployed land force, then sustaining it in the face of staggering combat losses, that aviation was largely eclipsed. With the exception of Colonel (later Lieutenant-General Sir) Sam Hughes, Canada's Minister of Militia and Defence until he was dismissed by Borden in November 1916, no Canadian politician grasped the potential of military aviation until very late in the war. Nor did the relentless quest by Canada for recognition in high British

councils of the significant Canadian land commitment to the war spawn a parallel push for recognition of the substantial Canadian contributions to the British flying services, or even a lobby for their relative autonomy overseas. The modest beginnings of Canadian military aviation are best exemplified by the random attempts of a relatively small number of young Canadian men to enter the British flying services, after flight training obtained at their own expense at schools in both Canada and the United States.[19]

Hughes had, however, formed a Canadian Aviation Corps on September 16, 1914, while he was busy assembling the First Contingent at Camp Valcartier in Quebec. This mighty force, consisting of one well-used Burgess-Dunne biplane purchased in the United States, two officers, and one mechanic, accompanied the 1st Division to Britain, where the aircraft was unceremoniously dumped on Salisbury Plain. It never flew again, and the Aviation Corps was stillborn. Ironically, in early 1915 the British Army Council suggested to the Canadian government that complete air units for service with the RFC might be raised in Canada. Apathetic Canadian politicians let this suggestion lie dormant for the next three years. When it was finally acted upon, the Armistice was imminent, and it was too late for an independent Canadian airforce to participate in combat.

British recruitment in Canada of suitable candidates for its flying services was delayed for a number of reasons. First, there was no shortage of volunteers from Britain itself at the outset, and the services' initially modest needs had not yet been well defined. Second, the British were slow to appreciate just how much rough-hewn potential talent was available in the air-minded Canadian population, especially considering its substantial numbers of single immigrant men. Third, the British pursued an elitist, class-based policy with respect to their conditions of service. Acceptable candidates had first to possess an aviation certificate from the Aero Club of America or a similar institution, an expensive proposition at the time. They were also to be British subjects of pure European descent. A December 1914 report suggested that "an almost ideal combination for an Aviator is that obtaining in a man who has had a British public school education, a good all-round engineering training, and has outdoor sporting tendencies."[20]

Further British bias can be seen in the selection tests for temperament, particularly for emotional self-control and pugnacity. The British officer who proposed these tests did not think it necessary to measure self-control in British candidates, since he felt that quality was inherent, but the tests were useful in evaluating "the more emotional Latin type." Pugnacity could be tested by making disparaging remarks to the candidates, and particularly prompt responses were considered acceptable. This élitist view was probably best exemplified through the words and impressions of Lieutenant-Colonel C.J. Burke, the RFC's recruiting officer in Canada at the end of 1915. Burke had serious misgivings about the social suitability of most Canadian candidates and the blurring of Old World social distinctions. His criteria for refusing two candidates are telling, for he did not feel them worthy of RFC service, let alone for holding the King's Commission. "Two people I saved you from are examples," he reported; "one had been a Berkshire farm labourer two years ago and another ran a newspaper stand in Regina. Suitable material for the RFC!!!"[21]

Still, if British recruitment of Canadians for the air services was muted during the early war years, it occurred nonetheless. Although there were confusing and competitive policy changes between the RFC and the RNAS with respect to commissioning and flight experience requirements, Canadian airmen could be recruited in three ways throughout most of the war. After obtaining the requisite flight training at their own expense, they could proceed to Britain, again at their own expense, and make direct application. They could also request transfers from the Canadian Expeditionary Force, the British Army, or branches of the Royal Navy. And, finally, they could be considered after graduation from RFC/RNAS-approved Canadian or American flying schools, the costs of which would be absorbed initially by the candidate. In February 1915 the RNAS approved the establishment of a flying school for embryonic military pilots at Toronto, to be run by a Canadian branch of the Curtiss Aircraft Company. This training cost each candidate at least $400 — a small fortune at the time — and it bought only 400 minutes of total flying time.

Despite the financial obstacles, the Curtiss School was popular and it graduated 129 student pilots in 1915 and 1916. In most cases, successful graduates received partial rebates for their expenses from the British services. All the flying was dual, except for the qualification examinations that were administered at the end of the course, and training was usually conducted in the early morning to avoid windy, gusty conditions. The examinations consisted of three solo flights, two of which involved flying a series of figures-of-eight around two posts spaced 500 metres apart. Power-off landings were to be within 50 metres of a predetermined touchdown spot. The third mission required the student to climb to at least 100 metres, then cut the engine and glide to a successful landing. Passing candidates were issued with certificates in the name of the Royal Aero Club of Great Britain.

By the spring of 1915 the Toronto Curtiss School was already full to capacity. Since the British did not care where the certificate was obtained, enterprising individuals started exploring alternatives. Along with courses offered by the American Curtiss and Stinson schools, a popular option was training at the Wright School in Dayton, Ohio, which, by August 1915, was processing the largest class in its short history. In all, twenty-five Canadians of independent means had been simultaneously drawn to this school, and its two Wright Pusher aircraft were in near-continuous operation throughout the autumn. A newspaper article of the period provides insight into the conditions and scope of this early training. It was similar to that received at the Toronto Curtiss School, although the amount of actual flying time offered was considerably less than on the Toronto course.

The Wright training grounds are located about five miles east of the city. Many of the youths from the Dominions are getting plenty of experience at sleeping out, for as many as can be accommodated have cots in the hangar and never leave the grounds, except to walk up the road to a nearby farm house at meal times. Others are living in the city and go out to the grounds every day by traction.

The course provides for a training of 240 minutes actually in the air. For this course, reasonably expected to take six weeks, the student pays $250. At this rate, the cost to the student is $1.05 for every minute in the air. Straight away flying, turns, dips, spiral glides and other maneuvers are taught by the instructors,

Lloyd Breadner (left)
in training during 1915 at
the Wright School in
Dayton, Ohio

as they gradually familiarize the men with the use of the aeroplane.

The men are given regular turns, accompanying the two instructors into the air, but practically all are to be had on a moment's call, as they are eager to complete the course. Two aeroplanes are being used.

Taken in regular turns, the men don heavy sweaters and gloves for protection from the wind, reverse their caps in aeroplane fashion, and after taking their seat beside the instructor, apply the power. The machine trundles along the ground for a couple hundred yards and then rises gradually from the earth.

Soaring back and forth continually forming the figure eight, the aeroplane is never allowed beyond a certain altitude during the progress of the instructions. The roar of the engine precludes the possibility of the instructor indulging in any oral explanations and suggestions, but actual operation of the machine, under the careful guidance of the trained aviator at his side, is enough to impress upon the student various lessons of control and operation.

The machine remains in the air only a few minutes and then descends when other students flock about and hear a short talk on experiences gained during the flight just completed. As one machine descends, the other is taken aloft on its canvas wings, the idea apparently being to have only one machine in operation at a time.

Every student, before he is granted his pilot's licence, must take the entire course of 240 minutes in the air and then pass the aviator's test, which demands certain knowledge and ability to successfully operate the machine alone. The coveted pilot's licence is awarded only after the student has displayed a certain degree of perfection in three distinct branches of aeroplane flying. Figure eight flying, rising to an altitude of more than 300 feet, and then spiral gliding with the power shut off, and finally the making of a proper landing are the determining factors in the awarding of the licence to fly.[22]

"Red" Mulock (right),
one of the earliest
distinguished Canadians
in the RNAS

The Canadian invasion of American flying schools was so pervasive between mid-1915 and mid-1916 that over half the flying certificates issued by the Aero Club of America during that period went to Canadians seeking to serve in the RFC and the RNAS.[23] Assuming these American-trained fledglings passed the other entrance requirements, they were normally commissioned or given provisional officer status and sent for further flight training with the RNAS or the RFC. The flight certificate was really just a licence to learn, since much more training was necessary before the pilots could be sent into combat.

The trickle of Canadian aircrew that characterized the first year of the war soon became a steady stream and ultimately a torrent. In 1915, 350 airmen enlisted by all methods. That number increased to 905 in 1916, 3167 in 1917, and 7782 in 1918.[24] At least thirty-seven Canadian airmen served operationally as either pilots or observers in 1915, sixteen with the RNAS and twenty-one with the RFC. These young men were noteworthy, for they were all pioneers at the cutting edge of this newborn military technology.

In the opening year of the war, Canadians who joined the RNAS logged many firsts in the air. Redford M. Mulock of Winnipeg, for example, eventually became one of Canada's most diversely distinguished military aviators of the Great War. He sailed with the First Contingent in 1914, quickly applied for transfer to the RNAS, and in due course became a probationary flight sub-lieutenant. After pilot training in early 1915, he made the first interception of a German airship, the LZ 38, over England. Flying an Avro 504, Mulock encountered the behemoth at 2000 feet on the night of May 16-17, but his Lewis gun jammed after firing one round. Somewhat later, he became the empire's second airman to bomb a submarine. Mulock possessed a tremendous zeal for flight and aerial combat. A true jack-of-all-trades in that early era of pre-specialization, he also bombed a Zeppelin shed by himself at Berchem Ste. Agathe near Brussels, after first accomplishing a remarkable feat of cross-country navigation in atrocious weather:

It was a large building painted green and
red and yellow so that from a height it looked
like the ground. He swooped down toward it
and the Germans opened fire on him with
dozens of guns, so that shells burst all around

him. Some of the shells were of a new type, which sent thousands of little balls of fire at him, with the idea of setting the aeroplane on fire. He dropped through them all and dropped a bomb on the building, then made another circle and dropped another one and then another, and all the time the bullets were spinning past him. One bullet went through the machine, but it did not hit him. Then he threw one more bomb and turned for home. The Zeppelin shed was on fire by this time.[25]

Mulock also became the first airman to spot for the artillery at night by using parachute flares. Flying with 1 Naval Wing from Dunkirk in early Nieuport scouts, he was actively involved in a number of early combats with German two-seaters towards the end of 1915 and in the first few months of 1916. Although the results were not always conclusive, they were claimed as victories under the guidelines of the day. By May 1916 Mulock had become the first Canadian to claim five air combat successes, and the first RNAS pilot to be credited with that distinction.

Other trail-blazing Canadian naval airmen of the period included J.A. Barron of Stratford, Ontario, the only Canadian selected for airship service in 1915. Flight Sub-Lieutenant H. S. Kerby of Calgary was the first Canadian airman to serve in the Dardanelles,[26] flying artillery-spotting missions in Voisin two-seaters from June onwards. James Harwood Arnold of the Queen Charlotte Islands was the first Canadian to be decorated for service in the air. Flying as an observer in Henri-Farmans and based in Southeast Africa, Arnold played a major role in directing the artillery fire on the German cruiser *Königsberg* which ultimately led to its destruction. These actions put Arnold and his pilot in grave peril, but they survived. Arnold was awarded the Distinguished Service Order (DSO) for this July 11, 1915, combat.

A. Strachan Ince of Toronto was one of the first two graduates of the Curtiss School there, arriving for service with 1 Wing at Dunkirk in October. He went into the record books on December 14 as the first Canadian to shoot down a German aircraft. Although a qualified pilot, Ince was serving at the time as an observer in a Nieuport two-seater. Their quarry was a large German seaplane intent on bombing a British ship stranded on a sand bar.

Ince sent the German raider spiraling down in flames, but the Nieuport developed engine trouble and had to be ditched. Fortunately, Ince and his pilot were picked up by a passing minesweeper, and Ince became the first Canadian to be awarded the Distinguished Service Cross (DSC) as a member of the RNAS.

The RFC also had its share of colourful Canadian pioneers, though by the end of 1915 only ten of the twenty-one Canadian pilots and observers who had been posted to the front were still serving there.[27] Captain Frederick A. Wanklyn of Montreal, an RMC graduate, became the first Canadian airman to be employed operationally with the corps. Awarded his pilot's certificate in 1912, by November 26, 1914, he was a flight commander with 4 Squadron in France at St. Omer, flying reconnaissance missions over the lines at Ypres. Wanklyn was then posted to 5 Squadron in May 1915, flying the Vickers Gun Bus. He was gazetted for a Military Cross (MC) and awarded a Mentioned in Dispatches (MiD) in June 1915.

Lieutenant Stanley W. Caws, relatively old at thirty-six to be actively flying, became the first Canadian airman to be killed in action. A jovial extrovert with arresting good looks, he had a disconcerting habit, while dining, of picking up all the table knives within reach and throwing them across the room into the woodwork of the mess door. Given the structured social behaviour of the period and the sheltered neophyte British officers with whom he came into contact, Caws undoubtedly left an indelible impression on his youthful colleagues. As Sydney S. Wise observes: "Perhaps his peculiar social graces help to explain how Canadians in the RFC got their reputation for unorthodoxy and mild rowdyism in a service where unorthodoxy and mild rowdyism were a way of life."[28] Flying BE2cs with 10 Squadron, Caws was set upon by several German fighters while on a reconnaissance mission on September 21, 1915. He and his observer put up a stout defence, expending all their ammunition in a fight that lasted a full fifteen minutes. However, he was fatally shot while still at 11,000 feet and his observer was wounded. The Quirk glided down into enemy territory, where the observer, named Wilson, was taken into captivity. The nation paid Caws a tribute shortly thereafter:

Lieut. S.W. Caws, Royal Flying Corps, who was shot dead on September 21 during a fight

in the air, and was buried with military honours by the Germans, was the only son of Mr. Douglas Caws…Lieut. Caws went through the South African War as a Trooper in Paget's Horse. At the time of the declaration of war last year, he was on an important and remunerative expedition in North-West Canada, but he gladly relinquished all to serve his country, and came over to England with the 1st Canadian Contingent. In February 1915, he transferred to the Royal Flying Corps.[29]

Of all the early Canadian airmen engaged in operations with the RFC during the opening months, none was more colourful than Lieutenant Malcom McBean Bell-Irving of Vancouver.[30] A charming and determined young man, he paid his own passage to England soon after the commencement of hostilities and vowed to become an airman. Arriving at the RFC training station located on the Brooklands Race Track in September, Bell-Irving accosted a young subaltern named Cyril Newall, who took him up for a brief familiarization flight. Newall was very impressed by Bell-Irving's inherent abilities. Later, as Marshal of the RAF Sir Cyril Newall, he said: " I shall never forget to my dying day that flaming redhead walking towards the hangars so determined to fly."[31] By early October 1914, Bell-Irving had earned his Royal Aero Club certificate, and on March 7, 1915, he crossed over to France with 1 Squadron. He was soon flying the full spectrum of combat operations expected of RFC airmen at the time, including artillery cooperation, reconnaissance, and the precursor form of air combat then referred to as patrolling.

Until at least the middle of 1915, revolvers and rifles were the main form of armament on RFC squadrons; it took considerable persuasion on the part of squadron pilots and their commanders to convince the higher echelons that light machine guns would be of considerable value to Allied airmen. Meanwhile, Bell-Irving's aggressive determination to engage the enemy with whatever armament he possessed led to some inconclusive and frustrating results. Richard, Malcom's younger brother, recalled one such unspecified engagement years after the fact: "Finally he [Malcom] came up to a Hun from behind, a German single-seater, which as you know can be done without being seen or heard. He attempted to shoot the German but his revolver jammed so he threw it at him and hit him on the back of the head, which upset him but otherwise no known damage." Bell-Irving had a well-documented series of engagements in a Martinsyde Scout on April 28, 1915, which must have been extremely frustrating. In four separate incidents on the same flight, armed with only two automatic pistols, he engaged nine different aircraft, all to no avail. In reporting the combats to higher headquarters, his commanding officer noted: "It was impossible to arm Lt. Bell-Irving with a machine gun, since all three machine guns [held by the squadron] were out." The speed and the climb capability of the Martinsyde made it totally unacceptable for air combat. During one of the engagements, Bell-Irving took twenty minutes to climb from 3800 to 5800 feet, just to engage from a position of tactical parity.[32]

Eventually, better equipment provided Bell-Irving with the edge he needed for success in the air. He had a memorable day flying a Morane Bullet armed with a machine gun on December 19, for which he won the Distinguished Service Order, the first Canadian in the RFC to be so honoured. This action also constituted the first decisive victory for a Canadian in the RFC:

For conspicuous and consistent gallantry and skill during a period of nine months in France, notably on December 19th 1915, between Lille and Ypres when he successfully engaged three hostile machines. The first he drove off, the second he sent to the ground in flames, and the third nose-dived and disappeared. He was then attacked by three other hostile machines from above, but he flew off towards Ypres and chased a machine he saw in that direction. He overhauled it and had got to within a hundred yards when he was wounded by a shell and had to return.[33]

As the citation suggested, the award also recognized Bell-Irving's indomitable spirit over an extended period of time. Although he did not become a high scorer, he continued to engage the enemy in an aggressive and inspirational manner, adding a Military Cross and two Mentioned in Dispatches to his awards before he was grievously wounded the following summer.

Major Malcolm McBean Bell-Irving (second from left) and Major Arthur Kellam Tylee (centre) presenting trophies at Camp Borden later in the war

By the end of 1915, air warfare over the Western Front had changed dramatically. Elementary notes on air fighting distributed in February accurately reflected the limited offensive capability: "Suggested forms of fighting hostile machines included dropping steel darts, bombs, and even 'charging the enemy' if need be."[34] Less than two months later, aerial fighting became codified, recognized duties of the RFC squadrons. Aircraft progressively became more robust, more capable, and better armed, and the extent of aerial activity increased dramatically.[35] The stage was set for much more extensive bloodletting in the air the following year.

CHAPTER TWO

ASCENDANCY WON – AND LOST

1916

*"We are absolutely supreme in the air,
our artillery is much better and our
infantry never fail to take their objectives."*

— WILLIAM GEORGE BARKER, VC

By January 1916 approximately 120 Canadian members of the Royal Naval Air Service were either in-theatre or en route to the war. The RNAS frequently used the British home air defence organization as a graduate course for its neophyte pilots, before deploying them elsewhere. It was not unusual, then, for Canadians in the final stages of naval flight training in 1916 to be slated on a roster system for active air defence duty, particularly anti-Zeppelin patrols. Several Canadian RNAS eventual luminaries, including Flight Sub-Lieutenant Lloyd Breadner of Carleton Place, Ontario, Flight Sub-Lieutenant Raymond Collishaw of Nanaimo, BC, and Flight Sub-Lieutenant Grant Gooderham of Toronto followed this route. Both Breadner and Collishaw experienced combat in these circumstances.

Meanwhile, Flight Sub-Lieutenant "Red" Mulock of 1 Wing Dunkirk continued to distinguish himself during the early months of the year. On January 24, while flying a Nieuport scout on a reconnaissance flight to Ostend and

Douglas Haig, commander of all British forces on the Western Front since December 19, 1915, hoped first to generate a massive rupture of the German front lines and then fully exploit that break to the Allies' advantage. This great offensive, which would be preceded by softening-up operations on an unprecedented scale, was scheduled for mid-summer. However, the Germans pre-empted Allied war plans with an enormous offensive of their own, directed against the French fortress at Verdun in late February. They were determined to crush the French will to fight. Further, the new action soon extended to the British sector of the front as more and more *poilus*, the common French soldiers, were drawn into the abattoir of Verdun. To provide the beleaguered French forces a measure of desperately needed relief, Marshal Joffre made passionate entreaties to the British to launch their own offensive as soon as possible. In May, Haig agreed to a massive assault "athwart the

Opposite: The Avro 504K provided yeoman service, both in training and in combat.

Fokker Eindekker *

Ghistelles, he drove down
a German biplane, forcing it to land.
Two days later he scored again while protecting
a British flotilla that was bombarding shore batteries near Westende.[1]

Early in 1916 the Allies agreed on a massive, joint French-Anglo offensive designed to wear down the forces of the Central Powers. General Sir

Somme" beginning on July 1.[2] As it happened, the two greatest battles of 1916, Verdun and the Somme, were huge in dimension, though a little different in kind, compared with the battles that preceded them in 1914 and 1915.

* Readers should note that neither this nor subsequent colour side profiles are done to a particular scale.

During the first half of 1916 General Hugh Trenchard strove relentlessly to create an air weapon that was custom-tailored to the needs of an army on the offensive. Between January and April, the Royal Flying Corps was reorganized into brigades, each one specifically assigned to a numbered army: "Each brigade consisted of a headquarters, an aircraft park, a balloon-wing, an army wing of two-to-four squadrons, and a corps wing of three-to-five squadrons (one squadron for each corps). At RFC Headquarters there was an additional wing to provide reconnaissance for GHQ [General Headquarters]; and, as time went on, to carry out additional fighting and bombing duties."[3]

Artillery observation was now the primary mission of the RFC, with secondary roles of photography and general battlefield reconnaissance. Because of the high demand and the lack of time to perform other duties, the squadrons performing these tasks soon became specialized. The corps squadrons were also tied to a specific sector of the front, matching the corps they supported on the ground. With the heavy workload, squadron strengths rapidly became a problem. All RFC squadrons at the time were established for eighteen aircraft, but in the early months of 1916 none possessed more than twelve. Additional aircraft were acquired slowly over the coming months, with priority given to units that directly supported the ground offensive.

The year 1916 did not commence well for the Allies in the air. The German Eindekkers were at the height of their brief success against the lumbering Allied reconnaissance aircraft. As a precaution, and until such time as a scout aircraft superior to the Eindekkers could be fielded, formation patrols now became mandatory. Specifically, each reconnaissance two-seater operating over the front had an escort of at least three other aircraft. On January 23, 20 Squadron left Britain for France with the first of a new pusher biplane series, the FE2b.[4] A powerful two-seater equipped with a 160 horsepower Beardmore engine and armed with two Lewis guns, the FE2b was a significant challenge to the nimble Fokkers. Manoeuvrable, rugged, and heavily armed, its only notable drawback was its relatively slow top speed of 73 miles per hour (mph). Albert Earl Godfrey from Killarney, Manitoba, was an observer with 25 Squadron during 1915. Although he later became a successful scout pilot with four-

teen confirmed victories, he recalled the FE2 and its employment at the time:

Upon my arrival, offensive patrols were carried out with two machines, but this soon increased to three, and finally to five … The FE was a very practical machine, suitable for any kind of work. Its armament of two Lewis guns, one on a rest behind the observer to shoot over the top wing, the other in the nacelle which could be moved to any position required, together with its ability to manoeuvre, [meant that the aircraft] could hold its own against all comers. At this period, they were used for offensive patrols, the same way the scouts were used later on.[5]

In the United Kingdom, production was underway of a new single-seat fighting scout, the DH2,

DH2s at operational readiness. France, 1916.

designed by Geoffrey de Havilland, who had also created the FE2 series. Since the Allies still had no viable interrupter gear, de Havilland designed this aircraft in a pusher configuration. The pilot sat in a frontal nacelle, armed with a single Lewis gun, which had limited mobility in both elevation and traverse. Typically, the DH2 pilots field-modified this weapon to a preferred fixed location on the aircraft's line of flight, though British bureaucracy initially forbade this initiative.[6] Powered by either a 100 horsepower Gnôme or a 110 horsepower Le-Rhône engine, the DH2 was equal or superior to the Eindekkers in speed, manoeuvrability, and rate of climb. Faster than the FEs, it boasted a top speed of 86 mph, which matched that of the latest Fokker variant, the E IV. The DH2 was a sturdy ship, but sensitive to overcontrolling and prone to spinning with little warning. A number of pilots were killed

in this manner until the spin's mysteries and its aerodynamic corrective action were fully comprehended later in the year. The first DH2s, flown by 24 Squadron, reached the front in early February and were soon recognized as first-class fighters, noted for their manoeuvrability. Pilots, however, complained of the cold in their exposed frontal positions, at the complete mercy of the elements.[7]

The Martinsyde G100 "Elephant," first fielded in March, was a British single-seat, tractor-powered biplane scout of dubious capabilities. Armed with a single Lewis gun mounted atop the upper wing in a configuration similar to that of the Nieuports, it was a large, cumbersome machine. It quickly became outmoded and was superseded as a fighting scout once more effective types became available.

The RFC learned a great deal about the effective organization of air resources from the French in early 1916, owing to the rapid evolution of French military aviation during the Verdun campaign. Early on, the French concentrated six fighter squadrons in the region, most equipped with Nieuports. By the end of February, orders had been issued that offensive patrols, designed to seek and destroy the enemy in the air, were to be conducted in formations by units of at least three aircraft. The RFC im-

French artillery observation aircraft and bombers to work with relative impunity. The next German countermove consisted of barrage, or Luftsperre, patrols, whereby the German aviators flew up and down their own side of the lines, hoping to deny

The DeHavilland DH2

mediately followed suit, although several of the most successful and individualistic British and French aces were exempted from this policy. In response, the Germans brought their scouts closer to the front and grouped them into fighter detachments, called Kampfeinsitzerkommandos, which provided close support to attacking infantry. These new units, one of which was commanded by Oswald Boelcke, were very successful at the outset of the campaign. However, the French policy of massing offensive air resources had significant ramifications for the ground battle, since the aerial supremacy it afforded allowed

that airspace to the French Air Service. These patrols were conducted in two-seater aircraft and, employed in this manner, they were not effective in stopping enemy bombers. The Eindekkers, flying in their specialized Kommandos, were charged with attacking French aircraft that broke through the Luftsperre. In the final analysis, this tactic merely dissipated German resources without effectively denying the French observation and bombing aircraft access to the area. Later in the Verdun campaign, the Eindekkers, grouped in twos and threes, were sent on offensive sweeps over the front to clear the air for German two-seaters, and this tactic was more effective.

Trenchard assimilated three valuable lessons from the French experience at Verdun: the paramount importance to the ground war of fresh intelligence gathering through aerial observation and photography; the absolute necessity for the overall direction and coordination of fighter forces engaged in offensive missions; and the need for aerial

units that were adaptable to changing situations and could perform a variety of missions. Numerical superiority in the air during an offensive was essential, and, to deny enemy access to that airspace, fighters had to be employed in formation on continuous patrols over the enemy lines. This policy would unquestionably be costly, since carrying the fight over enemy territory frequently resulted in irrecoverable losses in both men and machines. Gradually the combatants came to realize that air superiority was only a temporary condition in this war, to be achieved by whichever side concentrated the most assets in a specific area at any given time. [8]

In terms of individual accomplishments, the outstanding German air heroes over Verdun were Oswald Boelcke, who scored ten more victories there, and Oberleutnant Freiherr Ernst von Althaus, whose five additional victories for the campaign brought his ledger to nine and won him the Ordre pour le Mérite. The French had several luminaries, and their first official ace was Jean Navarre, with seven decisive claims, followed by Charles Nungesser, with six. Both of these aviators were flamboyant figures who captured the imagination of an adoring French public. Navarre was the independently wealthy son of a powerful industrialist. A firebrand loner, he possessed a contempt for authority and a recklessness that bordered on insanity. He roamed the battle area in an all-red Morane Bullet and wore a silk stocking as a helmet. Nungesser, who eventually became France's third highest-scoring ace with forty-five confirmed victories, flew into combat wearing all his medals. He was the toast of Parisian society in an enormous German staff car that he had captured in a ground engagement. Both were unrepentant ladies' men and risk takers, and the public could not get enough of their mad exploits. [9] Both were granted roving commissions — the authority to hunt alone and of their own free will in their aerial battlefield.

Given the haphazard application of airpower during the early years of the Great War, aerial combat lent itself to the improvisational skills of a few notable individualists. This new breed of hunters, bolstered by the official fostering of an offensive spirit, preferred attack to defence, and the most successful at this game were those who unhesitatingly and relentlessly engaged the enemy on every possible occasion. This offensive spirit was not without cost, however. Most of the thirty German air combat losses associated with the seige of Verdun were achieved by individual French pilots, such as Navarre and Nungesser, in search of targets of opportunity. The Germans, in turn, shot down nearly one hundred French aircraft engaged in formation defensive tactics. Yet, owing to the overwhelming numerical superiority of the French, the Germans' barrage tactics failed to stop the main French effort in the air. Although the French suffered considerably more losses, they did so from the significantly larger resource pool they were willing to commit to the battle. The establishment of air superiority at Verdun provided tangible benefits to the land battle and justified the critical role of fighter aircraft. In particular, it generated a morale crisis among German troops.

During the first four months of the year, the air situation in the British zone was decidedly tame compared with that over Verdun. Only 148 aerial engagements were recorded for the period. Nine Canadians were involved in these engagements, of which five became casualties. The very act of flying was still exceptionally dangerous: eighty aircraft were lost in safety accidents, while only twenty-six went down in combat. On March 29, Second Lieutenant F.G. Pinder of Victoria, BC, a FE2b pilot with 23 Squadron, became Max Immelmann's twelfth victory. Pinder had been in France for only a fortnight.

In keeping with the air situation at the time, most combats occurred between opposing reconnaissance/spotting aircraft and enemy scouts.

led the first operational finger-four formation — one deployed like the fingers of an outstretched hand. This flight included a Bristol Scout, flown above and behind the main formation as an additional lookout. A second Canadian, Lieutenant C.E. Rogers of Toronto, also took part. These pioneers patrolled deep into enemy territory to position themselves favourably up-sun on the return flight. Although they were essentially goading the Germans to attack, no engagements occurred. Soon the British air services would reap the benefits of these innovative tactics and the temporarily superior fighter aircraft, which would constitute more than half the total of RFC aircraft on the Somme. By early summer, they clearly dominated German aviation in the area.

The entire rationale of the offensive stance was "to permit freedom of action to artillery, reconnaissance and other ground support aircraft and to deny such freedom to the enemy."[10] Air superiority by itself was considered immaterial, however, unless the ground forces could benefit. After several inconclusive operations using the finger-four formation, the newly acquired air superiority paid huge dividends during the Canadian Corps counterattack at Mount Sorrel in early June. Superb aerial photographs of the area allowed for a systematic and accurate bombardment of German positions which was so devastating that it shattered the Germans' capacity to defend the region.

A Bristol Scout C with an unsynchronized Lewis gun mounted on the engine cowling

Rarely did scout-versus-scout combats occur, nor were they deliberately sought out at this stage of the war. After the middle of January, however, Trenchard encouraged his air units to develop formation tactics applicable to air combat. The idea of patrolling in force, rather than individually, did not take hold quickly with the scouting units, though some of them experimented with different tactics. On April 30 Captain William Milne of Chamadaska, BC, flying FE2bs with 25 Squadron,

By April 1916 two new naval wings, No. 4 at Petite Synthe and No. 5 at Coudekerque, had been established, although they were still considered part of the Dover/Dunkirk Command, the Flanders lodgment. Meanwhile, 1 Wing was split into two squadrons of twenty aircraft and twelve pilots each and tasked with naval support missions. Along with photo-reconnaissance and fire-direction duties, the unit had a designated fighter role. Part of the wing was equipped with Nieuport scouts and assigned an active patrol sector stretching from Ypres to the North Sea along the Western Front and out over the fleet itself. Although 5 Wing was expected to perform both reconnaissance and fighter duties, its main mission was to be bombing. Similarly, 4 Wing was expected to carry out a mix of bombing and fighter sorties, so it possessed a few Nieuport scouts

Around this time, a new two-seater tractor biplane joined 5 Wing of the RNAS at Coudekerque — the superb Sopwith 1½ Strutter, armed initially with only a flexibly mounted Lewis gun for the observer. It performed so well that it was selected to be the first British type fitted with production examples of the new interrupter gear,

Below: Sopwith 1½ Strutters of 3(N) Wing, 1916

Bottom: Sopwith 1½ Strutter

designated for that purpose. RNAS fighters took the offensive whenever possible. On May 21, in retribution for German bombing raids on the city of Dunkirk, 1 Wing Nieuports swept various German airfields in the vicinity. Mulock destroyed one aircraft, and possibly another, at Mariakerke.

In terms of equipment and personnel, the British air services were making significant strides forward. The quest to develop a reliable interrupter gear continued. While the Fokker gearing was mechanical, activated by the engine via linked rods, the British favoured a hydraulic system invented by a Romanian engineer named Constantinescu. In March a Bristol Scout armed with a Vickers machine gun was fitted with one of the new Constantinescu gears and sent to France for service trials. Although many problems were encountered, they were remedied in short order.

which augmented the Strutter's armament with a potent, nose-mounted Vickers gun. This aircraft was initially introduced as an escort to the wing's

Breguet and Caudron bombers. After intense lob-
bying by the War Office and the army chain of command, a number of these Strutters were transferred
to the RFC. Subsequently, 70 Squadron equipped its
first flight with Strutters by May 24 and, within
two months, the entire squadron had transitioned
to the new aircraft.

By late May another scouting unit, 60 Squadron, was also in France, working out of Vert Galand,
a beautiful, historic farm located alongside the road
between Amiens and Doullens:

At Vert Galand, pilots of 60 Squadron enjoyed rather a country-club atmosphere. When
they were not working, they were lounging in
deck chairs beneath trees in the orchard,
whooping it up in the Officers' Mess or away
on an expedition down the road to Amiens, pil-
ing into Smith-Barry's ("A" Flight Commander) touring car, bound for a splendid dinner at
the Hotel du Rhin or a visit to the *estaminet*
where wine, women and song were readily available. But it was the calm before the storm.[11]

Morane Parasols
in the field

The bad news for 60 Squadron was that it was equipped with largely obsolete French Moranes, including Type N Bullet monoplanes, Type BB biplanes, and Type L Parasols. Recognizing the urgent need for modernization of the fighting scouts, the Nieuport factory was busily developing successful offshoots of its Type 11. In short order, Type 13 and Type 16 single-seat scouts were available to augment both 11 and 29 Squadrons, and, by May, the classic Type 17 entered service with Escadrille 57. A few of these aircraft also com-

menced operations with the British in 1 Squadron.

The RFC had a few Bristol Scouts fitted with Lewis guns mounted on the top planes. Also, a third DH2 squadron was posted to France in May, making the RFC's fighting scout units a formidable force of twelve full squadrons by mid-year. In addition, the RNAS formed a fighting scout unit early that summer from many of the Dunkirk Nieuports known as "A" Squadron at Furnes and tasked it with defending Channel coast supply ports. All three RNAS Wings were now routinely assigned fighter patrols to maintain air superiority over the Belgian and French lines, on top of their fleet protection duties, and before long this "two-way pull" characterized their operations for some time to come. "A" Squadron also took delivery of the first examples of two fine new scouting aircraft from the Sopwith stables: the Pup and the Triplane.

Along with numerical supremacy, the Entente air forces now enjoyed temporarily a measure of technological parity and perhaps even slight ascendancy over the Germans. The Fokker Scourge had been eliminated as a viable threat. As if to mark symbolically this turning of the tide, Max Immelmann was shot down and killed by an FE2b crew from 25 Squadron on June 18.[12] Later the same month, while preparations for the up-coming Somme offensive continued, Nieuport scouts, armed with Le Prieur rockets mounted on the interplane struts and fired electrically, waged an intense and concentrated campaign against the tethered German observation balloons, destroying eight of them in a two-day period alone.[13] By the end of June the FE2d, a further development of this doughty pusher series, powered by a 225 horsepower V-12 Rolls Royce engine, started reaching the front. A new single-seat pusher type, similar to the DH2 but known as the FE8, was issued to 29 Squadron to replace the rapidly aging Nieuport 16s and to bolster its DH2 force.

When the Somme offensive began on July 1, the RFC and the French Air Service had each concentrated roughly 200 combat aircraft against a total force of approximately 130 German machines in the region. Specifically, the British possessed sixty-six fighter types, grouped in indigenous scout units, mostly DH2 pushers and a squadron of Moranes (60 Squadron) in addition to half a dozen

Nieuport scouts and a small number of Strutters. The French could field a force of seventy-two Nieuports concentrated in six Escadrilles stationed near Cachy, of which several were the new Type 17. In opposition, the Germans could weigh in with only nineteen fighters in the British zone, consisting of Fokker EIIIs and EIVs and a few Pfalz EIVs. They also possessed a sprinkling of new Halberstadt DIIs, which had already been proven inferior to the best of the new Allied types.[14] The Germans were totally outnumbered and, unlike the specialized Allied air units, their fighter squadrons had a heterogeneous mix of equipment. Predictably, the result was Allied dominance of the air over the

The land battle, in contrast, was a disaster for the Allies from the outset. The plan was simple. The entire front of the 4th British Army, and the VIII Corps of the 3rd British Army on its left, would conduct a seven-day advance bombardment designed to destroy German barbed-wire entanglements and other established defences. The infantry would then advance in lines behind a rolling barrage over a predicted distance of 1 to $1^{1}/_{2}$ miles, taking permanent possession of the gained territory. On the first day of the ground battle the Allies suffered appalling combat losses in spite of these rosy predictions, which were founded on misplaced confidence in the effectiveness of the softening-up bar-

Somme during the early stages of the campaign. In July and August alone, the Germans lost fifty-one aircraft in aerial combat and became completely ineffective in the air over the battlefield.[15]

rage. Once the advance bombardment ceased, the Germans came out of their protective hiding and slaughtered Lord Kitchener's advancing forces. The 4th Army alone, which numbered 100,000 strong at the start of the day, suffered 60,000 casualties — nearly 50 percent in the first hour of combat. At Beaumont Hamel the Royal Newfoundland Regiment, attached to the British 29th Division, was all but wiped out in a magnificent display of disciplined, trained, and pointless valour. Every officer who went forward in the attack was either killed or wounded, and so were most of the men. To make matters worse, the German line held fast. In all, this prolonged struggle of attrition lasted until November and consumed well over 600,000 Allied lives in a seemingly bottomless cauldron of sacrifice, generated for a very few kilometres of mud at best.

The air plan was complex, and initially much more successful than the land campaign for the Entente. Allied reconnaissance, bombing, and support aircraft enjoyed significant fighter escort at all

The year 1916 was a crucial one in the development of air combat. If specialized fighters experienced their kindergarten at Verdun, the Somme was their finishing school. It was here that the great early aces from both sides developed the first codified dicta for air fighting. For the RFC they were refined and widely distributed as their *Notes on Aeroplane Fighting in Single-Seat Scouts* of November 1916, and *Fighting in the Air* of the following March. Here, the RFC clearly established the pre-eminence of formation tactics over individual engagements, and henceforth a codified escort system for two-seaters became virtually mandatory. With respect to actual engagements, attacks made by more than one machine working in concert had a much better chance of forcing a decisive combat, especially when they worked as

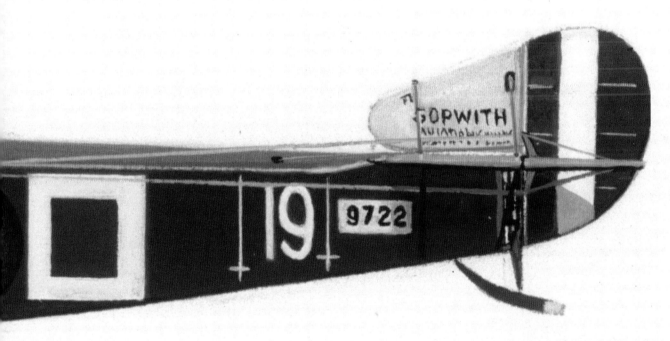

Sopwith 1½ Strutter

times. Also, on a concerted basis for the first time, scouting aircraft conducted deep offensive patrols over and behind the German lines. During the initial weeks of the Somme offensive, Allied fighters totally swept German opposition from the sky. Although the Allies suffered substantial losses due to anti-aircraft fire, they were virtually unimpeded by enemy fighter opposition when flying behind the German front.

coordinated pairs. Together, they exemplified mutual support and cooperation, providing at least a second pair of eyes to scan each other's vulnerable flanks and rearward approaches. While multiples of aircraft grouped together provided increased support and allowed the leader to devote his attention to offensive manoeuvring, formation size was generally felt to be limited to a maximum of seven aircraft, after which the unit became too unwieldy.

The earliest classic formation was the "Vee," consisting of the leader at the apex, with others flying to his left and right in stepped-up echelon. Often an experienced "floater" would rove freely between the extended arms of the Vee, providing an additional measure of lookout and protection. Rejoin or rallying locations were pre-determined in the event of one member's dislocation from the main formation, since radio communication was not yet available. Precautionary commands to the formation, such as preparation for attack or a specific manoeuvre, were conveyed by the leader through signals such as porpoising the aircraft, wing rocking, designated hand signals, or firing of specific flares. Formation leaders always attempted to fly at less than top speed, so any member of the formation could overtake the leader to get his attention if the need arose. This procedure also ensured that all the trailing formation members were able to keep pace with the leader.

Formation flying and station keeping were very demanding, particularly during violent manoeuvring with frequent and unexpected changes of direction, and required the intense concentration of all involved. Staggering a formation in altitude provided some measure of protection to attack from above: a logical extension of this concept led to the "stacking" of multiples of formations with up to 4000 feet of vertical separation between them. When opposing forces deployed in this manner joined in combat, it often resulted in a pitched battle in several distinct layers. Frequently, opposing forces engaged from squadron-size formations, and all too often formation integrity disintegrated after the initial turns. It rapidly developed into what the Germans called a *Kurvenkampf*, resembling nothing more than bees swarming a honey pot in the classic image of the early dogfights.

The amount of regimentation on missions varied considerably. On one extreme was the fixed escort provided to friendly bomber and observation aircraft. On the other was the free-roving mission, called *chasse libre* by the French and a "roving commission" by the British, flown either individually or in pairs. These fighters could roam at will, their small or solitary numbers capitalizing on surprise. The greatest of all the "lone wolves," men who preferred to stalk and kill their prey alone, favoured roving commissions right until the end of the war.

The British emphasized offensive patrols, and at least two out of three combats took place behind the German lines.[16] Aircrew from both sides soon learned to exploit their favoured environment whenever and wherever they could. The Allies

Alan Duncan Bell-Irving (right)
and his brother Roderick, an infantry officer

preferred a fighting initiative. In carrying the fight east, however, they allowed the Germans to exploit the rising sun in the early mornings by placing it at their backs for an attack. Many Great War airmen from both sides fell victim to sun masking, never seeing their attacker. Fighting generally over their own territory also gave the Germans advantages with respect to fuel, advance warning, friendly anti-aircraft artillery protection, claims verification, and optimum use of the prevailing winds out of the west.

By the start of the Somme offensive, the Eindekkers were relatively easy prey for the new Allied scouts, and Canadians would factor in the downfall of several of them. On July 29, Lieutenant A.M. Thomas of Toronto in a 22 Squadron FE2b met eight enemy aircraft, including several Eindekkers, over the Bapaume-Peronne road. Thomas successfully attacked one of them and left it spin-

ning out of control. Three weeks later, on August 23, Lieutenant C.S. Duffus of Halifax, again from 22 Squadron, engaged five Fokkers attacking a photo-reconnaissance FE2b over the 4th Army Front. "We dived at the HAs [hostile aircraft], opening fire at about 500 yards. The HAs immediately split up their formation, diving and making off in all directions. We closed in on one machine firing two drums into it and actually set it on fire but after a few seconds the flame went out. The HA then dived rapidly for the ground."[17]

Although the RFC enjoyed a temporary aerial supremacy during the first few weeks of the Somme, not all its aircraft were performing admirably, and some of the newer or offshoot types proved unworthy or disappointing. On the positive side of the ledger, the Nieuports and the Strutters

gave a good accounting of themselves, both types scoring victories on repeated occasions. The DH2 also acquitted itself well, and 24 Squadron alone claimed nine enemy machines destroyed out of a composite total of twenty-five encountered in two separate engagements.[18] The first of the great Allied aces also began to establish their reputations: Albert Ball, a shy Nottingham boy of twenty, was the first British ace to garner widespread public recognition. Although personable, Ball generally preferred his own company on the ground, immersing himself in gardening and playing the violin. Flying Nieuports with 11 and later 60 Squadrons, however, he engaged the enemy like a man possessed and soon became the toast of the RFC. His preference for solitary hunting worked to excellent advantage in the early months on the Somme. He attributed many of his successes to closing on his enemies from their vulnerable blind cones to point-blank range and then varying the spray of his fire on them ("hosepiping") for maximum effect. By the time he was sent on leave to England in early October, he had already amassed thirty-one victory claims. Although some of these claims were inconclusive, his true worth lay in his contribution, through his aggressiveness and dash, to the morale of the RFC at a time when it was again being bested in the air by the enemy.

On the French side, dark, slender, and distant Georges Guynemer became an instant legend. Fighting alone or, more frequently, in the company of others, he was credited with twenty-three aerial victories by November 1916, and added a dozen more by the following spring. Again, his success was attributable to his unhesitating aggressiveness in combat, coupled with his superb shooting capability.

On the down side for the Allies during the Somme's early innings, 60 Squadron's Moranes proved to be exceptionally vulnerable. Their losses were so extensive in July and August that they were pulled out of the line for replacement with Nieuports. Duncan Bell-Irving, who had successfully changed trades from observer to pilot, joined the unit in late summer when it had completed only a partial conversion to the new aircraft. He was fated to suffer operationally with the Bullet, whose shortcomings were manifest and plentiful. Although the aircraft was streamlined, design flaws made it exceptionally difficult to fly. The mid-wing positioning blocked the pilot's view of the ground, the small wing surface made stalls in turns a routine occurrence, and, in the absence of ailerons, lateral control could be conducted only by wing warping. In short, pilots were more concerned with getting the aircraft back to earth safely than with its operational employment. In addition, the 80 horsepower LeRhône engine was very temperamental, especially the primitive magnetos, and it was prone to cutting out at the most inopportune times. The Bullets continued to use the deflector system with their Lewis machine gun, which was prone to jamming. The propellers needed frequent mending, since the deflector blades were often damaged. This mutilation in turn threw the engines off balance. Bell-Irving commented on the aircraft's sinister nature in a letter home from the period:

> I found my machine difficult to control the other day and had to turn very carefully. Next day I went up determined to find out what the trouble was. I did — or started — a sharp turn over the trenches. The torque absolutely took over the machine and I turned upside down and "arsy tarsy" for a bit and then started spinning downward with wings going in an opposite direction to the propeller. I switched off and came out of the spin O.K. but tried again several times but the same thing happened every time.
>
> I reported that my machine went out of control on turns. Another pilot went up to see if he could discover anything wrong. He did very gentle turns but even so couldn't control the machine and he crashed badly when he came down.
>
> I got a new machine and had it all fitted up the way I wanted and went out on patrol. On the way back my engine conked out over some high trees so I stalled pulling it over them and crashed into pieces on the other side. I was lucky to get off with a 4-inch cut on the forehead.[19]

Duncan Bell-Irving did not let the Bullet get him down and he scored his first victory in it by shooting down an LFG Roland CII escort and reconnaissance aircraft near Bapaume on 28 August, 1916. He spoke with a slight stutter, particularly when agitated or excited. Arthur Bishop recalled a

charming Bell-Irving anecdote related to him by Lord Balfour, himself a Great War airman. After crash landing his battle-damaged Morane in a tree on returning from a particularly harrowing sortie with extensive battle damage, Bell-Irving was confronted by a dim-witted senior official visiting from headquarters who asked if he had experienced some kind of trouble. Not one to suffer fools gladly,

The Morane Bullet, complete with deflector blades on the propeller

Bell-Irving stammered, "N-n-no you s-s-stupid b-b-bastard ... I a-a-always l-l-land th-th-that w-w-way!"[20] Bell-Irving eventually became the first accredited Canadian ace in the RFC after 60 Squadron's full conversion to Nieuports and was awarded both the Military Cross and Bar for gallantry. In November 1916 he was severely wounded in the legs and removed from combat.

The Morane scouts were not the only equipment disappointment for the RFC. That summer both 19 Squadron at St. Omer and 21 Squadron at Fienvillers received the BE12, a single-seat derivative of the ubiquitous BE2. Its sole redeeming feature was a forward-firing Vickers gun equipped with an interrupter gear. Amazingly enough, the lumbering BE12s, of which over a thousand were

built, managed to bring down a few German machines before their shortcomings exceeded their limited merits. They turned out to be moderately more successful when employed in home defence duties. By September, however, to prevent their total obliteration, Trenchard was forced to order the BE12 squadrons in France to stop operating as fighters.[21]

During the early months of the Somme, the German Air Service was at a distinct numerical disadvantage. It was also suffering from poor morale due to flawed, unproductive tactics, such as the barrage patrol, and from an excessively rigid organization and lack of cooperation with the ground forces. The German high command was loath to divert the air service from the offensive operations on the Verdun front to the British relief operation at the Somme. There can be no doubt that the RFC prevailed until late in the Somme offensive, partly because the Germans did not reinforce this air sector until the end of August.[22]

The British success was also attributable to Trenchard's unshakable belief that continual offensive aerial activities, including offensive patrols and bombing missions, were the most effective way of protecting their own artillery spotting and photographic reconnaissance aircraft. This aggressive offensive posture characterized RFC/RAF operational policy for the duration of the war. Trenchard later stated that offensive fighter patrols "were designed to find, engage and destroy enemy aircraft whenever possible, while bombing raids would spur German air commanders to seek air cover, which will result in the withdrawal of aeroplanes and anti-aircraft artillery from the battle area."[23] This offensive spirit soon affected most Allied formation tactics with its overriding philosophy of attack first. It had several advantages: it assumed a position of moral ascendancy; it dictated the terms of combat; and it concentrated the formation's attention on the leader's opponent. This focus helped to keep the formation together and to preserve its all-important structural integrity for as long as possible in an engagement.[24] Initially not all RFC officers were enthusiastic about formation tactics, though Trenchard had little patience for those who did not embrace his beliefs. This reticence may well have been due to the limited flight experience of many of his crews, for in spite of numerical superiority, the quality of British aircrew was an issue. Trenchard was forced to dilute his

units with many men who had very limited or negligible combat experience. Haig demanded twenty-four fighter squadrons in June, four attached to each numbered army, and four attached as "floaters" to his General Headquarters (GHQ).[25]

In 1916 the single-seat scout came of age. In terms of armament, the British standardized their aircraft with .303 calibre ammunition, fired by either Vickers or Lewis machine guns. The Vickers gun, which was also used by the French, was a lightweight belt-fed version of the Maxim and was mated with interrupter gear as the standard forward-firing armament on Allied aircraft. The Lewis gun was a drum-fed weapon that was frequently mounted on the top plane of an aircraft and designed to fire over the propeller arc. The Lewis also became the standard weapon for observers in two-seater aircraft and was frequently mounted on a circular Scarff ring, to which a movable arm was attached for weapon flexibility. The German equivalent to the Lewis was the 7.92 mm Parabellum, and to the Vickers, the 7.92 mm Maxim LMG 08/15, normally in a twin-machine gun mounting. The Maxims became popularly referred to as "Spandaus," after the German city where they were manufactured.

In terms of airframe construction, both the Allies and the Central Powers used wire-braced wooden box girders covered with fabric. Later, they turned to new materials such as plywood as a means of covering and reinforcement. The Germans pioneered use of this material in creating semi-monocoque fuselages, in which the shell of the structure was integral to the chassis itself. They also experimented with sheet metal as a structural cover.

In engine developments, the British favoured light alloys. While both sides used in-line and rotary powerplants, the Germans concentrated on in-line engines, which gave many of their aircraft a "long-nose" look. Although the Allies developed in-line and "Vee" engines, most of their engines were rotary, with mechanical simplicity and good power-to-weight and size ratios. The main disadvantages were that they tended to shed cylinders and that they lacked a throttle, so had no proper method of varying the speed of the engine. Perhaps the greatest early engine advance for the Allies was the 180 horsepower V-8 Hispano-Suiza engine that powered the French Spad VII fighter.

Opposite: A Morane Bullet of 60 Squadron, flown by Captain Alan Duncan Bell-Irving on August 28, 1916. He is depicted here shooting down an LFG Roland C II escort and reconnaissance aircraft near Bapaume.

First introduced in the summer of 1916, it was also built in significant numbers for the RFC.

The German response to the new Allied equipment initiatives during the summer of 1916 was to field a succession of D-series biplane scouts from the Fokker works. The DI was a slow-climbing machine with an in-line engine that possessed lacklustre manoeuvrability. The DII variant was powered by a lighter rotary engine and was more manoeuvrable but no faster. Subsequent variants such as the rotary-engined DIII did not offer much in the way of performance improvements and had a relatively short operational life over the Western Front. However, two types were worthy of note: the Halberstadt DII and the LFG Roland DI. Both these aircraft were powered by tractor-type in-line engines. The Halberstadt possessed a modest top speed of only 90 mph, but it was exceptionally rugged and quite manoeuvrable. The Roland was streamlined, and, while not as agile as the Halberstadt, was much faster. Unlike any of the D-series scouts that preceded it, its armament consisted of twin forward-firing Spandaus, making it the most heavily armed single-seater of its time. This weapon configuration would become virtually standard in all downstream German scouts.

While the Halberstadt and the Roland were faster than their RFC contemporaries, the corps still held numerical superiority and a morale-boosting offensive spirit. However, yet another German scouting type — the Albatros DI — was introduced to the Western Front air war in 1916, and it proved to be a decisive factor in the re-establishment of German air ascendancy. While the handsome little Nieuport 17 was a decent performer as a front-line fighter, it was rapidly outclassed by the upstart Albatros, which made its combat debut in August. Of semi-monocoque plywood and fabric construction, the Albatros was sleek and powerful, equipped with a 150 horsepower Benz or a 160 horsepower Mercedes engine, and heavily armed with twin Spandaus.[26] It was rugged, fast (109 mph), and relatively manoeuvrable, and in a series of modifications it remained the predominant German fighter for most of the balance of the war.[27] Still, for all the combatant powers, there was now a considerable delay between the appearance of new prototypes and the date when they became available in general service. Also, new fighter aircraft were frequently given to the most successful aces to fly for combat evaluation and, particularly in France and Germany, to showcase their individual talents.

Although the Albatros carried nearly one thousand rounds of ammunition in twin, synchronized guns and was propelled by an engine nearly twice as powerful as those of the DH2 and the Nieuport, it did not immediately dominate the pusher aircraft of the RFC. The lower wing loading and better turning ability of the British types[28] meant they were employed in ever-increasing numbers and used more aggressive tactics. While not as fast as the Spad or as manoeuvrable as the Nieuport, the Albatros possessed a powerful engine, a superb rate of climb, and much greater firepower than the Allied types. The DII was a minor update of the DI, but the DIII, which appeared at the front in considerable numbers after January 1917, encompassed a new sesquiplane wing design. As in the Nieuport, its lower plane was much smaller than the upper plane and it suffered from similar structural deficiencies in its lower plane.[29]

Along with introducing new fighter types, the Germans had also grasped the connection between a dominant air force and success in the land battle. This link was driven home forcefully after an engagement on July 24, when four DH2s of 24 Squadron attacked a formation of eleven German aircraft, successfully gunning down three of them without loss. In the autumn of 1916, sweeping organization changes took place in Germany, culminating in the official establishment of the German Air Force on October 8. Fighter aircraft units became distinct entities from the other service types that conducted general duties, such as artillery coordination, observation, and photographic reconnaissance. These new units were named Jagdstaffeln, or Jastas, and were smaller than their British counterparts, established for fourteen aircraft in contrast to eighteen. By early September, seven of these new fighter units had been formed, of which Jasta 2 was given to the redoubtable Oswald Boelcke to command.[30]

Four of these new Jastas, including Boelcke's Jasta 2, were assigned to the German 1st and 2nd Armies on the Somme. Boelcke had returned from goodwill tours on the Eastern Front with two promising neophyte fighter pilots in tow: thirty-seven-year-old Leutnant Erwin Böhme and a young, aristocratic lieutenant of cavalry named Manfred, Freiherr von Richthofen. Boelcke drilled his subordinates relentlessly with his fundamental tenets and techniques for aerial combat. He preached that if you initiate an attack, you must carry it through to a decisive conclusion. He also firmly believed that aggressiveness and determination were the most significant keys to success as a fighter pilot.

After a frantic two weeks of preparatory training, during which Boelcke tested his own evolving tactics with early morning sojourns over the enemy lines,[31] Jasta 2 descended on the RFC. On September 17, 1916, near Marcoing, Boelcke's Jasta attacked a mixed formation of eight BE2cs and a half-dozen escorting FE2bs. In the ensuing battle, many of the British aircraft were shot down. Boelcke scored his twenty-seventh victory, while the novice von Richthofen drew his first blood in what would become an unprecedented Great War career. During the trimester of September-November 1916, Jasta 2 alone gunned down seventy-six Allied aircraft for a loss of only seven of its own. Along with the other Jastas in the region, it completely outclassed the opposition, reversing the Allied dominance in the air of the early summer.

At the start of the Somme offensive, approximately eighty Canadians were at the front serving with the RFC, of which roughly half were with corps, army, and headquarters wings that would be active and regular participants in the upcoming operation. Overall, they constituted one-tenth of RFC flying personnel at the time — a percentage of the total RFC operational force that would hold true for the remainder of the year. While there were no Canadian casualties in the fighter squadrons in July, this record would soon change. In August and September at least ten Canadian fighter pilots fell at the Somme. Nearly two-thirds of all Canadians in RFC fighter squadrons at the time were in action over the Somme front. Paramount among these units was 24 Squadron, led by Major Lanoe G. Hawker, VC, an early RFC luminary and a pioneer in formation tactics. Second Lieutenant R.H.B. Ker of Victoria, BC, one of the founding members of 24 Squadron in February, had left the unit in July to become a flight commander in 41 Squadron. In May, 24 Squadron had expanded from twelve to eighteen pilots, and with this augmentation came four Canadian second lieutenants: H.A. Wood and A.G. Knight of Toronto, H.C. Evans of MacLeod, Alberta, and A.E. McKay of London,

Ontario. All these men would have significant wartime careers, although some would be pathetically brief. Arthur Knight, a University of Toronto student and graduate of the Curtiss Flying School, flew throughout the Somme campaign, proving himself as a capable pilot. Officially credited with eight victories, he was decorated with a Distinguished Service Order, a Military Cross, and a Mentioned in Dispatches before he became von Richthofen's thirteenth victim on December 20, 1916.[32] Two of his citations provide a taste of his accomplishments:

MILITARY CROSS (*London Gazette*, November 14, 1916)

For conspicuous gallantry. He has shown great pluck in fights with enemy machines, and has accounted for several. On one occasion, when a hostile machine was interfering with a reconnaissance, he attacked at very close range and brought down the enemy machine in flames.

DISTINGUISHED SERVICE ORDER (*London Gazette*, December 11, 1916)

For conspicuous gallantry in action. He led four machines against eighteen hostile machines. Choosing a good moment for attack he drove down five of them and dispersed the remainder. He has shown the utmost dash and judgment as a leader of offensive patrols.[33]

The twenty-seven-year-old Evans was a British-born Alberta rancher who had seen service in the Boer War. He had also been badly gassed in September 1915, while serving in the trenches as an Alberta Dragoon. Officially he was credited with five enemy aircraft destroyed, four of them in a two-week period, and was awarded a Distinguished Service Order before being killed in action on September 2, 1916.[34] Alfred Edwin McKay learned to fly at the Wright School in Augusta, Georgia. He scored four victories during the Somme campaign, one of which he forced down inside Allied lines, and he received a Military Cross for these exploits.[35] Since 24 Squadron flew out of Bertangles, most of its combat experiences took place in a triangular area bounded by the German trenches at Pozières and Bouchavesnes, the Bapaume-Peronne road, and the Bapaume-

Opposite: The end of
Hauptmann Oswald
Boelcke, October 28,
1916. Canadian ace
"Jerry" Knight from
24 Squadron and his
wingman have just
been engaged by a
superior number of
Albatros scouts from
Jasta 2. Knight is
seen here executing
a violent evasive
manoeuvre in his DH2.
The Albatros DII
directly above him,
flown by Boelcke, is
about to clip the
undercarriage of
Boelcke's wingman,
Leutnant Bohme.
This will result in
catastrophic structural
damage to Boelcke's
Albatros.

Albert road. Flying DH2s in formations of four to six aircraft at around 10,000 feet altitude, these four Canadians were involved in at least twenty air combat engagements between the middle of July and the middle of September. The following action, fought in the late evening of July 20 over High Wood and opposite the right flank of the 4th Army, involved Evans, McKay, and two British pilots. In the ensuing battle, McKay and Evans were each credited with destroying a Roland:

Their patrol encountered five LVGs (presumably the C-II, the German Air Force's equivalent of the BE2c as maid of all work) escorted by three Roland D-IIs and three Fokker E-IIIs. The highly manoeuvrable DH2s were at their best in the confused melee that ensued: "Lieutenant Evans closed with a Roland and fired half a drum at a range of

Lieutenant (N)
Murray Galbraith

only 25 yards. The Roland went straight down apparently out of control, and Lt. Evans was attacked from behind by two Fokkers, but these nearly collided and Lt. Evans escaped them and attacked an LVG firing the remaining half of his drum." Meanwhile, McKay was having his problems: "A Roland dived at him from in front, but Lt. McKay outmanoeuvred it and attacked, firing the remainder of his drum. The Roland ceased fire and fell in a spinning nose dive. Lt. McKay was now attacked by a Fokker which he could not outmanoeuvre owing to his engine being shot, so to escape its fire, he descended in a steep spiral. Lt. Chapman observing this, dived to the rescue and attacked the Fokker at 1000 feet over High Wood. The Fokker fell into a spinning nose dive, hit the ground … and burst into flames. Meanwhile Lt. Evans attacked and drove off an LVG and a Fokker. All H.A. had now been driven off."[36]

And what of the RNAS? During the Somme offensive, the specific role of the Dunkirk forces was to divert as many German assets as possible away from the Somme through fighter patrols and interdiction missions. Notable Canadians of the period serving with 1 Wing were D.M.B. Galbraith of Carleton Place, Ontario, and H.R. Warbolt from Dartmouth, NS. In mid-July, Galbraith of 2 Naval Squadron had caused a minor sensation at the Admiralty for the tactics that he had employed during his first successful combat engagement. On July 15, 1916, while 10 miles out to sea and approaching Ostend at 12,000 feet in a Nieuport, he was attacked from his stern by a German seaplane. In desperation the Canadian applied full throttle and full aft stick pressure, putting his scout in a loop that positioned him directly on his former attacker's tail. At a range of 100 yards, he emptied an entire belt of ammunition into the seaplane, sending it plunging into the water engulfed in flames. A second German, this time in a large two-seater seaplane, fell to Galbraith's guns on September 28. Galbraith was subsequently awarded both the Distinguished Service Cross and the French Croix de Guerre in recognition of these achievements.[37] A third victory followed shortly after his squadron converted to the excellent latest offering from the Sopwith works, the Pup.

The delightful Pup apparently acquired its unusual sobriquet when an RFC general, seeing the diminutive aircraft parked alongside the much larger but structurally similar Strutter, said: "Good God! Your 1½ Strutter has had a pup!"[38] It became known affectionately by this name by all who flew it, as well as being renowned for its exceptional handling characteristics. Its operational ceiling was nearly 18,000 feet and its low wing loading made it very agile, even at high altitudes. Before long the Pup was reckoned a match for the new Halberstadt and Albatros scouts, and decidedly superior to the new Fokker DIII, which was promptly withdrawn from the front. Still, it was not without fault. The Pup was underpowered, and when the engine was throttled well back, the machine-gun firing rate was unacceptably slow until modifications were put in place.

A Sopwith Pup

At the end of August and in early September, the Allies noted a new surge in enemy aerial activity. Although Trenchard matched this increased enemy offensiveness, he needed more fighter-type aircraft. The RFC's systematic bombing of enemy airfields had been somewhat effective in diverting German resources from the actual battle zone, but the raids were of a nuisance nature and did little substantive damage. It was the fighters that bore the brunt of this offensive doctrine. Before the end of the Somme campaign, the combination on the German side of functional reorganization, better aircraft, and improved tactics had sounded the death knell for Allied air superiority, and the Alliance would not relinquish this ascendancy until well into the following year. German reinforcements were slowly

transferred from the Verdun to the Somme fronts and, by mid-October, nearly six hundred aircraft were concentrated there, of which nearly a hundred were Albatros scouts.

In concert with the gruesome land battle being waged towards the end of the year, local air superiority allowed the Germans to add to Allied soldiers' misery through repeated strafing attacks conducted with relative impunity. In air-to-air combat, however, German superiority was not as apparent. The Germans had only marginal superiority in numbers and technology, and displayed limited aggressiveness while engaged in battle. Sensing diminishing resolve from his fighter pilots after several disappointing encounters with the new German scouts, Trenchard exhorted them on September 19 that "driving hostile machines away from our line is not sufficient. The pursuit and destruction of hostile machines must be carried out with the greatest vigour."[39] By mid-autumn, as Allied air losses mounted, the strain of air operations was taking its toll on morale. Yet all was not gloom and doom. An innovation called "compass stations," strategically placed ground arrow markers designed to vector patrolling Allied aircraft towards their German counterparts, met with some success. Also, the mystery of the pilot-killing aerodynamic spin was solved in October by Captain Balcombe-Brown of 1 Squadron, when he applied full forward stick and full opposite rudder to the direction of the spin. Duncan Bell-Irving was largely responsible for bringing this technique to 60 Squadron that autumn, and pilots were soon spinning their nimble little Nieuports with great alacrity.[40]

From early September onwards, Generals Haig and Trenchard pleaded with the home authorities for more fighter air power, and the RNAS was called on to help the RFC at the Somme in a more direct manner than before. In spite of interservice rivalries, the War Office persuaded the Admiralty to hand over fifty-six of its fighters to the RFC, but when further aircraft were requested, the RNAS refused. The sailors cited extensive existing commitments, but the real reason for the intransigence was that 3 Naval Wing, which was based at Luxeuil and already possessed fifty combat aircraft, planned to quadruple in size to two hundred aircraft by the spring of 1917. Although the RFC's reinforcement crisis and RNAS parochialisms caused considerable initial friction between the two services, by October 26, 8 Naval Squadron had become a possession of the RFC on the Western Front. Each of the three Dunkirk wings allocated a flight to this initiative, with Pups coming from 1 Wing, Nieuport scouts from 4 Wing, and 1¹/₂ Strutters from 5 Wing. Collectively, they reformed as 8 Naval Squadron[41] and boasted six Canadians in the initial cadre. Along with Murray Galbraith, who would be the first of Naval 8 to score a victory on the new unit, they included E.R. Grange of Toronto, Flight Sub-Lieutenant G.E. Harvey of Edmonton, Flight Sub-Lieutenants A.H.S. Lawson of Little Current, Ontario, G. Thom of Merritt, BC, and S.V. Trapp of New Westminster, BC. Grange, Galbraith, and Thom had all previously scored victories over German seaplanes. By year's end, the Dunkirk Command had essentially assumed responsibility for all Allied fighter activities over the north flank of the Western Front, releasing French fighter assets to supplement those over Verdun. Naval 8 was particularly successful once it was deployed to the Somme at Vert Galand. Of the fifty-two enemy aircraft destroyed by the Command during the entire year, twenty-five of them were dispatched by 8 Squadron alone during November and December.[42] Although initially equipped with different types, by year's end the unit had completely re-equipped with Pups.

When Haig and Trenchard requested an additional twenty fighter squadrons by the spring of 1917, especially after Trenchard had forecast that only eleven of a quality comparable with the German Jastas would be available, the Admiralty was called upon to provide four more fighter squadrons as well as enough aero engines to equip six additional fighter squadrons. In the end, and considering the dire peril of the RFC, the RNAS was powerless to dispute the legitimacy of the corp's needs. Eventually the RNAS agreed to provide the four squadrons with fifty-five Rolls Royce engines and half of the 120 new Spad fighters on order from the French.

Many Canadians were by now in RNAS service, and pilot candidates were being enrolled in Canada at a rate of two dozen each month. By 1917 there were at least three hundred Canadians in service with the RNAS, including 230 of the total officer establishment of 2764 men. However, the majority of the pilots were serving either with 3

Wing at Luxeuil or as seaplane pilots at the British home bases. Relatively few were serving as fighter pilots at the front, although those that were, notably Red Mulock, were being progressively employed in positions of higher authority as they gained experience. Under Mulock's able leadership the following spring, 3 Naval Squadron of 4 Naval Wing, operating out of Furnes, would take a heavy toll of the enemy against only modest losses of its own.

Along with the introduction of the Sopwith Pup, two new RFC scout units were formed in France: 41 Squadron with largely obsolescent FE8s, and 45 Squadron with 1¹/₂ Strutters. Even the Strutters were now outclassed by the Albatros DI and its successor, the Albatros DII, which was also beginning to reach the Jastas. However, in skilled hands, the Strutters were still potent weapons, and 45 Squadron alone would claim eighty-eight victories with the aircraft in just eleven months of operations. Simultaneously, the French were introducing a new aircraft type of their own, the Spad SVII, which began to re-equip their Nieuport squadrons. This aircraft was actually evaluated by 60 Squadron, but as the British thought they would soon be replacing their Nieuports with some promising British types then under development, the Nieuports remained in service with the RFC far longer than they did with the French Escadrilles de Chasse.

Although outmatched by the new German types, the Strutters and the FE2ds were still able to acquit themselves well in combat, due in no small measure to the presence of the observer/gunner and his second gun. It was the single-seat DH2s, the BE12s, and the older RFC reconnaissance types that suffered particularly during this period.[43] Although the RFC was now losing many of its experienced pilots in aerial combat, the losses were not entirely one-sided. A severe blow was dealt to the morale of the German fighter community on October 28, 1916, when Oswald Boelcke was killed after having amassed an incredible forty aerial victories. Furthermore, Lieutenants Knight and McKay, flying DH2s with 24 Squadron on patrol between Bapaume and Pozières, played a part in his demise. During a vicious scrap with Boelcke's Jasta 2, which left the two Canadians manoeuvring for their lives, Boelcke and his protégé Böhme ended up pursuing the same enemy air-

Opposite: On the night of October 1, 1916, Lieutenant Wulstan J. Tempest successfully attacked Zeppelin L31 as it droned over the fogbound English countryside. Having succeeded in his task, it was only through violent evasive action that he escaped the plummeting German airship.

Lieutenant Wulstan J. Tempest, victor over Zeppelin L 31, October 1, 1916

craft. Suddenly, another British aircraft, closely pressed by von Richthofen, abruptly crossed their flight paths. Both Boelcke and Böhme were forced to bank evasively, and in doing so Böhme's under-carriage tore through Boelcke's upper port wing. Although the collision was not violent, it damaged the underlying wing structure and extensively tore the covering fabric. The aircraft entered a long spiral dive and, at one point, it appeared that Boelcke had regained control of his fighter. How-ever, the damaged wing totally collapsed and Boelcke plummeted to the battlefield below, leav-ing his Jasta gazing on in abject horror. So perished the greatest of the war's early aces.[44]

While Canadians were carving out a legacy against fixed-wing targets in the skies over the Western Front, significant events were occurring elsewhere. Lieutenant Wulstan J. Tempest and his brother, Edmund, had immigrated to Canada in 1910 and homesteaded near Perdue, Sask-atchewan. "My brother, Edmund R. Tempest and I, were homesteading and horse breeding about seven miles northwest of Perdue, Sask-atchewan, when war broke out in 1914," Wul-stan recalled. "I was on the strength of the 3rd Division of the King's Own Yorkshire Light In-fantry (Special Reserve), so of course had to hurry back to England to join up. My brother came with me. We sailed from New York on the *Franconia* and had a very exciting voyage as we were chased by the German cruiser *Hardesrue*."[45]

Both men subsequently transferred to the RFC. On the night of October 1, 1916, Wulstan Tempest, in a BE2c, intercepted Zeppelin L 31 at approximately 12,000 feet over London. Amid intense anti-aircraft fire and in spite of a failure of his mechanical fuel pump, Tempest persevered and punched round after round of shells into the dirigible until "it began to glow inside like an enormous Chinese lantern."[46] Roar-ing by like a runaway furnace, the blazing Zeppelin barely missed Tempest in its ensuing plunge to earth, ending up in a field near Potters Bar. With it, the L 31 had taken Kapitanleutnant Heinrich Mathy, the most

famous of all the German airship commanders, to his death. Tempest received a Distinguished Service Order for his actions. This episode marked the last time a German airship attempted to attack Lon-don.[47]

Canada's eventual three highest-scoring aces of the Great War were all involved in aerial combat in 1916. William Avery "Billy" Bishop served as an observer with 21 Squadron in RE7 reconnaissance two-seaters until injuries sustained in a crash sent him to hospital in England in May. Subsequently, he requested and received pilot training. William George Barker of Dauphin, Manitoba, had joined the 1st Canadian Mounted Rifles in Winnipeg in December 1914 and had served with this unit in the trenches from September 1915 until March 1916, when he transferred to the RFC.[48] He also began his operational flying career as

an observer, serving with both 4 Squadron at Bai- zieux and 15 Squadron at Marieux. Flying in BE2cs, Barker was in action from the first shots fired dur- ing the Battle of the Somme. Many of his missions were exceptionally dangerous, flown in direct sup- port of his former land brethren, and known as "contact patrols." In his own words:

Contact patrol was first successfully ac- complished in our offensive of July, 1916. The objective of this work was to establish contact between the foremost attacking troops and their headquarters. The reason for establish- ing such a service was that by the old method of runners, and signallers, much confusion was caused during an offensive, by these men becoming casualties, resulting in very impor- tant and necessary information not being com- municated to headquarters.

Aeroplanes detailed for contact patrol, in addition to being fitted with wireless, carried a powerful Klaxon horn and other signalling apparatus. The observer on these machines had to be very skilful and accurate in map reading. It was also necessary for him to have a thorough knowledge of trench warfare, and infantry formations, and to be familiar with the area.

During an offensive these contact machines would fly very low, often near enough to the

infantry to distinguish our khaki from the Hun grey. His main duty would be to find our foremost front line so that our artillery could be directed accordingly.

The observer would fly low over the lines, fire signals, blow his Klaxon horn, etc. Then the infantry would, in answer, show their front line by white ground signals, placed out on the ground, by signal lamps, and by ground smoke flares, which they would light. The observer would then make a note of the situ- ation on special maps, provided for the pur- pose, also add any other information that would be useful, then fly back and by means of a message bag drop that information to brigade or divisional headquarters.

There also is another very important duty for the contact machines, and that is to be on the lookout for enemy infantry formations or counter-attacks.[49]

It is important to grasp the symbolic bonding of the corps airmen to their land forces, as it accounts for many incidents of extreme, often reckless, sacri- fice by airmen to protect their earthbound cousins. This spirit was also no doubt fuelled by the fact that many RFC/RNAS members, including Barker, were first active in the trenches. Although Barker's contact, observation, spotting, and reconnaissance

The Maurice Farman Shorthorn, an extensively used RFC training aircraft

Bristol Bullet

patrols meant exposure to grave risk from the ground, airborne threats also abounded. On July 20 his Quirk was set upon by an enemy scout over Miraumont, but Barker, who was a crack marksman, succeeded in driving it off. It was the first of several occasions when he had to stave off enemy fighters while serving as an observer. By November he had earned the first of his many decorations, a Military Cross, and was sent back to England for pilot training.

Raymond Collishaw of Nanaimo, BC, had gone to sea at age fifteen with the Canadian Fisheries Protection Service and served there until the declaration of war. In due course, he joined the RNAS, and by early 1916 he was in England undergoing pilot training. Benefiting from excellent instruction from John Alcock, who with Arthur Brown would later make the first non-stop flight across the Atlantic, Collishaw graduated a better-than-average pilot. However, his training was not without colour. At one point, while attempting to deliver a note from a chum to a local girl, he crashed into a row of outhouses, totalled his aircraft, and covered himself in excrement and toilet paper. While such is the stuff of legends, the young lady was not impressed, nor were Collishaw's superiors.[50]

Fortunately, war made for short supervisory memories. After receiving his wings, Collishaw was posted to 3 Wing at Luxeuil flying $1^1/2$ Strutters in both the scouting and bombing disciplines. On October 2 he apparently shot down a Fokker over Obendorf,[51] and on October 25 he scored twice over Luneville. Nonetheless, he ended the year by being shot down on December 27, though he was able to glide to the Allied side of the lines near Nancy and crash land. By the new year, he was a flight commander under Red Mulock in Naval 3, where his star would shine brightly.

These future bright lights were the exception rather than the rule for the Allies in the air during the closing months of 1916. As if by tacit mutual agreement, air fighting over the Western Front essentially ceased for the year at the end of November. Of the twenty-four fighter squadrons that Haig had forecast as needed in June, the RFC was still seven short of that number in November. At that point Haig asked for a further twenty fighter squadrons, stating they were now essential for local air superiority. Without this dominance, the corps squadrons could not carry out their spotting, reconnaissance, and observation taskings. The fighter squadrons were suffering higher casualty rates than the general duties corps squadrons, tangible proof that they were aggressively seeking out the now superior foe. During the Somme offensive and including the period from June to December 1916, there were 583 RFC casualties, of which 65 are known to have been Canadian.[52] Two-thirds of this number came from the fighter and headquarters squadrons. In terms of total Canadian aircrew participation, at least 240 Canadians flew in combat over the Western Front during this period, although by year's end only 130 of them were on active duty there. This number would soon be significantly augmented as the trickle at last became a stream. During the winter months, however, the seven original German Jagdstaffeln would grow to a formidable force of thirty-seven, of which thirty-six would be garrisoned on the Western Front. And the losses incurred by the Allied air forces in 1916 would pale in comparison with the sacrifices incurred the following year.

CHAPTER THREE

TRAGEDIES
AND TRIUMPHS

1917

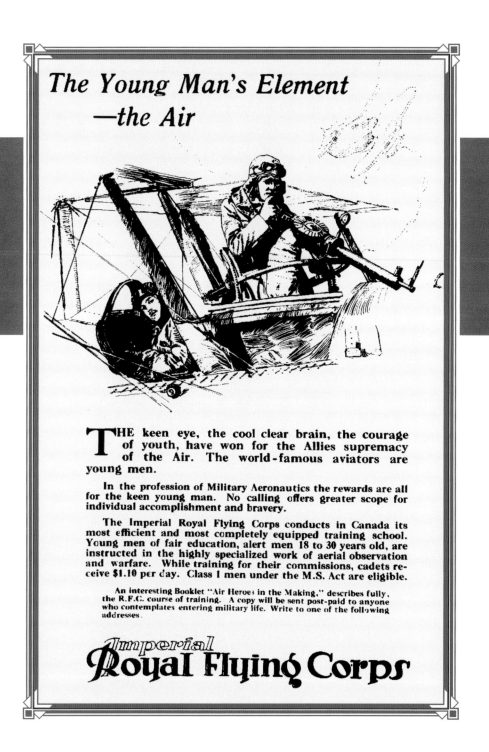
"A flaming meteor fell out of a cloud base by them and plunged earthwards. It was an aeroplane going down in flames."

— V.R. YEATES

To fully appreciate what transpired in the air above the Western Front in 1917, we must first understand the basic game plan for the Allied land campaign that year. French Général Robert Nivelle was a pivotal figure, for as Joffre's successor in overall command of all French forces, he intended to mount a massive offensive on the Aisne River in early April with all available French forces. This infantry assault would be preceded by a softening-up artillery barrage of overwhelming magnitude, intensity, and duration. The idea was to generate a French breakout within forty-eight hours, accompanied by a diversionary offensive by the British 3rd Army over the Scarpe River to the north. The British would eventually link up with the French after their breakout, somewhere in the vicinity of Cambrai. As part of the British subsidiary plan, the Canadian Corps, positioned north of the Scarpe with the British 1st Army, would seize and hold Vimy Ridge. There were, however, some ominous portents of impending failure.

The Russian Revolution, and the concomitant turmoil it created on the Eastern Front, posed a serious challenge to the strategic balance of forces. Unrestricted submarine warfare seriously threatened the North Atlantic supply lanes between the New World and Europe, and became a catalyst for American entry into the war as a declared belligerent. Closer to the battle itself, Général Nivelle ignored General Trenchard's cautions, and probably those of Commandant du Peuty of the Groupement de Combat on the Aisne (his own air command), that the Allies could not count on the air superiority they had enjoyed at the Somme. Nivelle's confidence was both unshaken and absolute: this massive assault, he believed, would destroy the Germans on the ground and force them to sue for peace, thereby bringing a rapid end to the war on the Allies' terms. No other outcome could be contemplated, let alone tolerated.

The effective use of massive artillery concentrations in this offensive was dependent on airborne spotting and control, which in turn demanded air superiority. The Germans also placed great stock in retaining control of the air and, by the start of the year, they had thirty-seven Jastas positioned on the Western Front to enforce their will. Most of the Jastas were equipped with Albatros DIIs, while the newer, faster DIIIs were also coming on board in significant numbers. The Germans had given up the notion of defending every square foot of ground, electing instead to thin out front-line positions and provide defence through strong reserve forces held ready for counter-attacks once Allied units outran their supporting artillery. As part of this more fluid defence plan, by March 1917 the Germans had withdrawn to the exceptionally well-defended Hindenburg Line, situated approximately 20 miles east of the old Somme front.[1] This new defensive line pivoted on the great bastion of Vimy Ridge, north of Arras, which dominated the Douai Plain below. It also eliminated two large and vulnerable salients between both Peronne and Soissons, and Arras and Bapaume. Vimy was effectively blocking an Allied advance into the industrial centres of Lille and Lens. Although the withdrawal adversely affected German morale, it greatly diluted the strategic justification for Nivelle's particular plan of attack.

The air plan for this spring assault was based entirely on Trenchard's unshakable faith in the

Raymond Collishaw in the cockpit, 1917

offensive. In a nutshell, the Allies were to acquire air superiority by taking the battle to the Germans over their own turf. Trenchard believed this plan would force the Germans to fight well behind the front, as opposed to over the lines themselves, and allow the army cooperation aircraft much more

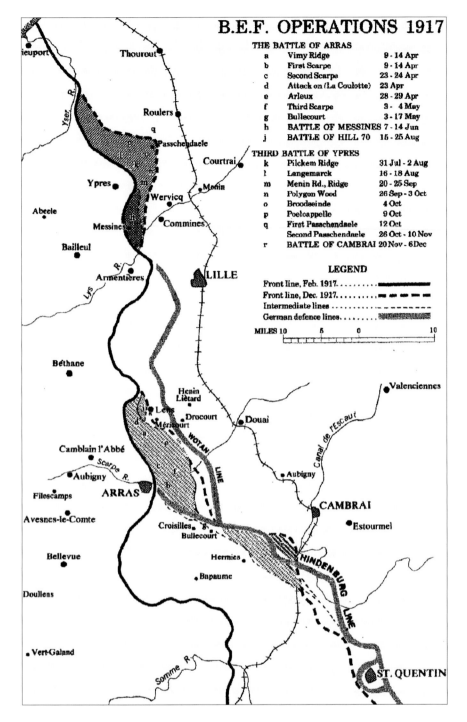

B.E.F. OPERATIONS 1917

THE BATTLE OF ARRAS

a	Vimy Ridge	9 - 14 Apr
b	First Scarpe	9 - 14 Apr
c	Second Scarpe	23 - 24 Apr
d	Attack on (La Coulotte)	23 Apr
e	Arleux	28 - 29 Apr
f	Third Scarpe	3 - 4 May
g	Bullecourt	3 - 17 May
h	BATTLE OF MESSINES	7 - 14 Jun
j	BATTLE OF HILL 70	15 - 25 Aug

THIRD BATTLE OF YPRES

k	Pilckem Ridge	31 Jul - 2 Aug
l	Langemarck	16 - 18 Aug
m	Menin Rd., Ridge	20 - 25 Sep
n	Polygon Wood	26 Sep - 3 Oct
o	Broodseinde	4 Oct
p	Poelcappelle	9 Oct
q	First Passchendaele	12 Oct
	Second Passchendaele	26 Oct - 10 Nov
r	BATTLE OF CAMBRAI	20 Nov - 6 Dec

LEGEND

Front line, Feb. 1917	▬▬▬▬
Front line, Dec. 1917	▬ ▬ ▬ ▬
Intermediate lines	▬ ▬ ▬ ▬
German defence lines	▨▨▨▨

MILES 10   5   0   10

developed in 1917 and 1918 into a war of attrition. No one can deny that it was the persistent policy of sending out small forces of British fighters to be overwhelmed by numerically superior hostile forces, that contributed in a major manner to the heavy casualties suffered by British fighter squadrons in France. It was the superiority of British production on the English home front in both aircraft and aircrew that saved the day for the British air arm in France. In practice, there was almost a complete lack of imagination in RFC operational control and the operation orders usually resolved themselves into an offensive patrol to endurance, at dawn and dusk. This process went on for years, as a kind of fixed idea. The German fighter control authorities were, of course, fully informed of this inflexible rule and numerous German autobiographies have since provided plenty of evidence that advantage was taken of RFC inflexibility of purpose, to send up numerically superior forces to overwhelm the patrols.[2]

In comparison, German air policy was tentative. Since December 1916, the German Air Force had modified its patrolling procedures. Hitherto, scouting patrols had been relegated to areas behind the German lines, but the new operating philosophy called for a presence directly above the lines.[3] This new approach proved to be a morale booster for the Kaiser's beleaguered ground forces, accustomed to maligning their air service for its absence over the battlefield. They could now see iron crosses, instead of only Allied roundels, when they looked skyward. Although patrols by lone aircraft searching out targets of opportunity still occurred, there was greater emphasis on massing aircraft together in formations.

And what of the RFC/RNAS equipment going into this air campaign? In December 1916, 54 Squadron became the first RFC unit to receive Sopwith Pups. In January 1917, 43 Squadron became the third and last unit to be outfitted with 1½ Strutters. With respect to the RNAS, 8 Naval Squadron had now been relocated to St. Pol, its place taken by Naval 3, re-equipped with Pups. Naval 4 also received the diminutive Sopwiths. The excellent new Sopwith Triplane went to Naval 8. This aircraft was a logical development of the Pup, with a third

unhindered freedom of movement. Nonetheless, even Raymond Collishaw, one of the most active and successful empire scout pilots of the period, later seriously questioned the wisdom of Trenchard's unrelenting offensive position:

While his conception gave lip service to the principle of war to sustain an offensive attitude, it conflicted sharply with the major principle of war, "to be the strongest at the vital phase." The general result of this policy was that all the enemy had to do was to count the number of aircraft on patrol and then to send up superior force to overwhelm them. The air war between the contending fighters gradually wing and a more powerful engine, and it had initially been planned for service with both the RNAS and the RFC. However, the Spad VII had also been ordered for both of the services via direct acquisition from the French and through licence-built construction in Britain. In a far-sighted attempt at equipment standardization and rationalization for operational and logistical reasons, an interservice agreement was concluded whereby the RFC took all the Spads and the RNAS acquired all the Triplanes. Consequently, both Naval 1 and Naval 8 received the new Sopwith in February and, by mid-month, Naval 1 had joined Naval 3 under the control of the RFC at the front.

The "Tripehound," as this new Sopwith was affectionately known, was compact and tiny. With the engine, pilot, and fuel cells closely concentrated, it was highly manoeuvrable. The narrow-chord wings afforded its pilot a good all-around view, yet the lift generated by the combined area of the three wings allowed it to outclimb and outmanoeuvre the Albatros. Simple to fly, it was essentially fault free and had no vicious flight tendencies. Although not as fast as the Spad or another new British type, the

SE5, it was still 15 miles per hour faster than the Albatros. Equipped with a rotary engine that produced significant torque to the right, Sopwith Triplane pilots would, in combat, attempt to place their aircraft as close as possible to an adversary, then commit him to turn to the right. The torque created from the mass of the rotating engine would aid the turn, allowing the pilot to gain continuously in terms of his nose position with the enemy. The air-

Two views of the National Aviation Museum's exact replica of Raymond Collishaw's Sopwith Triplane

craft was also so stable that it would eventually be used on trials to determine its structural tolerance to the force of gravity and concomitant effects on the human body. The "Tripe," as it was also called, was ideal for trials such as this, since if the pilot blacked out and lost control during a manoeuvre, the aerodynamically stable aircraft recovered itself automatically. Yet even this pleasing aircraft was not without its shortcomings, as Raymond Collishaw explained in a 1961 letter to an enthusiast:

> Looking back on triplane history, I now realize that the Sopwith Triplane was considerably underpowered and had it been fitted with more power, the resultant story would have been quite different. Increased horsepowered engines were available, but they were used later in new types, particularly the Sopwith Camel.
>
> Actually, there were three types of Sopwith Triplanes used in the Naval squadrons operating with the army in France. Sopwith sublet the manufacturing contract to two other firms. These firms produced faulty aircraft with skimpy-sized flying and landing wires; also cross bracing wires in the undercarriage. There were also two different types of engines used;

Sopwith Triplanes at RNAS Furnes, 1917

an English model and a French model, of which the French engine was far superior. It was the bad material types that caused all the trouble and ended the careers of the triplanes. [4]

By early March, 48 Squadron had arrived at the front with another new type, the Bristol F2a two-seater, commonly known as the Bristol Fighter or Brisfit, designed to serve a similar function to that of the earlier Strutters. This aircraft was powered by the first of the Rolls Royce V12 Falcon engines rated at 190 horsepower. The pilot fired a synchronized Vickers gun, while the observer had his own Lewis machine gun mounted on a Scharff ring. Fast, manoeuvrable, and affording the pilot excellent visibility, the Brisfits were initially inappropriately used tactically. As reconnaissance machines, they were told to stay rigidly in formation and to rely on their observers to fend off attacks by enemy scouts. The result was significant initial losses, until Brisfit pilots were encouraged to fly the aircraft more aggressively, akin to a single-seater, with the added bonus of a weapon pointing rearward. These tactics suited the aircraft perfectly. Flying a Brisfit, Canadian Captain Andrew McKeever of 11 Squadron would score all of his thirty-one

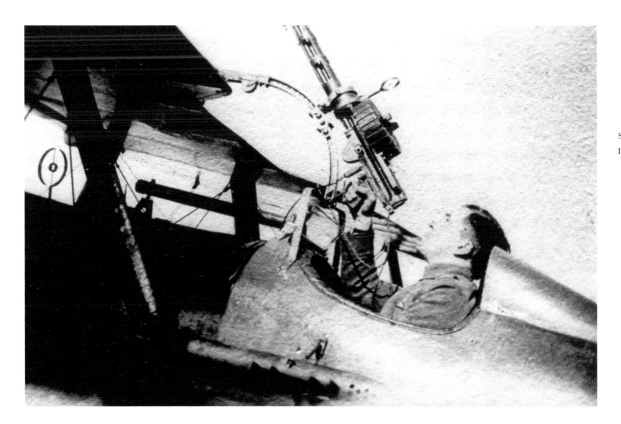

SE5a with close-up of Lewis gun and Aldis sight. The curved Foster mounting shows to good advantage.

SE5a in the field

confirmed victories in an F2a, making him the ranking empire ace of the two-seaters.[5] Later versions were fitted with 220 horsepower Falcon 2s, as well as Spanish Hispano-Suiza engines, and they frequently carried two Lewis guns for the observer.[6]

Breaking tradition with a stream of dreadful or at best mediocre combat aircraft, the Royal Aircraft Factory at last got it right with the excellent SE5. It was not as manoeuvrable as the Nieuports, owing to the high degree of inherent stability that stemmed in part from its in-line Hispano-Suiza engine, as opposed to a revolving rotary. However, it was ruggedly constructed, an excellent dogfighter, and it could climb and dive faster than most contemporary Allied types. It could also absorb extreme punishment in battle. Armed with a single synchronized Vickers gun and a Lewis gun on a Foster mounting atop the mainplane, it would eventually become a favourite for many of the empire aces. Its weakness lay in the absolute unreliability of the Hispano engine. However, once the Wolseley firm developed this engine into the 200 horsepower high-compression direct drive Viper series, the aircraft became the definitive SE5a, and the engine problems were solved. Still, the Lewis gun mounting left something to be desired, as Harold Molyneux, a Canadian ace and Distinguished Flying Cross winner explained: "To reload the Lewis, you pulled down on the mount, held empty drum overhead to be carried away in slipstream, reached down for full drum in rack between your feet, clamped it on and pushed it up on mount again. Quite a trick if you were in a dogfight!"[7]

One peculiar British scout introduced in 1917 was Geoffrey de Havilland's single-seat DH5. It had unusually staggered wings, with the main-plane set back approximately 2 feet. This design gave the pilot an excellent view to the front and above, but terrible visibility rearward. The DH5 was nimble but difficult to land, and its perfor-mance fell off rapidly above 10,000 feet. Eclipsed by other new types, it excelled low to the ground

and was used extensively for trench raids and other ground-strafing duties.

To complete the British air roster for the upcom-ing spring offensive, by mid-March 66 Squadron, a Pup unit, had also arrived at the front. In addition, 29 and 40 Squadrons would soon exchange their aging DH2s and FE8s for Nieuport 17s. The FE8 had been particularly disappointing in combat, suf-fering crippling losses as late as March 9. On this date, nine FE8s from 40 Squadron were severely thrashed by von Richthofen's Jasta 11, resulting in the direct loss of five and varying degrees of dam-age to the survivors.[8]

Geoffrey de Havilland's less-than-stellar DH5

Although the Germans, with their predominately Albatros-equipped scout fleet, possessed an overall performance advantage over most of the Allied aircraft types, they were still at a significant numerical disadvantage. During the first week of April, the British alone possessed 754 front-line aircraft, of which 385 were single-seat scouts. There were also French and Belgian assets. In opposition, the Germans could field 264 operational aircraft, of which only 114 were single-seat fighters grouped in depleted-strength Jastas. However, this force ratio is misleading. Trenchard had started the year with thirty-nine operational squadrons, but only twelve

could be classified as suitable for air combat, offensive patrols, and escort work. Of this number, only five units, those equipped with Nieuport 17s and Sopwith Pups, could be considered capable of meeting the Germans at close to technological parity. Also, the new types previously described would not be available in great strength until later in the year. Perhaps the brightest spot in the British air order of battle was the significant fighter augmentation that had recently been provided by the RNAS.

The land campaign in the British zone, collectively known as the Battles of Arras, began on April 9. However, it was preceded on the 4th by an all-out precursor aerial assault. The Germans, who were wisely selective in their offensive air tactics, had few difficulties in penetrating the Allies' air screen with small, flexible formations. By concentrating on the support aircraft and generally ignoring Allied scouts whenever possible, they wreaked havoc on the vulnerable reconnaissance and artillery aircraft. On the ground, the only battle of the campaign that was completely successful was the Canadian Corps' attack on Vimy Ridge on Easter Monday, April 9. A masterpiece of innovative preparation and planning by General Sir Julian Byng and Canadian Lieutenant-General Sir Arthur Currie, the capture of Vimy, although costly, was a decisive, proud, and important victory for both the Canadians and the Allies. It has often been said that Canada truly became a nation at Vimy Ridge through the courage, resourcefulness, and sacrifice of her fighting men. Four Victoria Crosses won there in one terrible day, along with the dreadful casualties, are telling testimonials to that claim.[9]

The generally accepted loss figure for RFC and RNAS forces seconded to the RFC in April 1917 is 316 airmen. Although accurate figures are impossible to determine for countless reasons, aviation historians Norman Franks, Frank Bailey, and Russell Guest more or less verify this figure. Specifically, they categorize 211 as killed in action, missing in action, or died of wounds received, while a further 108 were taken prisoner. This total does not include those killed in aircraft accidents. An additional 116 airmen were wounded in action, a figure that does not include those wounded and subsequently captured. In all, 245 RFC/RNAS aircraft were lost during Bloody April. The two-seaters took a hellish beating. BE2s topped the loss lists with seventy-five, followed by the FE2 force with fifty-eight. Of the single-seaters, Nieuport scouts were particularly hard hit with forty-three casualties.[10] Yet the air war was not without some rays of light for empire airmen in April 1917. At Furnes, Red Mulock's Naval 3 performed so well during the period that he was singled out by Trenchard for rare tribute: "The work of Squadron Commander Mulock is worthy of the highest praise. His knowledge of machines and engines and the way in which he handled his officers and men is very largely responsible for the great success and durability of the Squadron."[11]

scout ace, commented on the problems of these aircraft, as well as virtually all the offerings of the Royal Aircraft Factory:

What a misfortune it was to fly REs! Why did they use the wretched things? Probably because they were the product of the Royal Aircraft Factory, which, for one successful machine, the SE5 and 5a, turned out lots of deadly BEs, REs, and doubtful FEs … The Germans, largely through the skill of the Dutchman Fokker, had once obtained a great ascendancy in the air, but fortunately the

His Majesty King George V during a wartime visit to 3(N) Squadron

Almost as if to prove that the excellent SE5 was a fluke rather than a new standard of aircraft excellence, significant and demoralizing losses were further incurred on the two-seater community through the introduction of yet another lacklustre offering from the Royal Aircraft Factory, the RE8. Intended to replace the now-antediluvian BE2s, this mundane new aircraft acquired a fearsome reputation as easy prey for German fighters and for frequently catching fire on crash landings. V.M. Yeates, a British

inventors of the Bristols, the de Havillands, the Sopwiths had enabled the British to fight back. But still RE8s, with their RAF engines puffing out clouds of smoke from the chimneys over the centre-section, propelled at a maximum speed of ninety miles an hour, trundled lugubriously over the lines on their business of artillery observation, where they ought to have been shot down at once, or they killed their pilots by spinning into the ground.[12]

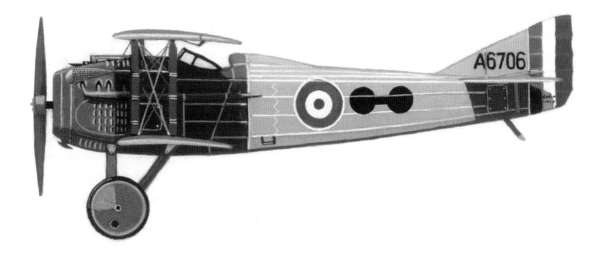

Spad VII

Why did the empire's air forces lose so many aircraft and aircrew during Bloody April? First, the concentrated forward fire from twin synchronized machine guns, now standard on virtually all German scouts, provided a thousand continuous rounds of ammunition. Even such excellent Allied scouts as the Pup and the Spad were significantly disadvantaged in this regard. Second, the relentlessly offensive posture of the Allies in large numbers on reconnaissance duties provided a target-rich environment for the Germans. Rates of scoring for the Germans were four to five times that of the RFC/RNAS, and the Germans frequently avoided combat when it was not advantageous for them to engage. For example, they did not rise to the bait when a large force of Sopwith Triplanes and Bristol Fighters over flew Richthofen's Jasta 11 base at Douai, attempting to taunt them into combat. The Germans adopted a new tactical emphasis, based on the urgent and predictable reconnaissance needs of the Entente. Hitherto the "lone wolf," or solitary hunters, had achieved prominence on both sides, stalking the air for suitable victims. Now both camps began to hunt in larger packs or formations. Mass engagements, or dogfights, began occurring regularly from mid-April onwards, exemplified by the melee on April 29 when von Richthofen led four separate Jastas into battle against a large mixed force of Sopwith Triplanes, SE5s, and FE2bs.[13] This concentration of forces by the Germans actually allowed the RFC observation machines, protected by massive scout umbrellas, to work with much less interference than before. The third reason for Allied air losses during Bloody April was that German tactics, once the decision had been made to engage, were now much more aggressive and effective. Typical formations used by both sides included two pairs in a rough diamond formation or the classic Vee. Fourth, the lack of reliable British engines at the time and the resulting blind faith in French engines caused a lot of Allied losses. The rotary LeRhônes and Clergets of 110-130 horsepower may have been marginally sufficient for light single-seaters, but were patently inadequate for larger, heavier types, such as the Strutters. Also, many of the British air-cooled stationary engines were copies of Renault designs, notoriously unreliable and underpowered. Fifth, RFC losses would probably have been less had there been more operational and developmental flexibility regarding the use of the two-seaters. For example, had the crew positions of the pilot and the observer been switched in the BE2s, the observer, now in the rear, would have had a much clearer field of fire.

Finally, overall technological inferiority invariably leads to a higher casualty rate, and such was the case for the empire during Bloody April. Trenchard's policy of the offensive at all costs may have been unduly vigorous and unrealistic for the corps at his disposal during the spring of 1917. But, in the final analysis, the RFC did everything that Trenchard demanded of it during all periods of German air supremacy, even in the face of daunting losses, and it never seriously faltered in maintaining its offensive spirit throughout. This attitude proved invaluable during later encounters with the evolving mass formations of enemy aircraft, and also during the extensive ground-strafing operations, which had now become a legitimate and frequent tasking for scout pilots on both sides. Those ground attack sorties became even more commonplace during the last year of the war.

However, the bloody assaults around Arras, which had originally been planned as a diversion for the main French thrust on the Aisne, were prolonged well into May. This delay was due to the utter collapse of the French effort, a debacle exacerbated by widespread mutiny among the troops. Nivelle was soon replaced by Général Henri-Philippe Pétain, the hero of Verdun, who promptly adopted a defensive posture for the balance of 1917 while he rebuilt the morale and fighting spirit of his decimated troops.[14] As a result, responsibility for further offensive action during the 1917 campaign season fell to the British. A limited success at the Messines Ridge in early June fuelled enthusiasm for a major offensive in Flanders, commencing with a push against the German defences in the Ypres salient. However, inclement weather, poor planning, inappropriately optimistic battle objectives, and inefficient, diffused use of resources easily overcame the great courage and skill of empire fighting men on the ground. In short, "while the great Flanders offensive petered out in the mud and degenerated into limited, expensive but largely vain attempts to gain minor tactical advantage, the struggle for air superiority went on unabated."[15] Furthermore, the British aircraft industry continued to introduce significantly capable new combat machines as the year progressed.

If one British scout aircraft manufacturer shone above all others in 1917, it was the Sopwith works. Close on the heels of the Pup and the Sopwith Triplane came the legendary Camel, brought to France to succeed the Pup in July. In was the first British aircraft to carry twin synchronized Vickers guns, the protruding breeches of which gave the aircraft its distinctive humpback appearance and nickname. The torque generated by its large rotary engine, coupled with its short, compact body, made it unstable but exceptionally manoeuvrable. However, it was not particularly fast, nor could it climb or dive as quickly as the SE5. The Camel was perhaps the most difficult aircraft in the RFC to fly. It was prone to spinning, especially to the right, and had no tolerance for an inexperienced hand. It was light on the controls and immoderately tail-heavy, which made it difficult to land. With a tendency to side-slipping, it had "a list of vices to emasculate the stoutest courage." At one point, nearly 30 percent of all pilot trainees crashed the aircraft on their first solo flights. However, it was a delightful aircraft once, and if, its pilot had a chance to get used to it. This training took approximately three months: "At the end of that time you were either dead, a nervous wreck, or the hell of a pilot and a terror to Huns, who were more unwilling to attack Camels than any other sort of machine except perhaps Bristol Fighters. A Camel was a wonderful machine in a scrap. If only it had been fifty percent faster!"[16] Peerless in a right-hand turn, the Camel seldom held the option to accept or decline combat, owing to its relatively modest top-end speed.

Camels turned out to be exceptionally well suited to ground strafing, and they were extensively employed in this role. They also became the leading destroyer of enemy aircraft in the air, with at least 1294 falling to their guns before the Armistice. One Canadian pilot who flew Camels with distinction on ground-attack missions was John M. Maclennan from Kelowna, BC. This Distinguished Flying Cross winner recalled that the Camel's big

rotary engine aided pilots in right-hand turns, but also subjected them to castor oil baths — a nauseating feature the British were not able to correct. "The poor chap behind them was half-blinded and more than half-sickened by a constant mist of castor oil lubricant which the engines spewed out in great quantities. The oil wastage was terrible."[17]

Sopwith Camel

Next out of the Sopwith works was the Dolphin — a formidable scout that has been underrated over the years. Also powered by a direct-drive Hispano engine, the Dolphin was relatively fast and, in the hands of several well-known pilots, particularly in 19 and 79 Squadrons, it established an enviable combat record. It was unusually configured, somewhat like the DH5, with a set-back mainplane, but the pilot's head projected through the wing centre section, thereby affording him excellent visibility in all directions. It was also heavily armed, with twin synchronized Vickers guns augmented by a twin Lewis mounting on the mainplane. Over 120 Dolphins had been delivered to front-line units by the end of the year.

The Germans did not accept these Allied technological advances without challenge. The outstanding capabilities of the Sopwith Triplane had greatly unsettled them, resulting in a frantic race to develop their own triplane. Fourteen designs for triplane fighters were submitted, but the clear winner came from the Fokker Flugzeugwerke, the brainchild of the brilliant chief designer, Rheinhold Platz. While slow, the Dr.I was exceptionally manoeuvrable, owing to its stubby wings, and was blessed with a dramatic rate of climb and descent. Although the Dr.I will forever be identified as the final mount of Manfred von Richthofen, many other great German aces scored heavily with the aircraft, including Werner Voss, Lothar von Richthofen, Ernst Udet, and Erich Lowenhardt. When it was introduced in August 1917, an initial construction flaw caused it to shed its mainplanes in flight, but full reliability was soon restored.

The Albatros was also improved in 1917, and both the DV and DVa variants entered service that summer. They were found to be little better than their predecessor, the DIII, and the DVa suffered badly from wing flutter. Still, it was produced in vast numbers and remained in front-line service until the end of the war.

The Pfalz Flugzeugwerke in Speyer had acquired extensive experience in building other firms' aircraft under licence, particularly the LFG Roland fighters. In September it fielded the natty little DIII, which, though slightly inferior in performance to contemporary Albatros and Fokker offerings, was robust and manoeuvrable. Like the Albatros, the Pfalz DIII had a streamlined wooden monocoque fuselage. The DIIIa had an uprated

180 horsepower Mercedes engine, rounded wingtips, and an attractive rounded vertical stabilizer.

The Germans were also evolving tactically. By June 1917 the decision had been made to amalgamate four Jastas under von Richthofen's command as a self-contained Jagdgeschwader, or hunting group, that could be moved rapidly to whatever area of the front needed a robust fighter presence.

Groupings of this kind were also made on a temporary basis for major offensives when they occurred. Jagdgeschwader I became known throughout the RFC/RNAS as "Richthofen's Circus," owing to its mandate of touring the front as mobile troubleshooters.[18] Dogfights between the Circus, other large German formations, and countering formations of Allied fighters, either on escort duties or on offensive patrols, became commonplace. These forms of engagements, as well as regularized trench strafing, would characterize fighter operations for the rest of the Great War.

By the beginning of 1917, the nature of the air war over the Western Front had become relatively well defined along boundaries that generally held true for the balance of the conflict. Organizationally, the combatants had matured into units formed for specific purposes and tasked with the support of specific ground units. However, air combat was no longer the only role for the scout pilots. Ground attack missions, such as trench strafing, were becoming routine for both sides. These missions were exceptionally dangerous, as the front was

now aggressively defended by many types of anti-aircraft weapons. Most pilots viewed these assignments with extreme trepidation. While the RFC emphasized the offensive, the Germans were generally content to, in their own words, "let the customer come to the shop." Overall, base locations and combat areas had become static and a certain routine had developed, punctuated by infrequent periods of dynamic changes during the various offensive operations. Technology had rapidly evolved, with aircraft types introduced in 1917 that would set the standard for the rest of the war. As air combat became more sophisticated and codified, the risks also became greater and more easily defined.

With respect to scout or fighter aircraft, two-seaters often made up in firepower what they lacked in agility and manoeuvrability. A few were lucky enough to have it all, such as the Brisfit. Most authorities, however, have conceded that single-seat scouts best answered the needs of the

role, provided they were fast, rugged, aerodynamically stable, quick in climbing and diving, well armed, and manoeuvrable.[19] Machine guns were considered the optimum armament for air combat. The French had introduced the LePrieur air-to-air rocket system, but it was deemed effective only against relatively large, stationary, or slow-moving targets, such as dirigibles or observation balloons. The standard machine-gun shell was from the .30 calibre/8 mm class with a firing rate of 600 rounds a minute. Ball ammunition was standard, but during the last eighteen months of the war incendiary rounds were used with increasing frequency, particularly against the highly flammable observation balloons. Tracer rounds were also used to adjust aiming patterns. By 1917 most fledgling fighter pilots were taught the art of deflection shooting, or "leading" a target, in the three-dimensional world of aerial combat, but only the best appeared to master this shooting art. Those pilots skilled in dynamic marksmanship, such as skeet shooting or game bird shooting over a variety of atmospheric conditions, enjoyed a distinct advantage in this environment. For most, the favourite method was to fire directly from the rear and directly aligned with the flight axis of the enemy aircraft.

Air combat tactics were first tentatively codified by the RFC in November 1916, and amplified in the March 1917 handbook, *Fighting in the Air*.

Flying Suit Advertisements

These guidelines included a number of attack options, based on whether the foe was a single-seater or a two-seater, and whether the attacker or the selected target were accompanied by other aircraft. These options outlined only the initial offensive and defensive moves, and not the dynamics of a typical air combat engagement. The outcome of the encounter depended on a host of variables, including weapons reliability, reaction of the target when attacked (assuming the attack had even been observed), weather conditions, relative airspeed and manoeuvring capability, and altitude advantage. Air combat was exceedingly stressful and dangerous, and repeated exposure to these stresses resulted in widespread combat fatigue. By 1918 probably two-thirds of those classified as permanently unfit for further air operations were psychological rather than physiological casualties.[20]

What were the attributes required of a successful fighter pilot during the Great War? He needed to be able to manoeuvre his aircraft throughout its entire performance envelope with both competence and confidence. Other desirable qualities included excellent eyesight, the ability to see the enemy first, coupled with excellent shooting prowess, a knack for flight path prediction, and the ability to visualize where aircraft would be both in time and space relative to the present position. Perhaps, above all, the pilot had to possess determination or gumption, the willingness to engage born of a brave heart. He also needed luck, for chance was by its nature depressingly random. Many pilots were philosophical: you either had good luck or you did not. Others hoped to cheat death or to charm it away, often becoming profoundly superstitious. Many coped with their fears by setting short-term goals for survival and frequently renewing those goals, dealing with their fate a week at a time. A distinct lack of imagination or speculation, together with an ability to accept life on a day-to-day basis, appeared to help. As British ace Cecil Lewis recalled, "We lived supremely in the moment … Our preoccupation was the next patrol, our horizon the next leave."[21] He said that he and his mates would often dreamily discuss what they would do after the war, but in the same tone as speculations about winning the Derby Sweep. Some men had a distinct premonition of their fate. Alfred William Carter, a seventeen-victory ace from Calgary, recalled just such an event relating to John "Punk" Manuel, a thirteen-victory winner of both the Distinguished Service Cross and the Distinguished Flying Cross, from Edmonton:

That late afternoon it was Punk's turn to lead. The Orderly said he couldn't wake him as he was sleeping very soundly. I went back to our Flight Commander's hut and shook him awake. He sat up startled and said quite loudly "I am going to be killed." I was taken aback but said something like — "Not you, Punk old chap. What nonsense. Come on. Let's get going." He came on down to his flight and agreed that it was his turn to lead but would prefer to follow this time. In the end, away he went. Manuel led the squadron in a long climb to the lines and crossed around 16,000 to 17,000 (feet), as was our usual practice. Well over the lines we saw a formation of about a dozen or so EAs a few thousand feet below us. Manuel stalked them, very properly manoeuvring to attack from the East, from which direction they would not be expecting an attack. As he led the formation down, he was overshooting a bit and I saw him do a rather abrupt turn to the right. His right wingman, Lt. Dodds, a newcomer to Punk's flight, flew right into him. The two Camels locked together and spun slowly down. Jenkins, his other wingman, an experienced fighter pilot, was devastated. We were all very upset, particularly myself. He was a schoolboy friend and we were so pleased to be serving together. As I said at the time, "No enemy aircraft could defeat Punk. He knew the answers to success in combat."[22]

Socially, the British upper and middle classes were somewhat overrepresented in the flying services. Public schoolboys were drawn in particular to the scouting units, where they exerted a great deal of influence. Yet the RFC, and later the Royal Air Force, appeared officially to place very little emphasis on an applicant's social standing or cultural background. There was an extensive mixing of classes in this newest branch of service, perhaps less encumbered by traditions and biases. Outside Britain, however, recruitment suggests that a certain amount of class selection based on service requirements was inevitable. With respect to dominion aircrew, a popular misconception in Britain held that the bulk of Canadians in RFC / RNAS service were "wild colonial boys" from rural backgrounds. In fact, three out of four came from urban backgrounds, where exposure to engines and other mechanical conveniences, the benefits of a higher education, and more frequent exposure to recruitment propaganda drew them to the flying services. Canadian historian Allan D. English noted the desired characteristics in a 1917 Canadian RFC recruitment campaign:

> The RFC's ideal candidate was expected to demonstrate "gentlemanliness, educational attainment, mechanical aptitude, and physical excellence, with a measure of recklessness thrown in." Recklessness was to be found in a candidate who "had ridden horses hard across country," or had "nearly broken his neck motoring or … playing hockey." An interest in "motoring" as proof of recklessness may seem curious today, but it would have seemed logical at the time, because, like an interest in horseback riding, it was a criterion for identifying social class. Automobiles did not become widespread until mass production in the 1920s, and during the war few people had access to a motor car. Knowing how to drive, therefore, often implied wealth and high social status.[23]

Within the international fighter pilot community, individualism was at least tolerated, if not encouraged. The personalizing of aircraft through distinctive unit or individual markings usually had official sanction. Examples are legion, from the specific names and personal emblems given aircraft of the French and Italian air services to the distinctive individual and unit paint schemes favoured by many German aviators. Under the influence of von Richthofen, the German Jastas were displaying a certain panache in the air. In a stroke of genius for unit morale, he had his Jasta 11 aircraft painted red, though all except his had some secondary colour as an individual marking. It was also a public relations coup: soon, many German front-line aviators followed suit with their own distinctive colour schemes. However, there were limits to acceptable individualism, and some nations discouraged it more than others. The British were much less flamboyant than other nations, generally preferring drab khaki, brown, or muted silver finish, except for the national markings in distinctive roundels and fin flashes. Still, there were many exceptions. Albert Ball's aircraft sported a

A Sopwith Camel, probably from one of the naval squadrons, in "gaudy dress"

Murray Galbraith
of Carleton Place,
Ontario, beside his
colourful Camel,
"Happy Hawkins"

garish. Trenchard and other British officials felt that the German and French custom of painting aircraft "in gaudy dress" was in poor taste. Some pilots suggested it was akin to shooting birds of paradise and that they "spoiled the sky."[25]

British leaders, with their public-school background, were loath to let individuals diminish the collective image and identity of the group. Squadron relations were not uniformly harmonious: jealousy and animosity were exacerbated by the forced closeness of the fraternal unit. Within units, extreme individuals — those who exclusively kept their own company — usually did not thrive, unless they were great aces. These men were frequently shunned as misfits: the Frenchman Navarre was difficult to get along with, so was Bert Hall, a remarkable American flying with the French Lafayette Escadrille; and later, his distinguished countryman, Frank Luke, acquired the same reputation. The Canadian Billy Bishop was to an extent similarly categorized, owing to his relentless determination to engage the enemy and his openly transparent personal ambition. Eccentric behaviour abounded, particularly among the loners, though they were obviously skilled, effective, and courageous warriors.

While the risks were great, the potential rewards had to be commensurately high to spur performance. Historian Lee Kennett has argued that the quest for glory, the recognition manifested in snippets of coloured silk ribbon and citations for valour, existed in every country. Today, society views such behaviour with cynicism, but it was real during the Great War, and many men were killed furthering these ambitions.[26] Decorations were causes for joyous celebration, their announcement being shared with admiring colleagues. They were tangible recognition of a warrior's tenacity, courage, and success. Others derived pleasure from the sheer sport of aerial duelling, which they often compared to the sport shooting of birds. They were the hunters rather than the hunted. Reactions to the deaths of friend and foe alike varied from outright horror to bloodthirsty glee, depending on the individual. The majority of airmen seem to have taken no particular pleasure from the killing of a fellow human being, unless that killing was motivated by revenge. Most fighter pilots seemed to accept that destroying as many enemy aircraft as possible, or at least denying them the ability to

distinctive red spinner on the hub of his propeller. Billy Bishop, during his first combat tour, featured a bright-blue cowling and spinner on his Nieuport. When his unit re-equipped with SE5s, his personal mount was even more distinctive, including much more blue on the fuselage, vertical stabilizer, and wheel covers.

The RNAS was generally more tolerant of these initiatives than was the RFC. Raymond Collishaw's "B" Flight of Naval 10 was known as Black Flight, since their Triplanes' engine cowlings, and top and side fuselages were painted a distinctive gloss black for ease of identification. "A" and "C" Flights of this unit used red and blue colour schemes, respectively, in a similar manner to identify their aircraft.[24] In fact, the markings of some RNAS units and individuals were outright complete their own missions, was their essential function. Donald Roderick MacLaren of Ottawa, who would end the war tied for fourth place on the empire scoring list with fifty-four confirmed victories, elaborated:

> Many of my friends have asked me if I ever felt any remorse for the men who went down with them. The first time I saw two Germans being carried away from their machines, which we had brought down behind our lines, I did feel it very keenly. But the feeling that was uppermost with us was a great love of our own fellows, and we knew well that every Hun who got away might kill one or more of our comrades later on. We had not asked for the war, and we were there for one purpose — to kill the Hun … It was my experience that our bravest air fighters, those who always fought to a finish, were the most courteous to captured airmen, and the most deeply grieved when one of their own men was killed. Those who were at all squeamish about the Hun were usually comparatively indifferent to the death of a comrade.[27]

Donald MacLaren in a very weather-beaten Camel

The great aces became fiercely competitive with each other for top honours, though this was not the dominant urge in all Great War fighter pilots. Most were simply driven by a desire to do their duty to the best of their individual ability, come what may. The select minority who were impelled by dreams of greatness were often reckless. Frequently, their relentless desire to engage in battle contradicted extreme fatigue and clouded their judgment, occasionally with disastrous results. This self-destructive trait is well documented, for the greatest of the aces also had the poorest overall survival rates.[28]

The relatively static conditions that characterized the front in 1917 made a significant impact on the lives of airmen. Units tended to be garrisoned for long periods in fixed locations, and the relative comfort of their living conditions frequently fuelled resentment among the troops in the trenches. Virtually all the empire scout pilots were commissioned officers, so they were automatically assured quarters of a certain gentility. Normally, two or three squadrons would share a common airfield location, with an officers' mess for dining and socializing, and occasionally accommodation. These quarters varied considerably in quality depending on location and circumstances. They could range from the relative splendour of a requisitioned chateau, manor house, or large farmhouse to a series of prefabricated huts. Often it was a combination of both: a larger building for common functions and huts for living quarters.

Food and lodging was based on the British officers' mess system. Regular meals were taken in the mess, the quality of which varied greatly depending on the resourcefulness and initiative of the president of the mess committee. Mess dues would usually average fifty to sixty French francs a week, but they could be substantially higher if a major celebration had been planned. Normally, the mess had a separate room for dining and an anteroom, often with a fireplace, for games and the bar. Junior officers regularly shared huts with three other colleagues, or rooms with at least one brother officer. A typical hut might have several small windows, heating from a tortoise-style stove, and contain a gramophone and a table for bridge. Popular recorded songs of the day included "Any Time's Kissing Time," "Three Hundred and Sixty-Five Days," and "The Bells Are Ringing for Me and My Gal."

Senior officers had more space and privacy. The messes and the sleeping quarters tended to be furnished through scrounging, rather than an organized support system.

Meals could include lobsters in mayonnaise, oysters, veal, lamb, and a great variety of salads, sweets, and cheeses, though normally it was more modest fare. Frequently, squadron members would dine out at local *estaminets* on simple meals such as eggs and chips, or head for a nearby urban centre when the mood struck for something more splendid. Alcohol, unlike good food, was plentiful on the Continent, and airmen partook extensively of fine wines and liqueurs. Excessive drinking was probably the single greatest antidote to the horrible stresses of combat, and it was encouraged at all rank levels. Flying while intoxicated, let along hungover, was not uncommon. "Whisky was nourishing stuff. No need to eat breakfast after drinking the distilled essence of an acre of barley."[29]

Post-dinner activities were punctuated by games such as billiards or Slippery Sam, much singing, perhaps a toasting fire, and a great deal of drinking and storytelling. There was much cynical talk and rancour about the war profiteers and the politicians, and speculation on how the world should be governed once the war was over. The mess often got quite rowdy: a life of inebriation, noise, foolishness, and irresponsibility, fashioned to help men forget the horrors of war, a kind of desperate *carpe diem*. Many craved the gentleness of a woman's touch to counterbalance the violence in their lives, and they were none too discriminate where this comfort was obtained. When comrades were killed or captured, their own friends sanitized their belongings for offensive materials unfit for the scrutiny of next of kin. Replacement aircrew were generally treated with aloofness by the experienced squadron veterans, who often appeared to resent their presence because they usually signalled the loss of a friend.

Some of the men faithfully recorded their life at the front in diaries. Robert Dodds, a ten-victory Brisfit pilot from Hamilton, Ontario, mixed domesticity and ground routines with the perils of combat in a curious, and perfunctory manner:

Officer's Mess
10(N) Squadron,
Droglandt, 1917

Tues Aug. 21 1917

Fine. MO called at 10:02. Fixed my ears & CO speaks to me about getting up sports. Wrote letters to H.F. and made out claims sheets. Went to sand dunes with Tuffield for revolver practice. Up on high patrol and didn't land until 8:30 PM.

F2b of 11 Squadron

Wed Aug. 22 1917

Fine. Up at 8:00 & went as bait over Ghistelles Aerodrome for Naval Wing. Attacked by many Huns and brought one down and Naval Wing didn't come. Millman's observer Price was very badly wounded. Went up again with Capt Letts for Gothas over Sea (North) and Power's observer was killed. Rec'd 3 letters from Can. Test gun on 7222 at 7:30 PM.

Thur Aug. 23 1917

Fine. Up on high patrol at 6:00. Had sleep after return. Rec'd new Pass Book from Bank. Wrote letter home. French Spad crashed on aerodrome. Up again at 6:30 PM on OP. Very cloudy, had to fly at 7,000' & very dark when we returned. Crocker my tent mate sick with Scarlet Fever. [30]

Leave in England was normally granted to only one squadron member at a time. Even in London, food shortages abounded, and it was difficult to get tickets to any of the popular musical shows such as *Maid of the Mountains* or *Chu Chin Chow*, or access to any of the favourite nightclubs. War profiteering was shamelessly abundant. "Everyone was still doing well, from newspaper owners and prostitutes to hot gospellers and cabinet ministers. An officer on leave, especially one with flying pay, was charged double for everything." [31]

Dressing down was common on an empire squadron in 1917. The fashion was to wear old regimental badges with one's wings, and very few

men wore the RFC tunic and cap. This individualism prevailed, even after the formation of the Royal Air Force and the introduction of distinctive new uniforms in April 1918:

There was a queer mixture of uniforms; or rather there was no uniform, and the new RAF outfit was intended to impose order on this chaos. But as no outfit allowance had been made, and the uniform was generally disliked, progress was not rapid. The typical RFC bloke still wore his wings on his dirty regimental tunic edged with leather at the cuffs and scented and stained with castor oil, a pair of oily but elegant breeches or slacks, a soft-topped cap pulled on with infinite rakishness, and an expression of hard-bitten sardonic wisdom …[32]

A typical fighter sortie on an empire squadron could range from a solo effort to a patrol by the entire squadron. The most common patrols were generally conducted in flights of three or more aircraft. Weather permitting, the average line pilot could expect to fly several times a day. Normally, there would be a cursory pre-flight briefing, which would detail the purpose of the mission and any significant details not considered standard procedures, along with special cautions and guidance to new and inexperienced flight members. The crews would then head to their respective aircraft, noting the colour of the streamers attached to their flight

41 Squadron pilots
on the Western Front;
the acme of sartorial
splendour

commander's interplane struts, which allowed for his rapid identification in the air. The aircraft starting sequence was extremely simple. First, for a Camel, the mechanic called "Switch off, Petrol on," which was repeated by the pilot, who pumped up the fuel pressure, fastened his safety belt, and then wagged the joystick and kicked the rudder to ensure that the controls had free and proper travel. He pulled up on a device called the CC Gear Piston Handle while the mechanic turned the propeller and the LeRhône rotary engine backwards to suck in gas. The mechanic called "Contact," which the pilot repeated as he placed his starter switch on. The mechanic swung the propeller, the engine fired, and the pilot made fine adjustments with his throttle. The mechanic removed the wheel chocks and, because aircraft of the day had no wheel brakes, he held the aircraft by the rear struts to help the pilot turn. Once airborne, the sortie could last from a half-hour to two hours or more, depending on the nature of the mission.

While most of the glory fell on the top aces, all aviators shared common dangers during the Great War. First, the aircraft, while significantly more robust than they were in the early days of the war, were still relatively frail. Production flaws

accounted for frequent and varied structural weaknesses. The pace of the war allowed for little aerodynamic testing and evaluation. Engines, although improving, were still often unreliable. Instrumentation was spartan and armament was subject to frequent jamming, usually at the most inopportune moments. Operational aircraft were not equipped with radio, and they were cold and noisy. Brooke Bell, an ace from Toronto, recalled that the cold demanded special precautions at altitude when he was flying Pups during the autumn of 1917: "Later in the day, I had my first experience of 'high flying' when our patrol went up to 21,000 [feet]. My nose and cheeks were frozen as I hadn't enough sense to put whale oil on them to prevent frost bite."[33] Protective clothing was far from standardized, and it had not yet become regular issue. A "gentleman" was expected to purchase appropriate flight clothing from reputable merchants or clothiers, as one would other items of dress. Lloyd Breadner of Carleton Place, Ontario, an RNAS pilot who was eventually credited with ten official victories, wrote to his mother about the problem:

It is frightfully cold up high [in] this weather and we are having a hard time of it from frost bite. It is getting to be a serious proposition. You know, we are the first to fly at the height we do, in winter-time. Yesterday one of the boys took a thermometer up with him. The maximum reading was 60° of frost, or 28° below as we Canadians speak of it. You can't imagine what it is like up there. When you are shifting through that atmosphere at 100 miles per hour it is certainly cold. We would all be very thankful to anyone that would send a Balaclava or scarf along.[34]

Pilot training, though greatly improved, was still rudimentary. The Wings badge was not now awarded until some simulated wartime missions had been conducted. However, little in the way of combat experience was passed on from returning veterans on a systematic basis, and what was done in this regard was anything but uniform. Learning to fly competently was stressful in itself. As experience increased, stress decreased. Training accidents were legion, in part due to the fact that stunting was officially encouraged in the belief it would inculcate an offensive fighting spirit. Of the 1388 official Canadian aircrew fatalities during the Great War, only 417 were killed in action. A full 451 were killed accidentally, and another 225 were killed with no cause provided, while 106 died with no cause provided. If nothing else, these statistics speak volumes about the inherent dangers of flight at the time.[35] Formation flying was particularly demanding and tiring, with the leader seldom flying a straight line in the combat zone. Meanwhile, those following had to concentrate intensely, anticipating regular course changes while also scanning the ground and the sky around and tending to the frequent needs of the aircraft.

The aircrew lifestyle was responsible for a considerable amount of stress. The competitive nature of air combat brought with it a pressure to excel, while the range of tasks required competence in air and ground firing, bombing, and reconnaissance. Food and quarters, while superior to those of the fighting men in the trenches, were not of a uniform standard. Further, when a unit was on the move, such as during a major offensive, the quality of both plummeted. During such times, the pilots lived in dusty, wet, uncomfortable tents that they shared with all kinds of insects. Food on the move could be a wretched meal of dog biscuits and bully beef. Virtually everyone drank too much and did not get enough sleep. Sickness was common, exacerbated by the lifestyle, the diet, and the

An Albatros DVa, immediately after capture. It may have been brought down by Canadian ace, Captain F.R. McCall.

climatic conditions in the air and on the ground. Besides actual combat, the cumulative effects of cold, anoxia (lack of oxygen), G forces, and unusual flight attitudes took their stress toll. And then there was the curious dichotomy of their lifestyle. Sholto Douglas, a fighter pilot during the First World War who became a senior air commander during the Second World War, felt that one of the greatest strains on airmen was the constant change from the civility of mess life to the extreme violence of aerial combat. And that change could occur in minutes. He attributed much of the insomnia, nightmares, and gastro-intestinal tract disorders, including the ulcers that plagued airmen during the Great War, to this phenomenon.[36] Fighter pilots, except for two-seater pilots, always flew solo, without the psychological support of another crew member. They fought and died alone, and many of their actions went unnoticed and unappreciated by their colleagues. Since so much independent action characterized the fighter pilot's world, initiative and a willingness to engage were definite prerequisites to success.

For the two-seater crews, the risks were similar, but the crew concept provided some measure of comfort through shared perils. Crews relied enormously on each other and also developed mutual respect. F.C. Farrington was gunner/observer to thirty-five-victory ace Frederick McCall of Vernon,

Captain F.R. McCall

BC. Although McCall scored the majority of his victories in single-seat SE5as, he cut his combat teeth in two-seater RE8s, and undoubtedly owed much of his later success to lessons learned while working with Farrington. "It was my great privilege in 1917, whilst serving with No. 13 Squadron, to accompany Freddy McCall as his observer on his first trip over the lines, and afterwards to become his regular observer."[37] Still, a good-natured banter war developed between the two-seater and the single-seater fighter communities, exemplified by this incident involving Canadian Brisfit ace Andy McKeever:

A Canadian fighter pilot recalls an occasion on which McKeever intervened in a dogfight between Scout Experimental 5as and Albatroses. It had been an even fight, but the SE5as were far from home and dangerously low on fuel. The enemy seemed to sense their advantage and to be pressing it fully — until the sudden appearance of a Bristol in their midst. 'Naturally we were grateful for any kind of help ... but it was damn humiliating for SEs to be rescued by a two-seater!'[38]

However, of all the stressors dealt with by aircrew of the Great War, perhaps none held a more mind-numbing fear than that of fire in the air:

A flaming meteor fell out of a cloud close by them and plunged earthwards. It was an aeroplane going down in flames from some fight above the clouds. Where it fell the atmosphere was stained by a thanatognomonic black streak.[39]

The thought of being shot down in flames. That was my one trouble. We had no parachutes. If we were on fire, we'd had it, and you got 16 gallons of petrol sitting on your lap.[40]

One's heart beats more quickly when the adversary, whose face one has just seen, goes down in flames.[41]

Faced with this most dreadful of all aerial fates, a Great War fighter pilot had very limited choices. He could resign himself to roasting alive in his cockpit, step smartly over the side and plummet to his death, or shoot himself with a service revolver. While many pilots are known to have stayed with the aircraft, others jumped rather than burn, an occurrence witnessed regularly by both sides. The trauma from such a crash usually obliterated any evidence of the third choice, but many, including the high-scoring Irish ace Mick Mannock, vehemently maintained they would exercise this option if necessary and carried sidearms aloft for just that purpose. Mannock was shot down in flames on July 26, 1918. What makes this death in a hell of blazing petrol even more reprehensible was the exceptionally callous attitude of the British Air Board with respect to the non-issue of suitable parachutes, which were available by the summer of 1916. In the autumn of 1915 the Air Board had made the following shameful declaration on the subject:

> It is the opinion of the Board that the present form of parachute is not suitable for use in aeroplanes and should only be used by balloon observers. It is also the opinion of the Board that the presence of such an apparatus might impair the fighting spirit of pilots and cause them to abandon machines which might otherwise be capable of returning to base for repair.[42]

In short, the Air Board did not trust its pilots to do their duty. Even later in the war, when a Calthrop "Guardian Angel" parachute, suitable for even small aircraft, was successfully demonstrated in early 1917, the Air Board did yet another cold side-step on the issue. Although it was true that some refinement of the device was still needed, the board flatly rejected the issue of parachutes. It stated that safety was not considered particularly important and that the ignorance of pilots, coupled with the fact that many accidents occurred at low level on takeoff, landing, or while stunting, mitigated against their acquisition and development. By the spring of 1918 the Germans had successfully used parachutes in combat aircraft. One of the lives saved by this device was the great ace Ernst Udet, who parachuted to safety on June 29, 1918. Sholto Douglas said he was disgusted when he discovered it had been official British policy to deny aircrew the use of parachutes, even when they were available.[43] As it transpired, it was not until the mid-1920s that an Irwin free-fall parachute of American design was introduced into Royal Air Force service. Strangely enough, while it

is true that some pilots vilified their seniors for withholding parachutes during the war, there was a macho bravado from others that scorned their use. While these sentiments may have been doubted privately, they were publicly expressed, and they played a hand in stifling any organized pressure on the system to provide parachutes.

The British method of dealing with aircrew who succumbed under the weight of stress harked back to the Victorian concept of self-control. Any mental illness or neurosis was viewed as a cowardly, hereditary weakness that denoted immorality in an individual.[44] Although British authorities had accepted the few psychological casualties in the opening rounds of the war, the large number of

Scout pilot with 41 Squadron SE5a, Western Front

such cases that were appearing by the end of 1915 raised serious questions about the moral fibre of the entire British Army. They accepted the term *shell shock* as a legitimate diagnosis, and victims were provided, in most cases, with the same care and attention as those who suffered physical wounds. In due course, *flying stress* became recognized as a subset of shell shock. This flying fatigue, or ex-

Bristol F2b

haustion due to combat stress, often made a tired pilot lethargic, to the extent that he could not even manoeuvre in his own defence. While the RFC and the RNAS treated such cases separately, many of the treatments were similar, though the RNAS tended to dedicate many more medical officers to the care of aircrew. Most medical officers felt that treatment should be simple and conducted as close to the front lines as possible. One RNAS medical officer, Sheldon Dudley, criticized the practice of granting leave at fixed periods "because … given the nature of flying stress this was illogical. Instead, he suggested a policy of judicious and generous granting of leave when individual fliers needed a rest, even if only to special cases selected by the MO and squadron commander, to get more hours of operations flying out of the combat flyer."[45] An RFC medical officer, James L. Birley, also determined that virtually every airman would eventually become a psychological casualty if he remained in action long enough.[46] Although no overall flying stress casualty statistics are available from the Great War, it was not uncommon for the malady to

permeate entire units, particularly if leaders such as the squadron and flight commanders suffered combat burnout.

The major combative powers had vastly different ways of processing and awarding victory claims for aerial combat. Both the German and the French authorities were quick to seize on the propaganda and morale value of this new breed of individual warrior, the fighter ace. In doing so, they kept careful track of the rising scores of their luminaries and devoted extensive publicity to their exploits. The British, however, were uncomfortable with individual glorification, because it contradicted their public-school values of teamwork and unit solidarity.

Under the German system of claims accreditation, only one pilot was allocated a specific victory, meaning there were no shared credits. Further, accreditation was not awarded for merely damaging an enemy aircraft, but only for its destruction or capture. To become an "ace," or Aberkanone, by German accounting, an airman had to destroy ten or more enemy aircraft — and the Germans would

eventually declare 375 of their airmen to be aces.[47] They required physical evidence of a combat victory, proof they could normally obtain because most air combats took place behind German lines.

The French system also demanded proof of capture or destruction, and, after mid-1915, enemy aircraft forced to land behind their own lines were no longer counted. Unlike the Germans, however, the French allowed all the members of a successful flight to share the claim. Under the French system, 159 scout pilots were recognized as aces, which, by their rules, required the vanquishing of only five enemy aircraft. An individual could be proclaimed an ace for having participated in the destruction of an enemy aircraft in five or more decisive engagements, in which the victory may have been shared many ways.

The British adopted the most complicated and also the least accurate national scoring system. Accreditation records were scrupulously maintained, and British aviators were allowed to count enemy aircraft they had "forced to land" (FTL), "driven down" (DD) behind German lines, and "driven down out of control" (DDOOC), as well as those that were actually destroyed or captured. Shared victories were also permitted. This system made sense, given that the main British objective was to deny the enemy the ability to complete its mission, whether or not that intervention resulted in actual destruction. These moral victories were in step with the British philosophy of team results rather than individual aggrandizement. By 1917, as better armament led to a far greater proportion of decisive victories, credits were limited to aircraft destroyed, captured, or driven down out of control, where there was little likelihood of the victim recovering. Credit was also given for a forced-to-land claim behind Allied lines, where an aircraft could subsequently be captured, but the mere driven-down category was no longer deemed admissible.[48] Daily communiqués issued by Headquarters RFC France included the majority of the air combat claims. After May 1918 the driven-down-out-of-control category was not listed, owing to its sheer volume, though it continued to be processed as a victory. In terms of processing, the squadrons filled out combat reports, which were sent to the wing headquarters to which the squadrons were attached. The wing commander allowed or disallowed them, and passed them all up to brigade headquarters. By 1918 wing commanders were consciously attempting to eliminate duplicate claims and limit the amount of out-of-control submissions. Brigade review and approval procedure tended to mirror that performed by the wing, but it was not uncommon for a decision by the wing to be overturned by the brigade.

The main weakness in the system was the lack of any centralized review process. Two or more patrols from different units engaged in the same fight individually claimed all the enemy aircraft attacked. By 1917 the scale of air fighting had become enormous, and it was not uncommon to have thirty or more empire claims made in a single day. By 1918 fifty-plus claim days were numerous. It was also difficult for the Allies, who deliberately fought the bulk of their engagements over enemy territory, to confirm the ultimate results. In the circumstances, empire forces alone claimed over seven thousand victories from the middle of 1916, from an Allied wartime total of nearly twelve thousand claims. German tabulations, in contrast, allow for only three thousand aircraft losses on the Western

KNIGHTS OF THE AIR

Front. The true figure probably falls somewhere in between.[49]

Why the great disparity? German record keeping could be capricious, and many Jastas did not list their non-fatal casualties.[50] In addition, most surviving German records appear to be extracts from longer documents, so it is not possible to counterbalance the losses incurred by one side with the opponent's declared victories. From the British perspective, no ground witnesses and no specific air witnesses were required, although other aircrew members or ground observers could add confirmation statements to a claim submission. There was also an arrogance to the British system, which in this respect trusted their pilots and crews, unlike the French and the German systems, which required witnesses or ground confirmation. Reliable sources have claimed that only 325 of the 863 empire aces would have qualified under the rules of the Second World War.[51] Moreover, none of the other combatant nations included unconfirmed claims in their fighter pilots' official scores.

There is no doubt that some squadron commanders and wing commanders were conscious of scores, of how these statistics would reflect on the reputations of their organizations. They made isolated efforts to increase individual scores as much as possible, though there is no evidence of widespread fraudulent activity in this regard. Rather, there may have been some tendency to grant an individual the occasional benefit of the doubt, based on a known record and observed past performance. Christopher Shores maintains that the reasons for particularly zealous reporting range from boosting morale to fostering an offensive spirit, often in times of dire peril. These claims may also have been made to justify the award of decorations, which were based on tangible success in aerial combat. For empire two-seater crews, the pilot received credit for a victory whether it came from his or his gunner's weapon. The gunner received credit only for victories achieved with his own weapon. All the combatants accorded the destruction of an observation balloon a similar weight of importance as the destruction of a heavier-than-air aircraft.

The final comment on this complex, often emotional subject is that the Great War triggered the first of history's air combat engagements. Although it has become enormously popular to second-guess

the motives and methodology of the claims verification processes, little thought was devoted to these issues at the time. No one expected that historians and enthusiasts would pore over statistics once the war had ended.

The marriage of the scout aces to the wartime propaganda apparatus became a match made in heaven. With the demise of the idolized cavalrymen, the public ached for new heroes, but the collective anonymity of the carnage on the Western Front tended to mask feats of individual heroism. Submarine captains and scout pilots became the exceptions: their individual victories were easily tabulated, and the public identified with these warriors from the lower ranks.[52] From 1916 on, the air aces received vast press coverage. They caught the public's imagination as a new type of warrior: solitary aerial duellists who became the modern version of the jousting knights. The attention afforded these knights greatly outweighed their physical contribution to the war effort, for the impact made by air power during the Great War was anything but decisive in the larger sense. In the province of national morale, however, their impact was significant.[53] Photographs, postcards, and biographies of them flooded home markets, and they were encouraged to write autobiographies. These books sold exceptionally well, especially those dealing with Georges Guynemer, Manfred von Richthofen, Silvio Scaroni, and, eventually, Billy Bishop. Society's élite vied shamelessly with each other to be seen in their presence and to cater to their every whim. The great aces were frequently banned from further combat, as governments feared the effect their demise could have on public morale. When they were killed, they were normally granted state funerals worthy of kings and emperors, and the public mourned accordingly.[54]

The German high command was particularly quick to exploit its individual heroes, for it gave the German people something to think about beyond the dreadful stalemate on the Western Front and the drain it was exacting on their male youth. Propaganda issued by the Imperial General Staff portrayed the air aces as models of the highest German values — intelligence, decency, sense of duty, and courage. The official versions of events, as dictated to journalists, were often utter fabrications or at least distortions of reality.[55] Successful warriors in Germany were idolized and placed on the highest rung of the societal ladder, particularly the winners of the coveted Blue Max, the Ordre pour le Mérite.

The British, in contrast, stubbornly refused to publicize the exploits of their successful airmen. The air commander, General Sir Hugh Trenchard, insisted that "special treatment would be invidious and likely to cause jealousy both inside and outside the RFC."[56] He did not realize, according to Arthur Gould Lee, a decorated scout ace with 46 Squadron who later became an air vice-marshal, that human beings need heroes, particularly in time of war, to sustain courage, to stir pride and admiration, and to inspire patriotism.[57] The British press at the time could mention the achievements of empire airmen, but not the specific aircrew responsible for them. The sole exceptions to this policy were the posthumous tributes paid to young Albert Ball. By mid-1917 the War Office began to give grudging permission to publish limited articles on the leading British airmen, though this public recognition never approached the formidable press coverage given to air heroes in Germany, Italy, France, and the United States. Canada, Australia, and the other dominions opposed this official reticence and eventually chose to honour their own men in their own way.

Within both the RFC and the RNAS, Canadian airmen greatly distinguished themselves over the Western Front as scout pilots in 1917, particularly during the latter half of the year. However, some exceptional performances were also being recorded during the early months. Captain Carleton Main Clement of Vancouver would score eight of his fourteen official victories, all with 22 Squadron, in obsolete FE2bs, including one in 1916, before converting to Brisfits in July. At the time of his death from ground fire on August 12, he was by far the most successful member of his squadron. Between March and May, Lieutenant R.G. Malcom, flying FE2ds with 24 Squadron, destroyed eight enemy aircraft in short order. Most of his victories were over Albatros scouts, and Malcom was awarded the Military Cross for his efforts. Another Canadian FE2d pilot, Lieutenant Harold Waddell Joslyn from Sintaluta, Saskatchewan, claimed seven Albatros DV scouts while flying with 20 Squadron between June and August. A skilled and tenacious air fighter, he was killed in action on August 17, 1917, in the Halluin area.

Captain Reginald Theodore Carlos Hoidge of 56 Squadron, stationed at Vert Galand, was one of the earliest SE5 pilots. Flying this aircraft and its SE5a successor, Hoidge scored twenty-seven of his twenty-eight officially confirmed victories in 1917. Awarded a Military Cross and Bar, Hoidge consistently displayed great dash, keenness, and devotion to duty. On September 14, for example, he experienced severe engine and gun malfunctions after attacking a large formation of enemy aircraft. In the ensuing battle exit, Hoidge was driven down from 7000 feet to 600 feet, and was also carried 5 miles behind enemy

Captain R.T. Hoidge in his SE5a. Note the elaborate windscreen for the period; a local modification.

On the evening of September 11, 1917,
Canadian ace Captain Reginald
Theodore Carlos Hoidge and Major
James McCudden of 56 Squadron were
involved in a complex dogfight with
various Albatros DVs. These enemy
scouts were most probably from
Jasta 5, the Green Tails, and they
were frequent adversaries.

Hoidge is seen in SE5a B4851 and
McCudden is in his usual mount,
SE5a B4863. Note the addition
of a heightened cockpit fairing
on McCudden's aircraft, which
reduced turbulence in the cockpit.

Opposite: Captain
A.T. Whealy, a
27-victory ace, and
his Sopwith Camel.
Note the 25-lb.
Cooper bombs by
the wheel.

Below right: Lloyd
Breadner, future
Chief of Air Staff,
in the cockpit

lines. It was only through his determination and skill that he was able to bring his badly shot-up scout back to home base. Hoidge was also innovative on the ground, as one of his squadron mates, British ace James B. McCudden, VC, recalled: "The cold weather was now coming on, and we began to make our quarters and Mess more comfortable. Hoidge, who was before the war an architect, designed a wonderful brick fireplace, for which we had to enlarge the Mess specially, and the fireplace took weeks to build. Eventually, shortly after it was completed, we, needless to say, received orders to move."[58] On September 23, in the company of McCudden and many others, Hoidge was one of the participants in the epic last air battle of German ace Werner Voss. The British ace, Lieutenant A.P.F. Rhys-Davids, was actually credited with the victory, but not before the pilot of the silver-blue triplane with the painted face on its cowling put bullet holes in all the opposing SE5s!

The RNAS boasted a disproportionate number of Canadian scout aces in 1917. Joseph Stewart Temple Fall from Vancouver Island was officially credited with thirty-seven victories, all of which would be attained that year. Flying both Pups and Camels with Naval 3 and Naval 9, Fall became the only Canadian to win the Distinguished Service Cross and two Bars to the award for gallantry in the air. He became a most able flight commander, exceedingly generous in sharing his aerial victories with the rest of his flight. He also had triple-victory engagements on two separate occasions during 1917. His combat report for one such event provides an excellent description of the fighter pilot's war at the time:

When BEs were attacked at Cambrai, I attacked HA [hostile aircraft] head on at about 8,000 feet. I saw many tracers go into his engine as we closed on one another. I half-looped to one side of him, and then to about 4,000 feet and fired about 50 rounds when he went down absolutely out of control. I watched him spinning down to about 1,000 feet, the trail of smoke increasing. I was immediately attacked by three more Albatros which drove me down to about 200 feet. We were firing at one another whenever possible, when at last I got into position and I attacked one from

above so close to him that the pilot's head filled the small ring in the Aldis sight. I saw three tracers actually go into the pilot's head; the HA then simply heeled over and spun into the ground. The other two machines cleared off.

After flying west for about five minutes I was again attacked by a Halberstadt single-seater and as he closed on me I rocked my machine until he was within fifty yards. I side-looped over him and fired a short burst at him. He seemed to clear off, and then attacked me again; these operations were repeated several times with a slight variation in the way I looped over him, until within about five minutes of crossing the lines (flying against a strong wind), when he was about 150 yards behind me, I looped straight over him and coming out of the loop I dived at him and fired a good long burst. I saw nearly all the tracers go into the pilot's back, just on the edge of the cockpit. He immediately dived straight into the ground.[59]

John Joseph Malone of Regina was an early star with Naval 3 and may well have been the first RNAS ace. Malone scored all his victories in Pups and won the Distinguished Service Order in the process. On April 24 he forced an enemy two-seater down, and was then obliged to land beside it when his own engine failed. He helped pull the wounded enemy observer from his cockpit, though the German died shortly thereafter. Eventually, the Canadian and the German pilot ended up reliving the engagement back at Malone's squadron mess, where the German confided that he thought he was actually landing behind German lines![60] This Canadian was killed on April 28, 1917, by the future high-scoring ace Leutnant Paul Billik of Jasta 12, while escorting FE2bs on a reconnaissance mission.

Arthur T. Whealy of Toronto was an eventual twenty-seven-victory ace who flew Pups, Sopwith Triplanes, and Camels with both Naval 3 and Naval 9 in 1917 and 1918. He scored eight of his total in 1917 and was eventually honoured with a Distinguished Service Cross and Bar, a Distinguished Flying Cross, and a Mentioned in Dispatches. Frederick C. Armstrong also flew Pups and Camels with Naval 3 in 1917 and 1918. Of his total of thir-

teen air combat victories, seven were attained in 1917. Flight Commander Fred Everest Banbury of Wolseley, Saskatchewan, flew Pups and Camels with Naval 9 in 1917. Ten of his eleven total wartime victories were achieved in 1917, commencing in May.

Alfred William Carter from Calgary flew Pups and Sopwith Triplanes with Naval 9, and was scoring from April 6 onwards. Nine of his total wartime score of seventeen were claimed in 1917, the remainder when he was flying Camels the following year with Punk Manuel. "Nick" Carter enjoyed contour flying, usually at about 20 feet above the ground. At one point in a dive, his aircraft was suddenly thrown onto its back, where it jolted to an abrupt stop. It had struck a balloon cable, which shattered its propeller, and the cable wound around the propeller shaft. The cable tightened while the balloon, acting as a parachute, let the aircraft down gently. Both Carter and the two startled occupants of the balloon escaped without a scratch![61]

On April 23 Lloyd Breadner, or "Bread," as he was popularly known, flying a Pup with Naval 3, became the first Allied airman to fell one of the

huge Gotha bombers — a GIII from Kagohl III/15 near Vron.[62] Having downed the mighty bomber, Breadner landed in a field beside it, intending to capture the crew. That feat had already been accomplished by ground troops, but he returned with a sizable strip of fabric bearing the Maltese Cross, which promptly adorned the wall above the fireplace in the mess at Naval 3. He was accredited with ten aerial victories during the Great War, all of them attained during 1917.

Stanley Wallace Rosevear from Walkerton, Ontario, flew Sopwith Triplanes with Naval 1 in 1917, scoring ten times. In October he wiped out an entire German company while flying close support for a British infantry attack in Flanders. As he wrote of the event in a letter home from the period:

> I caught them on the march along a road and swept them three times, leaving many of them lying on the road. The others jumped into ditches and I gave them some more.
>
> It was a very hot day's work, and we got some hot receptions. I could not begin to explain what an awful hell a barrage is. At times I could not hear my own engine or my machine gun. Several times I distinctly saw large shells

zip past my machine. We were heartily congratulated by the General for our great help in making the push a success. However, we paid for it in the pilots missing. [63]

Rosevear was destined for continued successes the following year, when, flying Camels, he would account for a further fifteen German aircraft, eleven of them in one month alone.

While most public perceptions of Great War aerial combat centre around swirling dogfights between opposing aircraft, the war against enemy observation balloons evolved dramatically during 1917. Albert Earl Godfrey, by now a Nieuport pilot with 40 Squadron, describes the successful evolution of this highly dangerous mission, which involved coordinated attacks by two distinct forces:

> These attacks were very good object lessons in the value of surprise. Our Squadron Commander, Major Tilney, first thought of this idea several weeks before an attack was carried out. All the pilots put forth their suggestions as to how the attack should be made. To begin with, everyone practiced contour chasing until they became very efficient. The first

Opposite: The Sopwith Pup was a nimble fighter used to great effect by many Canadian fighter pilots in the Royal Naval Air Service during late-1916 and 1917. Lloyd Breadner of Naval 3, flying his Sopwith Pup N6181 named "Happy" on April 23, 1917, has just successfully attacked Gotha GIII 610/16. It subsequently force-landed and the crew was imprisoned.

RNAS Canadian Scout pilots McDonald and Shearer in front of a diminutive Spad VII

attack was made just before the Canadian Corps attack on Vimy Ridge. Several flights of Nieuports and Triplanes were sent on patrol with orders to make attacks on six balloons at a given time, and, during the attack, to riddle them with machine-gun bullets. The idea of these attacks was to force the balloons down. Timed to coincide with these attacks, six additional Nieuports took off from an advanced landing ground armed with two drums of Buckingham ammunition, each machine with orders to attack one balloon by contour chasing from the advanced landing ground to the balloon, and when within 500 yards of the balloon, to open fire. If the balloon failed to burst into flames, a second attack with a second drum of ammunition was to be made. Everything worked accordingly, the balloons were driven down by the high attacks; six Nieuports aimed at their targets and six balloons went down in flames with less than a drum of ammunition used by each machine.[64]

Canadian pilots were also carving a niche for themselves in Spads during 1917. Lieutenant George Marks gained eight victories in these aircraft flying with 23 Squadron between June and August. Even more successful was Marks' squadronmate, Captain Douglas McGregor, who scored twelve times between May and September. McGregor also garnered a reputation for fortitude in pressing home attacks against ground targets, best exemplified by a June 6 dawn attack on a German airfield at Château du Sart. Captain Arthur B. Fairclough, with an eventual score of nineteen confirmed, accumulated the first nine during the month of December 1917, flying Spads with 19 Squadron. He added a further ten victories the following year, flying Dolphins with both 19 and 23 Squadrons. Captain Frank Soden from Petitcodiac, NB, won his spurs flying Nieuport 17s and SE5s with 60 Squadron, scoring eleven of his eventual twenty-seven claims with that unit in 1917. He particularly distinguished himself, apart from air combat venues, during the autumn Battles of Passchendaele, when his skilful reconnaissance work in atrocious weather and violent defensive fire provided essential information to the leaders of the land campaign.[65]

Andy "Hawkeye" McKeever set records for scoring in Bristol Fighters, flying with 11 Squad-

ron out of Estree Blanche during the second half of 1917. According to Eric R. Dibbs of Newport Beach, New South Wales, Australia: "Andy McKeever was a bright, wide-eyed young man of medium height and good physique. He had a friendly nature but tended to keep to himself a good deal. He was never involved in men's gags or binges. To my knowledge he neither drank nor smoked. He was modest and unassuming, and I liked him." The twenty-two-year-old Listowel, Ontario, native was paired most frequently in combat with gunner Sergeant L.A. Powell, who was subsequently decorated and commissioned for his fine war efforts. Perhaps their most memorable day was their last combat mission, on November 30. McKeever and Powell duelled alone with two enemy two-seaters and a covering force of seven black Albatros scouts. In the ensuing melee, McKeever gunned down two of the Albatros with his forward-firing Vickers, while Powell accounted for two more from the rear, badly damaging another. With their Brisfit now holed like a sieve and both guns out of ammunition, McKeever calmly engineered their escape from the incensed German survivors by feigning a crash landing. "McKeever therefore tried a ruse which, if it didn't work, would put him in an even worse position. Pretending to be hit, he switched off the engine and began to glide down. The ruse worked. Within twenty feet of the ground, McKeever switched back on and zoomed away to safety!"[66] McKeever received the Distinguished Service Order to add to his Military Cross and Bar for the exploit. Powell received a Bar to his Military Cross.

Camel aces abounded during the latter half of 1917. Francis Granger Quigley accounted for thirty-three German aircraft overall, every one while serving with 70 Squadron. Nine of those victories occurred in the October-December 1917 period. Like McKeever, Quigley received the Distinguished Service Order as well as the Military Cross and Bar for his courage and resourcefulness in the air.

The navy was also exceptionally well represented by Camel aces. Stearne Tighe Edwards, yet another Carleton Place native, garnered seven of his sixteen official victories in 1917 during service with 9 Naval Squadron. Wilfred Austin Curtis of Havelock, Ontario, was another significant scorer in 10 Naval Squadron, a unit replete with star performers. During a seventy-five-day period that autumn,

"Wilf" would claim ten of his total wartime score of thirteen victories, winning the Distinguished Service Cross and Bar along the way.

The honours for being one of the highest-scoring small units on the Western Front during the summer of 1917 must surely go to Black Flight of Naval 10 and its five Canadian members under the command of Raymond Collishaw. Returning to the front on May 30, Collishaw was posted to the squadron as a flight commander, and was soon flying Sopwith Triplanes out of Droglandt in support of preparations for the upcoming Messines offensive. Their opposite numbers were the cream of the German Air Force, including von Richthofen's Flying Circus, Jadgeschwader I, and they soon locked in a period of ferocious, unrelenting combat. In the two months from June 1 until July 27, "Collie" claimed thirty enemy aircraft destroyed, all but six of them Albatros scouts. Double and even triple victory days became regular events for him. On June 15 he accounted for four enemy aircraft, and three weeks later, on July 6, he was credited with six victories in one engagement near Menin. Yet his accomplishments were only part of a larger whole, since, collectively, Black Flight was credited with a remarkable sixty-eight enemy aircraft destroyed during the period against a loss of only two of its own.

Owing to British reticence in publicly acknowledging its heroes, the exploits of this remarkable and charismatic group did not become widely known until much later. Collishaw and his four colleagues — John Edward Sharnan of Oak Lake, Manitoba, Ellis Vair Reid of Belleville, Ontario, William Melville Alexander of Toronto, and Gerald Ewart Nash of Stoney Creek, Ontario — flew highly distinctive Sopwiths into battle. These aircraft were not entirely black, as they have frequently been misrepresented. In Mel Alexander's words, "I can't tell you why Collie called it the Black Flight, but I have a humorous idea. All of a sudden we just found our machines painted. Painted black to the back of the metal work (engine cowling to cockpit). And the wheel covers were black, [but] the struts were not black, nor were the wings black. Additionally, the five original

Opposite: On July 27, 1917, Raymond Collishaw engaged three Albatros DVs north of Menin. In the ensuing battle, one scout was seen to come apart in the air after a telling burst by Collishaw to the cockpit area. He then gunned down a second machine in a daring, head-on attack. He is depicted here in Sopwith Triplane N533, one of only five examples equipped with both the 130 horse power Clerget 9b engine and twin Vickers guns, built by Clayton & Shuttleworth.

members of the Flight had their tactical names painted in small letters near the cockpit: Black Maria (Collishaw), Black Roger (Reid), Black Death (Sharman), and Black Sheep (Nash)."[67] Collishaw added, "The name 'Black Maria' was painted in white on both sides of the cockpit just forward of the pilot's seat. I fancy that the letters were about three inches high. The idea of the Black Flight was in affinity with the need for distinguishing features. The main reason why squadron markings for triplanes became necessary emerged when the German triplanes appeared on the scene."[68] Alexander continued: "Perhaps Collie called his machine 'Black Maria' because he knew something about Black Marias (police cars). Probably in some of his mischievous days, he'd been in one!"

The fabled luck could not hold out forever. On June 26, after attaining six official victories, Nash was the first of the original group to fall when he became Leutnant Karl Allmenröder's thirtieth victory. Allmenröder was a high-scoring ace with Jasta 11 at the time, but Nash cheated death and became a prisoner of war. Sharman was also lost on July 22, shot down and killed by ground fire. He had scored seven out of his wartime total of eight victories while serving in Black Flight and had been awarded a Bar to add to his Distinguished Service Cross, won during a previous tour. Ellis Reid scored nineteen times during the period, and was also awarded the Distinguished Service Cross and Mentioned in Dispatches for his remarkable string of victories. Mel Alexander claimed eight times as a member of Black Flight and four times later in the year. Before the war ended, he obtained twenty-three confirmed victories, the Distinguished Service Cross, and 557 hours of flying time, most of them involving combat. His praise for Collishaw's leadership was unqualified, and he strongly believed that one of the keys to their collective success was Collishaw's inherent ability to keep a positive attitude, even when the going got rough: "This fellow Collishaw: I never saw him down; never once. No matter how bad things were — and they were pretty bad sometimes — he could keep built up. That was his strong point. Talk? He could talk his head off. Laugh? He was a wonderful fellow."[69] Still, the strain of near-continuous combat took its toll. Alexander found the anticipation of combat more stressful than the combat itself: "Just before attacking ... butterflies

in your stomach is what you call it — nervous tension. You're almost panicky, but when you get your guns firing ... I used to clear up just like that. My brain worked clearly."

Great War aerial combat was very dynamic by 1917. Collishaw reflected on some of the tactical fundamentals as he remembered them:

It was commonplace for contending antagonists to meet "head-on." This introduced the most hair-raising experience for fighter pilots. At a distance apart of about 1200 feet both opponents would open fire. Each pilot could see his own and his opponent's tracer bullets intermingling and he could feel his aircraft shudder from the impact of bullets, while the near misses reacted harshly upon his ears. In about $3^1/2$ seconds of fire, the intervening 1200 feet interval was covered and the contending pilots tried to dodge collision, over or under. There was no rule of the air. Escaping collision, each pilot had the same idea, how quickest to turn about and get on the other fellow's tail. Almost invariably this resulted in another head-on encounter.

A so-called "air dogfight" was the most exciting experience possible to the contestants. Dozens of waltzing couples could be seen in all directions. If one contender became disengaged and saw a likely opponent, it was highly likely that still another intervener would assault him from the rear. No individual could do more than dodge his attackers and attack in turn. As the contending adversaries approached one another, each was possessed of the same idea, how to get on to the other fellow's defenseless tail and at the same time, prevent the other fellow from doing it. Thus, when opposing air fighters met, it almost invariably resulted in a waltzing match. Tightly gripping his opponent in a spinning waltz and sharply banked, each pilot could watch one another's face very closely.[70]

Excerpts from both Collishaw's and Alexander's official combat reports and summaries give a clear picture of just how close and personal air combat could be:

6.6.17 — Shot down two Albatros scouts in flames and drove down a third OOC, while

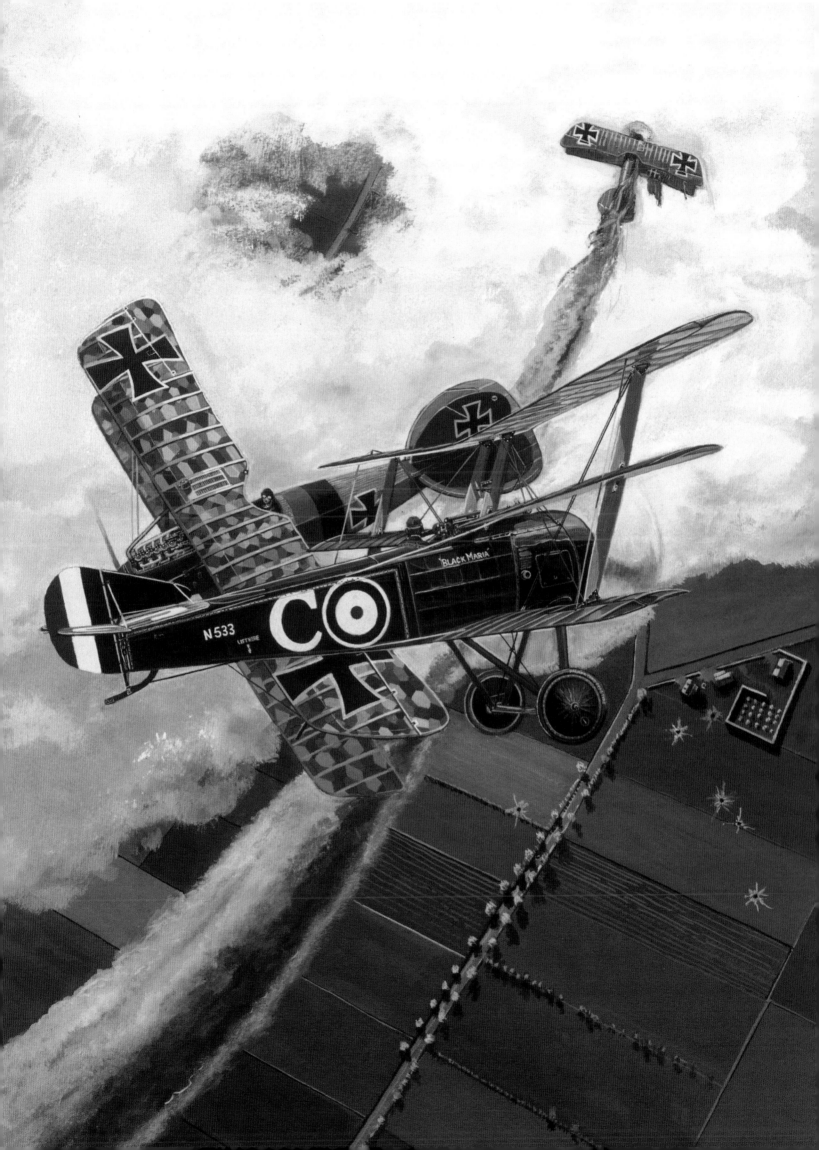

F/S/L Nash destroyed a two-seater Albatros and drove down an Albatros scout OOC. [Collishaw]

15.6.17 — Attacked an Albatros near Moorsledge, and fired one burst at close range out of the sun; the EA spun and stalled. Later went to the aid of Reid being attacked by a scout and drove off the EA attacking him, firing 100 rounds and seeing the right hand planes carry away and the EA fell in pieces. Later shot down yet another EA and was in several indecisive combats. [Collishaw]

25.6.17 — In a general attack on 12 or 15 scouts near Moorslegde. Dived on a 2 seater and fired 30 rounds at close range and saw tracers hit, some striking the observer in head and chest until he fell over. [Alexander]

27.7.17 — North of Menin dived on three scouts; one folded up and went down in pieces after tracers had hit the cockpit. Attacked a second, tracers again hit and the EA went down OOC. Also in six indecisive combats. [Collishaw]

Second Lieutenant L.P. Watkins, dirigible victor, June 17, 1917

6.7.17 — Shot down an EA near Deulemont, diving to 75 feet from it and firing 25 rounds. Saw tracers enter the pilot's back, he fell against the side of the fuselage and the EA fell OOC. Then attacked another, fired 20 rounds at 200 yards and saw it go down in a spin. [Alexander][71]

On July 28, 1917, Collishaw was ordered back to Canada on leave. However, he later returned to the war on the Continent, and his personal ledger of scoring against the enemy continued.

Canadian pilots also achieved successes against enemy dirigibles during 1917. During the period extending from July 1915 until August 1918, twelve German airships were shot down by Allied airmen. In a strikingly disproportionate manner, Canadian airmen either accounted for, or played a leading role in, the destruction of half these menacing giants. On May 14, 1917, Robert Leckie, a transplanted Scot who had taken Canadian citizenship seven years before the war's outbreak, piloted a large H12 Curtiss flying boat with the RNAS on anti-Zeppelin patrol out of Great Yarmouth. Near the North Sea island of Terschelling, flying at 6000 feet, Leckie spotted a Zeppelin 10 to 15 miles ahead of him and approximately 2000 feet lower. He skilfully manoeuvred the big flying boat into a line-astern position from which his navigator/gunner, C.J. Galpin, poured many rounds of incendiary ammunition into the airship from the twin bow Lewis guns. After a slight glow was noticed inside the airship, it was soon a flaming mass, plummeting towards the sea with no suvivors. Just before the Zeppelin burst into flames, Leckie and Galpin noted the number L 22 on her bow. Leckie, who received the Distinguished Service Cross for this engagement, shot down a second German airship the following year — the only Great War airman to do so.[72] During the summer of 1917, Lieutenant Loudon P. Watkins of Toronto flew antiquated BE12s with 37 Home Defence Squadron out of Gold-hanger aerodrome in the south of England. On June 17 he gunned down the L 48 at 13,000 feet over Harwich. The blazing airship fell into a field and, miraculously, two of the crewmembers survived. Watkins received the Military Cross for this feat, but was killed in action over the Western Front the following year.

The RFC was present in every theatre in which the British Army was committed to battle, so inevitably Canadian airmen also flew in every theatre of war. Seventeen Canadian airmen are known to have participated at some time during the Mesopotamian campaign, while in the Egypt-Palestine theatre at least nineteen Canadians flew operational missions. Several of these airmen were decorated for their services, including F.F. Minchin, an original member of the Princess Patricia's Canadian Light Infantry, who won a Distinguished Service Order and a Military Cross while flying over Palestine.[73] This theatre, a backwater campaign from an air combat perspective, was interesting to scout pilots because it witnessed the only operational deployment of an excellent little mid-wing monoplane scout from the Bristol works, the Type 20 M1.C. Fast, manoeuvrable, and an absolute delight to fly, the Bristol's only vice was the fact that it was a monoplane. Before the outbreak of the war in 1914, the War Office had decided that monoplanes were structurally dangerous and were therefore not to be acquired for His Majesty's airmen. This predisposition against monoplanes seriously impeded British aircraft performance advancement not only during the remainder of the Great War, but for nearly two decades thereafter. All 125 production models of the Bristol were sent to Basra, Mesopotamia, Palestine, and Salonika, commencing in September 1917. There they flew rings around the opposition, and at one point caused an entire Kurdish tribe to surrender and switch allegiance to the Allied cause.[74]

Although at least twenty Canadians flew with the RFC and later the RAF during the Macedonian campaign, the most important "sideshow" theatre for the corps was Italy. For over two years before September 1917, the Italians had campaigned doggedly but in vain against the Austrians in an attempt to secure Trieste on the Adriatic Sea. Interventions by both the British and the Germans in this theatre resulted in massive losses for the Italians at the Twelfth Battle of the Isonzo — the Capporetto debacle — in late October. The British then ordered two divisions to be sent into the theatre from France. Significant air assets were also deployed, including three Camel units — numbers 28, 45, and 66 Squadrons. By early December, 28 and 66 Squadrons had established themselves at Grossa, to the northwest of Padua, while 45 Squadron shared Istrana aerodrome to the west of Treviso with two RE8 units. One of the flight commanders

Major A.B. Shearer in a Sopwith Camel in Italy

in 28 Squadron at the time was Captain W.G. "Billy" Barker, fresh from France, where, flying RE8s and Camels, he had acquired several victories as a scout pilot and had also added a Bar to his Military Cross. Barker's new fighting home was a sharp contrast to the drab squalor of France. Located on the Piave River and with a backdrop of snow-capped Alps, this beautiful vista included the pastoral, rustic Venetian Plain and, 40 miles to the southeast, the Gulf of Venice. Barker wrote of his initial impressions in this theatre, including recent recollections from his pilot tour in France:

I suppose you will be surprised to hear I am on the Italian Front. Arrived here a few days ago but have not been over the lines yet. When we do I am out to get the first enemy plane down for the RFC in Italy.[75] Will let you know how I get on later. I came out on a small single-seater scout called the Camel. It has two Vickers shooting through the propeller and I like it very much. I was only flying for a few days in France & enough too, for we were up against the Hun traveling circus, or in other words, their picked squadron. They fly red coloured, black and white, etc., Albatros scouts. We had some furious battles and after 8 days of this I had lost all my Flight — some killed, some prisoners & some wounded. I managed to destroy 8 myself; 4 down in flames, 3 with wings shot off & 1 crashed out of control. I drove a good many more of them down but I don't think any of them crashed. All my above were confirmed by Archie (anti-aircraft) and other pilots …The above included 3 enemy patrol leaders in red machines. They fought well but I could out-manoeuver them & I seldom fired at more than 30 yds. range & my two Vickers are pretty deadly at that range. I like my little bus very much. It is a rotary engine & is very fast. Also sensitive in turns. I will probably be out here another 5 months — certainly not more — and should have a squadron before then. I am then going to take it easy.

Had quite a nice trip around the Alps. Went up to 16,000 feet & was then just above the peaks by a few feet — got some good snaps.

I cannot speak this lingo yet but you can always find people among the educated classes

A Bristol
F2b Brisfit
in Italy

who can speak French and so I get on reasonably well. We will probably give the Huns and Austrians a shock when we start. Our crack corps is here & a goodly number of planes.

Will now close as I have to take up two buses for tests.[76]

Barker became the most successful Allied scout pilot on the Italian front. He is best known for a spectacular solo dogfight in France the following year, which earned him the Victoria Cross, but he was by no means a dedicated lone wolf. He was a very responsible leader who took great pains to indoctrinate and shepherd inexperienced new arrivals to his squadron. Although he would

emerge from the war as Canada's most decorated airman,[77] he was not a trophy hunter. Like Collishaw, he was exceedingly generous in sharing his victory claims with others in his formations. Excerpts from his combat report for an offensive patrol undertaken on December 3 highlight some of his qualities as a fighter pilot and leader, including his apparent taste for low-level attacks — a rarity in the RFC:

Lt. Cooper, Lt. Woltho and I crossed the river Piave at a low altitude and attacked a hostile balloon N.E. of Conegliano. I fired about 40 rounds into it at a height of 1000 feet and it began to descend. I then observed an Albatros scout about to attack Lt. Woltho. I immediately engaged the EA, drove him down to 300 feet, and then succeeded in getting a burst of fire into him. He dived vertically, crashed, and the wreckage burst into flames. I then re-attacked the balloon, and after firing at very close range, saw it in flames on the ground. I broke up a party of enemy who were at the balloon winch. A large covered car proceeding E. from Conegliano turned over into a ditch when I attacked it. Later I attacked small parties of the enemy and dispersed them.[78]

Audacious and determined, Barker soon exemplified the RFC's mode of offensive action. Captain James Hart Mitchell, MC, DFC, a Yorkshireman, eleven-victory ace, and, like Barker, a flight commander on 28 Squadron, described a subsequent event:

On Christmas morning, 1917, Barker arose early and took Lieut. Hudson with him on a visit to Motta Aerodrome, which was 10 miles across the lines. Barker had a large piece of cardboard with the following inscription on it: "To the Austrian Flying Corps from the English R.F.C., wishing you a Merry Christmas." This he dropped in front of the hangars and then proceeded to shoot up the people on the ground and fired into the hangars.

This evidently annoyed the Austrians, and about 7 a.m. on Boxing Day they came over to Istrana Aerodrome with 15 machines and proceeded to bomb it from 200 feet. They did considerable damage to Italian machines and wiped out 2 R.E.8s and killed some Italian mechanics. Two Italian pilots put up a good show by running out to their Hanriot scouts whilst they were being bombed and took off and shot down two Austrian machines on the aerodrome. Some of the other machines were met by our pilots on their way out to the lines, and Archie accounted for two; finally, out of the 15 raiders, 13 of them were shot down and remained on our side of the lines, including one Gotha.[79]

In fact, the "Austrians," who were actually German airmen, lost only six aircraft on this reprisal raid, but the captured crews from some of them were found to be quite inebriated![80] A short time later, Barker was awarded his first Distinguished Service Order.

Other seasoned Canadian scout pilots were in Italy with Barker at year's end, 1917. One of them was Thomas Frederick Williams, an Ontario native.

Williams gunned down a total of fourteen enemy aircraft during the war, the majority on the Italian front. He also shot down four German aircraft over the Western Front during October and November 1917 while serving with 45 Squadron. His first victory came during a spectacular lone engagement against seven Albatros scouts on October 24 near Menin. Williams got the enemy leader and also acquired the lifelong nickname of "Voss," owing to the similarity of this fight to the great German ace's spectacular last engagement. Williams started his Italian service with 45 Squadron, but soon joined Billy Barker at 28 Squadron. Both men had many scores to settle with the Central Powers over Italy during the upcoming year. The stage was set for the final bloody rounds of the Great War, and airpower played a significant role during those closing battles.

Throughout much of 1916 and 1917, the Borden government in Canada was hobbled with problems

A crashed Austrian DFW on the Italian front

of war funding, the erosion of Conservative support in the provinces, bankrupt railways, widespread discontent in the military, and general public discontent with the war effort. The proud but costly Canadian triumph at Vimy Ridge in April had temporarily helped to galvanize a war-weary nation to the Entente cause, but the Conscription Act of August 29 was even more divisive. In October the Canadian Corps received orders to relieve the shattered Anzac forces around Ypres and to prepare to capture Passchendaele — a task the British had been unable to accomplish themselves. General Currie protested that this order could not be accomplished without incurring horrendous casualties, but was overruled by Haig. In a series of attacks lasting from October 26 until reinforcements arrived on November 6, in waist-deep mud, violent rainstorms, and incessant German shelling, the Canadians took Passchendaele and grimly held on to it. When the battle was over, the corps had prevailed yet again, but four-fifths of the actual attackers were dead or wounded, and Currie's prediction of 16,000 casualties had been chillingly accurate.[81]

Henceforth, Canada demanded much more input into the closing innings of the war. The nation had paid for this right with a disproportionate amount of Canadian blood. Borden made this point to Lloyd George during the spring of 1918: "I want to tell you that if there's a repetition of the Battle of Passchendaele, not a Canadian soldier will leave the shores of Canada as long as the Canadian people entrust the government of their country to my hands."[82]

Shortly thereafter, a viable alternative to this ghastly strategy of attrition was demonstrated in a brilliant British victory at Cambrai, won by the extensive use of tanks and by fluid, surprise tactics. The 1917 Battle of Cambrai was also a particular source of pride for Canadians, as the Canadian Cavalry Brigade and the Royal Newfoundland Regiment both fought with distinction while attached to British forces there. However, Haig did not have the reinforcements to exploit his initial success, and the Germans were soon able to rally and check the attack. Nonetheless, the tank had proven its worth in battle. Its use, along with innovative employment of fighter-bombers and fluid tactics by smaller fighting teams that bypassed major areas of enemy resistance, became the hallmarks of the drive to victory in 1918.

The horrors provided by Flanders and Passchendaele in 1917 had thrown Canada into a deep fit of war depression. Canadians needed a charismatic hero to help buoy their spirits. They would find one in William Avery Bishop.

CHAPTER FOUR

THE INCOMPARABLE BILLY BISHOP

"Think of the audace of it."

– MAURICE BARING

Air Marshal William Avery Bishop, Victoria Cross, Companion of the Most Honourable Order of the Bath, Distinguished Service Order and Bar, Military Cross, Distinguished Flying Cross, Mentioned in Dispatches, Chevalier of the Legion d'Honneur (France), Croix de Guerre avec Palme (France), was certainly audacious.[1] He was also an imperfect human being with both strengths and weaknesses, contrary to the perceptions of an adoring public that all but deified him. And Bishop played on those perceptions. He was proud, ambitious, covetous of recognition, occasionally self-obsessed, a risk-taker, and an embellisher of the truth. He was also a loving husband and father, a fiercely loyal friend, a resourceful, skilled, and courageous warrior who could be gracious in his praise for his contemporaries, including his enemies. He was very much a product of his circumstances, a war-weary British Empire in need of a hero.

Bishop was born on February 8, 1894, in Owen Sound, Ontario. A "disinterested student with poor grades,"[2] young Bishop was an enthusiastic outdoorsman who preferred solitary sports, such as swimming, riding, and shooting, to team efforts. Although he was the class clown at Owen Sound Collegiate[3] his friendships with girls, his dancing lessons, and slight lisp made him the butt of many practical jokes. In self-defence, the pugnacious young Bishop developed formidable fighting skills and won the respect of his peers with his fists in numerous schoolyard scraps.

In 1911 he followed his older brother Worth to the Royal Military College in Kingston. A poor grade record had kept him out of the University of Toronto, but admission to RMC depended on an entrance examination. He managed to pass this exam, rating forty-second out of forty-three applicants[4]. Although his tenure at RMC was far from stellar, he was not, as the rumour goes, threatened with expulsion for cheating when war loomed in 1914. The stories appear to have originated with Bishop's son Arthur in *The Courage of the Early Morning*, a biography of his famous father. They were probably related by Bishop to his son, who recorded them for posterity.[5]

Ross McKenzie, the assistant registrar of RMC and curator of the RMC Museum, has attempted to sort out what really happened to Bishop during his cadet years.[6] The academic dishonesty apparently occurred during Bishop's first year (1911-12). While the exact nature of his offence has not survived the years, he was only temporarily suspended, or "rusticated," as punishment and required to repeat the academic year. According to the RMC Regulations of 1912, rustication was awarded for "use of any improper means of obtaining information relative to an examination." Bishop's sins were not taken lightly, but he was deemed worthy of a second chance. In the repeated class, he showed remarkable improvement, placing twenty-third out of forty-two. The following year, however, his marks again took a nosedive. From the contemporary surviving literature it is clear that he was a popular prankster, best known for his active pursuit of local females. In the spring of 1914 he and a classmate "borrowed" an RMC canoe for a nocturnal rendezvous with two girls. That sojourn ended in a capsizing and twenty-eight days of restricted leave. In brief, Bishop's performance during this academic year appears to have been characterized by high-spirited antics and little academic application. His scholastic standing was a dismal thirty-third out of thirty-four, with number thirty-four being the only class failure. It was, in fighter pilot parlance, a "low pullout," but a pullout nonetheless.

There is no record of academic misconduct by Bishop at this time. Contrary to previous assertions, he did return to RMC on August 28, 1914, for the commencement of the 1914-15 academic year. And in spite of his poor academic standing, he was given some rank and deemed worthy of trust:

> On arrival, Bishop, now a senior, was appointed a Lance-Corporal;[7] of his other classmates, three received no appointment at all. One week later, on 7 September 1914, he was promoted to Corporal. These appointments were made by the Commandant, who stated, "Cadets so entrusted with authority should remember that upon their example and the manner in which their duties are performed, in a great measure depend the general conduct, gentleman-like, honourable and moral tone of the cadets."[8]

Three weeks later, on September 30, Bishop withdrew "at parents' request" — the annotation used for every departure from RMC except those

Left to right:
Gentlemen Cadets
Bert Mannsell,
Bill Bishop and
Doda Atwood
studying for exams
at RMC in 1914

Bishop's RMC
discharge paper

for normal graduation, expulsion, or academic failure. The conduct assessment on his RMC Discharge Certificate read "Good." It was a far cry from the highest character assessment of "Exemplary," but he was certainly not "the worst cadet RMC ever had."[9]

When Bishop withdrew from RMC, sixteen of his colleagues in the senior class had already left for war service. Most of the remaining members of the class would soon follow. McKenzie suggests that the earlier departure of some of his friends, who were awarded special commissions because of their high academic standings, possibly inspired Bishop to act on his own behalf. In all probability, Bishop left RMC motivated by a desire for war service in the name of King and country:[10]

Whatever Billy Bishop was at RMC, he was not an "RMC reject," nor was he "the worst cadet," nor did he leave one step ahead of expulsion. He may have been unhappy at times, he may have run afoul of regulations, he certainly wasn't a good student, and no doubt about it, he liked girls — but would that make him so different? There has been a Billy Bishop or two in every class![11]

Bishop was commissioned in Toronto's Mississauga Horse, a cavalry detachment of the 2nd Canadian Division. Here, his fabled good luck kicked in. Hospitalized with pneumonia, his unit embarked for Europe without him as a part of the Canadian Expeditionary Force and was decimated in hopeless charges against trenches armed with machine guns. On recovery, he was transferred to the 7th Battalion of the Canadian Mounted Rifles (CMRs), garrisoned in London, Ontario. Here he remained until the unit departed for England in June 1915.[12]

Shortly before embarkation, Bishop proposed to his long-time sweetheart, Margaret Burden, a granddaughter of Timothy Eaton, the department store millionaire.

Bishop quickly established a good name for himself with the 7th CMRs, displaying "excellent individual skills and leadership qualities, both of which were recognized by his fellow officers and superiors."[13] However, the Atlantic crossing must have given him pause for thought. For two weeks he braved storm-tossed seas and German U-boats on a requisitioned cattle ship, the *Caledonia*. On arrival in England, his unit was quickly deployed to Shorncliffe on the coast of Kent, a camp he referred to as "the worst hole in England." Here, unrelenting rain and the muddy terrain made living conditions particularly miserable.[14] It was not the great romantic adventure for which Bishop had gone to war. As they watched two RFC aircraft flying overhead their positions one day, George Stirrett, one of Bishop's soldiers, remembered Bishop remarking: "George, it's clean up there. If you were killed, at least you'd be clean."[15] On another occasion in July, an unexpected visit from a Nieuport scout proved to be the final catalyst:

It landed hesitatingly in a nearby field as if scorning to brush its wings against so sordid a landscape; then away again up into the clean grey mists. How long I stood there gazing into the distance I do not know, but when I turned to slog my way back through the mud my mind was made up. I knew there was only one place to be on such a day — up above the clouds and in the summer sunshine. I was going into the battle that way. I was going to meet the enemy in the air.[16]

In short order, Bishop made direct application to Lord Cecil at the War Office for transfer to the RFC as a trainee pilot. Cecil was apparently quite taken with the brash young Canadian, but stated that a pilot training vacancy would not become available for at least six months. However, if Bishop wished to go to war in the air as an observer, he could start training almost immediately. Bishop's commanding officer at Shorncliffe advised him to take the offer.

After a period of formal training and the awarding of his observer's badge, Bishop was posted to Number 21 Squadron at Netheravon, flying in antiquated RE 7 reconnaissance aircraft. He was subsequently posted to the front at St. Omer, France, in early January 1916, where he spent the next four months. Bishop flew many missions deep into enemy territory, conducting forward artillery obser-

Billy Bishop (right), while serving with the 7th Battalion, Canadian Mounted Rifles, at London, Ontario, in February, 1915

vation and photo-reconnaissance of the lines, and also fighting patrols designed to keep enemy aircraft at bay. He was by all accounts quite skilled at these tasks, but found an observer's lot tame and longed to fly as a pilot. Dogged by illness and accidents, Bishop was granted sick leave back to England in May. Fortunately, he avoided the carnage of the June Somme offensive, for 21 Squadron suffered heavy casualties in its obsolescent RE 7s during the Allied assaults.

While in hospital in England with a knee injury, Bishop met and apparently charmed seventy-year-old Lady St. Helier, a wealthy and influential hospital volunteer and socialite who had been introduced to Bishop's father on a visit to Canada before to the war.[17] The patronage of this kindly woman, whom Bishop came to call "Granny," would prove highly beneficial to him. She undoubtedly pulled some strings and arranged for him to have a period of convalescent leave back in Canada that summer. He had recently been diagnosed with a heart murmur, so could easily have remained at home, exempt from further war duty. However, he was more determined than ever to become a pilot. Returning to England in September, he was repeatedly rejected as being medically unfit, but, again, Lady St. Helier intervened and persuaded the doctors to give him a chance. By November he had commenced pilot training at Upavon on Salisbury Plain.[18]

A persistent myth that he was a dilettante, if not a poor pilot, has sullied Bishop's reputation. Yet Lord Balfour, one of the instructors who taught Bishop to fly, remembered him as "a good and apt pupil … an outstanding personality."[19] Canadian aviation historian Stewart K. Taylor called him a better-than-average aviator in comparison with his contemporaries: "A quick learner, he flew solo on only the third day of his pilot training, after a meager two hours and thirty minutes dual instruction on the Maurice-Farman Longhorn."[20] Bishop's pilot training advancement was rapid: he received his pilot's brevet on December 9, 1916, after only 18 hours and 30 minutes of solo flying time. In 1916 the average amount of time required to achieve this milestone was 25 hours.

Bishop was posted initially to home defence duties with 37 Squadron at Sutton's Farm in Essex, flying BE12as and conducting anti-Zeppelin patrols and night drills over southern England. Although this tour did not result in much combat, it was an excellent opportunity to hone his new-found flying skills. He experienced his first scrap with the enemy on January 7, 1917:

I had such an exciting time. I spent the day taking mechanics for joy rides, and then just about noon a Hun seaplane toddled over, and Headquarters ordered me to go up after him. I did and caught up to him at 1000 feet and had a terrific scrap … He had an observer and I was alone but I was in a BE12a and it is very fast. I must have hit him over and over again but didn't finish him. He hit my machine six times — three times, funny to say, in the propeller.[21]

Bishop longed to become a single-seat scout pilot, and in March he finally got his wish. Posted back to France for his second operational tour, this time for service with 60 Squadron, he arrived at the bleak, forlorn, half-deserted village of Izel les Hameau on March 17. He was joining a scout unit with a formidable fighting reputation and a history of resolute warriors, including the illustrious Captain Albert Ball, who had made his reputation with the squadron the previous year as the leading British scout pilot of the day. Bishop was eager to prove himself worthy of membership in this elite fraternity.

The airfield was located adjacent to the village on Filescamp Farm, the centrepiece of which was a picturesque but run-down old chateau, surrounded by decaying granaries, stock barns, and an enormous refuse pile. The airfield's buildings — barracks, cookhouses, and storage facilities — were strewn about in a random manner. Located 10 miles behind the lines near Arras, the continuous rumble of the guns left no doubt that the occupants were in a war zone. At this time, 60 Squadron shared Filescamp with 40 Squadron, also a Nieuport outfit, and 16 Squadron, flying Spads. Each unit normally had eighteen pilots, as well as twenty mechanics, an armourer, and other assorted support staff, including clerks, batmen for the officers, and drivers. Approximately 150 men usually lived at Filescamp, along with the French residents of the farm itself. Arthur Gould Lee, a pilot with 60 Squadron later in the year, recalled the airfield as follows: "A vast aerodrome in open countryside, with accommodation for three squadrons … Our quarters are most civilized, as we have a pleasant Mess, Nissen huts for officers and NCOs, a hard tennis court of sorts, and a badminton court in an empty hangar next door. And all this sited in a large orchard full of luscious fruit trees, which most of us have already raided."[22]

Bishop quickly felt at home in the comfortable mess, located in the orchard. Informality prevailed, and virtually any sort of clothing, uniform or otherwise, was acceptable. Drawings of scantily clad females adorned one wall, and pictures of aircraft and squadron members, the others. Combat trophies were everywhere, and the propeller from a Fokker shot down by Ball the year before had a place of honour above an enormous red-brick fireplace. Bishop was delighted to discover that an old RMC chum, E.J. Townesend, was one of the squadron's pilots, and within days they would be joined by Billy's friend from pilot training, Lieutenant Tim Hervey.[23]

The squadron commander, Major Jack Scott, was a wealthy London barrister who had been lamed in a training crash in 1914. The epitome of leadership by example, he became a determined and successful air fighter in his own right. Though in continuous pain, he walked with the aid of sticks and his batman lifted him into his Nieuport for flight. Courageous and tenacious, he was also ambitious, and determined that his unit would be the best in France:

He was a generous man, a father-figure warmly respected by the young pilots. He nurtured their loyalty and support by giving in return his own commitment to the squadron and its record. The young pilots knew they could rely on his support both personally and in his projection of the squadron's best image. Maj. Scott keenly encouraged his men to engage and shoot down the enemy, thus improving their own record as well as that of the squadron.[24]

William Fry, a contemporary of Bishop, found Scott to be very concerned with public relations. In this respect he broke with the traditional British Army outlook that shunned individual publicity of any sort. He used his impressive social connections to obtain victory credits and decorations for his pilots, and he was generous in recommending honours for those who excelled.[25]

Bishop returned to France at the start of the spring campaign, when his squadron still flew the nimble Nieuport 17. Although a formidable scout in 1916 when it first appeared at the front, by 1917 it was an outdated machine. The inherent structural weakness of the sesquiplane design caused it to shed its wings, particularly the lower planes, in high-speed dives over 140 miles per hour.[26] In the spring of 1917 this weakness was exacerbated by faulty production techniques of the manufacturers in Paris. Scott asserted that kiln-dried, unseasoned Canadian spruce was the main problem, compounded by the use of too many small screws in the main spars, jeopardizing their structural integrity.[27] In the fifth wing failure on squadron, Fry had a narrow escape on May 2 when his lower plane broke in flight and he was forced to make an emergency landing just west of Arras. This problem was a considerable source of angst to the Nieuport pilots, who had less than total faith in the structural integrity of their mounts. The issue culminated on June 7, when Second Lieutenant Roland Harris lost both his starboard planes on an air-to-ground practice firing mission, sending the aircraft into a vertical dive and the unfortunate Harris to his demise. In yet another example of his inspired leadership, "Major Scott immediately had himself helped into his Nieuport, whereupon he took off and continued the firing practice in an effort to restore confidence in the little biplane."[28] After this accident, a concerted effort was made to prevent further wing failures by advising the manufacturers of the suspected shortcomings in the production process, and by attaching an additional flying wire between the upper wing and the cowling.[29]

Although Bishop was quickly socially integrated into the squadron, his flying debut there was less than auspicious. The skittish little Nieuport was the antithesis of the doughty BE12as he had just left, and he was plagued by a series of landing accidents — a not uncommon event at the time. Again, hyperbole has played an unfair role in maligning Bishop's reputation. He did not "smash four aircraft" in his first twelve practice flights. Rather, he burst a tire, destroyed a propeller and broke a longeron, all minor and locally repairable damage.[30] Yet, for a few days, it seemed that Bishop might join that sizeable group that had been sent back to England for remedial training. The last mishap had literally occurred at the feet of the visiting 3rd Brigade Commander, who had been less than impressed.

In the final analysis, since qualified pilots were in very short supply at the time, Bishop was allowed to continue flying until a replacement for him arrived. He was assigned an old hack of a scout that had been on squadron strength since the previous year, and it was this aircraft that he first flew over the lines on March 22. Totally confused and unsure of himself, he had great difficulty keeping up with his flight, and was nearly killed in a dogfight. Captain Keith "Grid" Caldwell, his flight commander, was not impressed: "The Huns almost nailed you! You left formation and half a dozen V-strutters came out of the sun after you. They took off when they saw the flight turning back to help you."[31]

This engagement lit a fire in Bishop's belly, and he determined to excel in his new environment. Within a month, he was assigned Nieuport B1566, soon to become the most famous scout of its type ever flown. He flew this same aircraft "on regular patrols until the 24th of July 1917, for a total of 153 hours and forty minutes without one serious landing mishap. Few of his contemporaries could equal this." [32]

Bishop downed an Albatros for his first victory on March 25, but his engine subsequently failed and he had to force-land in the trenches. He was caught in an artillery duel and spent a very uncomfortable night. Having landed in an unhealthy spot, he quickly got into a dugout occupied by some field gunners and, with their assistance, moved his aircraft every half-hour to prevent the German artillery from shelling it. [33] This event, preceded by his first victory, solidified his place on 60 Squadron, and it made him the toast of the squadron's mechanics for taking such good care of the aircraft. Old sins were totally forgotten. Joe Warne, the squadron's historian, noted that on March 28, Bishop was invited to lead his first patrol, which turned out to be totally uneventful, "instead of being sent away for further training, which had proved necessary in many instances with new arrivals" [34]

On March 30 Bishop witnessed an event that would have a profound emotional impact on him. Leading a patrol for just the second time, his flight was decoyed into a numerically superior force of Albatros scouts, which scattered the Nieuports. One of his mates, Lieutenant W.P. Garnett, was shot down and killed by Leutnant Kurt Wolff of Jasta 2 over Fouquieres, while another, Second Lieutenant Frank Bower, pursued six of the enemy aircraft over Douai. In this engagement, Bower was hit from behind by an explosive bullet and his aircraft was thrown into a spin. He recovered it valiantly and flew westwards until he could no longer hear the anti-aircraft fire of the front lines. Suffering intensely and in a state of shock, with blood pouring from gaping abdominal wounds, Bower held his intestines in with one hand

Two views of the National Aviation Museum's replica of Billy Bishop's Nieuport 17 while flying with the other. Showing extreme fortitude, he landed at Chipilly and walked 40 yards from his Nieuport before collapsing. He died in hospital the following day and was Mentioned in Dispatches for his valour, the only possible posthumous award in the British system other than the Victoria Cross.[35] Bishop was profoundly moved by the loss of his friend. In a letter to his fiancée around this time, he admitted that "a blood-thirsty streak" had now appeared in him.[36]

While leading another patrol the next day, Bishop again lost two of his colleagues in yet another German ambush, but managed to claim a second victory over an Albatros near Gavrelle. Although he had not yet worked out any systematic tactics, he was congratulated by the 60 Squadron hierarchy on the relative success of these flights. High casualties, they said, were to be expected in wartime. Still, these losses shook him considerably, and he now vowed he would develop tactics to complement his natural fighting gifts. Scott felt that Bishop was successful largely because of his renowned eyesight and shooting ability, for he was probably never more than a moderately proficient

pilot.[37] Bishop himself insisted that shooting ability separated the chaff from the wheat — indeed, the living from the dead — in aerial combat.[38] While these factors were important, the official RFC view at the time held that the most exceptional fighter pilots possessed an unquenchable determination to aggressively seek and destroy as many of the enemy as possible. Albert Ball certainly had it, and Bishop not only had it but appeared to harbour a personal vendetta against the Germans.[39]

Bishop's strategy was to gain the upper hand in combat through both surprise and altitude. On the attack, he always tried to put the sun at his back, kill quickly, and promptly exit the combat arena. He became a master of the deflection shot, which, unlike the steady tracking shot, "led" the target so that quarry and shells met in time and space. He also developed an excellent sense of situational awareness (that is, his position with respect to enemy and allies in all dimensions) and how best to exploit a given situation to his advantage. Bishop adapted these tactics to suit both formation patrols and solo forays. Although he engaged initially regardless of the odds, he generally shunned foolhardy heroics.

Billy Bishop in front of his famous Nieuport 17. The manufacturer's serial number (B1566) appears to have been obscured by wartime censors.

A German
observation
balloon

He came to adopt the dogma expounded by British ace James McCudden of dictating the terms for combat with the enemy, instead of the other way around. In Bishop's opinion, reasoned aggressiveness behind enemy lines and formidable shooting ability explained his prolonged success in battle. The earlier and less successful baptisms of fire had left an indelible mark:

> I had now come to the conclusion that to be successful in fighting in the air, two things were required above all others. One was accuracy in shooting, and the second was to use one's head and take no unnecessary risks. Consequently, my plans from about this time forward were to take a minimum of risks, and wherever things looked doubtful or bad, immediately to make my escape and wait patiently for another opportunity. [40]

Bishop's tactics were built around surprise, which he considered the absolute essential. In no small measure they were forced upon him by the inferior performance characteristics of the Nieuport. Once surprise was lost, he usually broke off combat and, when that was not possible, "his heavy-handedness became a positive advantage in the rough-and-tumble of air combat." [41]

The precursory Allied bombardments and softening up of German positions in March led to a

significant increase in air activity. During Bloody April, the average life of a British pilot in France was approximately forty-five days, [42] and 60 Squadron suffered a 105 percent casualty rate. Thirteen of the original eighteen Squadron pilots were shot down, along with seven of their replacements. [43] Billy Bishop, Jack Scott, Grid Caldwell, and William Molesworth were the principal survivors of the period. The squadron registered thirty-five confirmed claims against the enemy that month, along with a number of unconfirmed claims for destruction, yet twelve of the confirmed claims were accredited to Bishop. Of the survivors listed above, Molesworth received two confirmed credits, Scott, one, and Caldwell, none. For most of them, it was an exercise in survival and the retention of sanity. For Bishop the hunter, it was a target-rich environment.

Bishop was awarded his first gallantry decoration, the Military Cross, for actions on April 7, when he destroyed an enemy observation balloon on the ground after destroying an Albatros DIII that had attacked him. Although he flew more than his fair share of formation patrols, he preferred stalking alone and pleaded with his commanding officer to be allowed more flights. Scott granted him a roving commission — official permission to range at will by himself behind enemy lines — in addition to his normal patrol duties. [44] Joe Warne points out that there were some advantages to these deep penetration solo efforts: clouds could be used in which to escape detection; aircraft encountered could automatically be considered hostile; and there were no friendly aircraft to be concerned about. Conversely, the Germans held significant performance advantages at the time, and the solo pilot lacked cross-cover and mutual support under duress. Also, return flights over hostile territory were normally made against the prevailing wind.[45] Scott, like Trenchard, extolled aggressive tactics. He hoped that Bishop's heroism and initiative would not only be inspirational to others, but would garner further recognition for the squadron. As for Bishop, in addition to his skill, determination, and courage, hopes of personal aggrandizement were also creeping into his conscious expressions:

> Some days I could have been accused of violating all the rules of a flying men's union (if we had one). I would fly as much as seven and a half hours between sunrise [and sunset]. Far from affecting my nerves, the more I flew, the more I wanted to fly, the better I seemed to feel and each combat became more and more enjoyable. Ambition was born in my breast, and although I still dared not entertain hope of equaling the record of Captain Ball, who by this time had shot down over thirty-five machines, I did have vague hopes of running second to him.[46]

Bishop flew the squadron rate of three or four patrols every day as well as his solo forays, and still he appeared inexhaustible in the quiet hours. Mess hijinks and games abounded, with Bishop always looking for new ways to relieve boredom and foster esprit de corps.[47] He was the squadron's clown prince, and he kept up the morale of most pilots with his practical jokes. William Fry, who joined the unit in late April, was detailed to C Flight, just after Bishop had been promoted to captain and given command of the flight.[48] Fry found Bishop to be "fair, strong, open and uninhibited, he was a success in the squadron and popular. He was friendly and I could not have had a better welcome … an extrovert to a degree … who took the lead in every off-duty activity."[49] Other squadron members of the period have equally fond, well-documented memories of him. Bishop pranks included painting most of Filescamp Farm's sows red, white, and blue, while decorating another of them with black Maltese Crosses and inscribing its flanks with the name "Baron von Richthofen." He also loved to feed brandy-soaked breadcrumbs to the farmer's ducks and drakes, then watch them wallow about the yard in a highly comical fashion. Scott turned a blind eye to these pranks, for he knew their forced urgency was essential to morale. Whenever off-duty time permitted, Bishop and his chums made the three-hour drive from Filescamp to Amiens, 70 miles north of Paris on the banks of the Somme. There the main attractions were Charlie's Bar and Le Hôtel du Rhin, where fine cuisine, wines, and accommodating young ladies could be picked up for a few francs.

Billy often went to Charlie's. On one occasion he was seen there with two vivacious women. He instituted a game in which each pilot who managed to charm a garter from a girl in Amiens would hang it as a trophy in the squadron mess. Included in it would be the lady's name and address. The airmen who brought in the most garters had almost as much prestige as the man who had shot down the most enemy planes. Before long, Billy led the squadron in both departments.[50]

Women gravitated to Bishop like moths to a flame, and most of his liaisons were frivolous affairs, a product of wartime urgencies. However, although betrothed to Margaret, he eventually developed a serious relationship with a beautiful young girl from Amiens named Ninette. In her he found a gentle woman who temporarily helped him forget the horrors of war. She supported him through some very traumatic periods, and Dan McCaffery speculates that, without Ninette, Bishop probably would not have survived. Bishop's old friend George Stirrett put it in a broader perspective: "Oh, he was a real womanizer back then, although I think his future wife was the only woman he ever really loved."[51]

Whenever weather permitted in April, Bishop flew, and he drove himself relentlessly. In spite of constant venturing over the lines, he often failed to engage the enemy through lack of contact. Still, he closed out the month on April 30 with a stunning display of fortitude and panache. On this particular day, in one flight, he had eight separate engagements with the enemy, though he would ultimately be credited with only one German two-seater. Scott was effusive in his praise of Bishop to RFC head-quarters over this arduous period:

I beg now to suggest to you that the subsequent conduct of this officer merits further distinction. On different dates between the 6th and 30th April he has destroyed 10 hostile aeroplanes and 2 balloons, while he has driven down 10 other German machines. In the same period he has 34 times engaged enemy machines. He often flies six or seven hours a day, two or three hours by himself looking for hostile aircraft. Comment is, I think, needless on this record of 24 days work, as the figures seem to speak for themselves.

One observation, however, I wish to add. By his gaiety and gallantry, and in particular by his example in treating the business of hunting H.A. as a sport, Captain Bishop has done a great deal to induce other pilots to regard this pursuit from the same angle. Where pilots have adopted this view the effect has been to enormously improve the quality of their work, they then find it much less tiring.[52]

Most 60 Squadron members were avid supporters of Bishop. William Molesworth, a gallant and successful warrior in his own right, was full of unbridled admiration for his Canadian colleague, who had acquired a distinctive nickname: "Our 'stunt merchant' is good at this game, and continues to add to his score, seldom coming back without firing his red light.[53] He works by himself a lot now, preferring to surprise the Hun by hiding rather than by trying to get him in a scrap. Wish I could do the same. I always feel so fagged after a patrol, that I haven't got the energy or the patience to sit up in the clouds waiting for a chance to bag a 'lone hun.'"[54] Molesworth's closing comment is of pivotal importance, for it underscores the fact that much of Bishop's success was due to his unrelenting pursuit of the enemy.

Yet praise for Bishop was not universal, even in the early days of his tour with 60 Squadron. For one thing, the jolly extrovert was also becoming a hardened warrior, a killer of men. Flippant remarks on viewing dead German infantrymen angered and alienated some of his colleagues. In a letter to Margaret, he fairly gloated over shooting down a Pfalz scout in flames, and again upon gunning a two-seater down in flames: "That made my heart feel good, sweetheart, because there is so much less misery that they will bring to the world." He

William Avery Bishop, VC

111

also admitted to forcing a two-seater down and strafing its helpless crew on the German side of the lines. While not a violation of the Articles of War, it was certainly viewed by some as a violation of the accepted etiquette of war. Neither did Bishop display any mercy in manoeuvring combat. On the occasion of his twenty-third victory, when a two-seat Rumpler's Parabellum gun jammed and the observer struggled to clear it, Bishop closed to point-blank range and raked the two men with fifteen rounds from his Lewis gun. He also freely admitted using the ghastly Buckingham incendiary bullets against an aircraft on at least one occasion — a forbidden procedure and a violation of the Articles of War. In fairness to Bishop, he may not have known of this specific regulation. Also, when the enemy aircraft was encountered, he may well have been loaded with these shells with the intention of going after enemy observation balloons, a legal and acceptable practice.

Bishop's increasing blood lust at this juncture may have been a product of the loss of so many close friends in battle. During one two-day period in April, ten of the unit's eighteen pilots were gunned down.[55] After April 14th, when his Australian chum Alan Binnie was downed and presumed killed, Bishop unashamedly wept and wrote of his distress to Margaret: "My heart is full these days. We are having the most awful time. Yesterday, Binnie, a friend of mine and three others were shot down and today,[56] four of my flight went under in a scrap. I'll pay a few of them for this, I swear I will. They were such good people and one was at RMC with me."[57]

Although Bishop had been deeply affected, other pilots were also having a dreadful time. Numerically, the losses to the squadron's core of originals were staggering. Some of the replacements were killed before Bishop even had a chance to meet them. This turn of events may well explain a downstream criticism that, after April, he was often aloof and, apart from Jack Scott, did not cultivate close wartime friendships. This strain generated by the losses took a staggering toll on the survivors. Fry recalls tempers being so frayed that anyone was likely to flare up at the most trivial or imagined provocation. Others sensed a tangible odour of fear that the wildest drunken parties could not eradicate. Bizarre behaviour abounded, yet no one thought it the slightest bit unusual. Bishop found

himself laughing uncontrollably in situations of dire peril. Scott himself became so distraught over losses that at one point he took off alone, shadowed by a worried Bishop, who "spotted his commander flying upside down above the heads of enemy troops. German gunners were blazing away furiously. The Major, who appears to have gone temporarily berserk, later claimed he had pulled the stunt to show his contempt for the Huns."[58] Some of the survivors were later plagued by stomach ulcers, alcoholism, and extreme mental disorders. Others simply quit: combat cowardice was a legitimate concern of squadron supervisors, who noted a great increase in mission aborts and early returns due to faked engine or armament problems. Still others drank before and during flight, to muster enough will to enter combat:

In neighbouring squadrons the situation was worse. One RFC officer refused to fly a mission, was confined to quarters and promptly blew his own brains out rather than face a court martial. And an entire squadron once defied an order, flatly refusing to embark on a dangerous mission. In fact, it was estimated by Flying Corps doctors that half of all airmen fell victim to serious neurosis problems before completing a tour.

Such statistics make Bishop's exploits during this period, the darkest in RFC history, seem even more remarkable. But it would be a mistake to believe the often-repeated take that he was a "man without fear." Bishop was under as much strain as anyone. He once admitted that his hands shook and his throat went dry at the sight of enemy planes. When his own machine was hit, he added, he always felt the muscles in his anus retract involuntarily. But he was better able to cope with his fears than many of the others.

That he was still able to maintain his fighting edge despite six weeks of daily adversity was amply demonstrated on May 7th when he drove two Albatros pilots down, gaining his twenty-first and twenty-second victories.[59]

Through this horrific carnival of destruction, Bishop's press-on spirit was a tremendously stabilizing force and a positive example in what was otherwise a sea of madness. He had few thoughts other than how best to engage the Germans to the absolute limits of his capability and endurance. He was rewarded with additional claims, as well as his second decoration, the Distinguished Service Order. Still, detractors of his motives and leadership ability surfaced. Some felt he was a personal glory seeker who cared little for the welfare of his colleagues — and there were occurrences to bear that contention out. At one point, charged with initiating Lieutenant R.B. Clark to combat against observation balloons, Bishop left the novice alone while he searched for quarry. Jumped by three German scouts and shot down in flames, Clark was hideously wounded by gunfire in the process. Through sheer force of will, he was able to nurse his blazing scout to a crash landing near an Allied field hospital, where he subsequently died of his wounds. On another occasion, 60 Squadron pilot Sydney Pope was particularly annoyed when Bishop left him to go off on a private foray. "Pope was taking photographs while Bishop provided overhead escort. They were operating deep behind enemy lines when Pope looked up for a moment and, to his astonishment, found himself absolutely alone and extremely vulnerable."[60]

Was Bishop ambitious to the detriment of his squadron associates, or did his burning desire to engage the enemy take precedence over more selfless actions? There can be no doubt that he was personally ambitious and covetous of fame.[61] His letters and conversations with others provide ample evidence of both. However, there is no documented reason to suppose that the quest for glory was anything more than a reasonable expectation derived from his obvious successes. His propensity to forage alone at occasionally inappropriate moments was probably due more to lapses in judgment than to wilful neglect of his peers. He may also have been the recipient of some anti-colonial bias. High-ranking Canadians had recently challenged British authority, and the feisty Canadian Minister of Militia, Sir Sam Hughes, had openly criticized British competence on the battlefield. Hughes had been particularly vociferous in his attacks on General Sir Edwin Alderson, the British Commander of the Canadian Corps. Sir Arthur Currie would later be highly critical of Field Marshal Earl Haig, as would Prime Minister Borden of his British counterparts, Herbert Asquith and David Lloyd George. Given Canada's disproportionate contributions to the war effort, they wanted to gain a greater say for the dominion in the conduct and planning of the war. Some of this

discontent may have filtered down to the unit level. There, in addition to the predisposition against individualism, Bishop was inordinately successful, while most of those around him were being killed, cruelly maimed, or captured. Some bitterness toward the young Canadian is not difficult to fathom.

For every Bishop detractor, however, there were many avid Bishop supporters. Jack Rutherford, a contemporary Canadian from Montreal on 60 Squadron, was very fond of him, as was J.B. Crompton.[62] Rutherford would later tell Arthur Bishop that none of them possessed Billy's confidence, a quality pivotal to his survival and success.[63] Caldwell was also a devotee. Jack Scott's admiration for him knew no bounds. He was also tremendously popular with the groundcrew, and his admirers on other units were legion.

In dire need of a respite from combat, Bishop returned to England on leave on May 7, the day Albert Ball was killed in action. Bishop wept at the news of Ball's demise.[64] The two had shared much in common, and when Ball visited 60 Squadron on May 5, the two aces are thought to have plotted an early morning raid together on a German aerodrome once Bishop returned from leave.[65] Trenchard, after all, had recently exhorted the RFC scout community to seize the initiative through offensive action whenever possible.[66] With Ball's passing, Bishop was now the reigning empire ace-of-aces, and a side of him thoroughly enjoyed the attention heaped on him by Lady St. Helier and others. Hobnobbing with London's élite must have been a heady experience for the young Canadian. The other side of him longed to return to his service home at Filescamp Farm, which he did on May 22. Henceforth, he did not mince words about his personal war aims. As he wrote later: "By this time I had become very ambitious, and was hoping to get a large number of machines credited to me before I left France."[67]

The Germans did not cooperate. They were nowhere to be seen, having moved further north to Flanders in anticipation of the upcoming Ypres offensive. Still, doggedly pursuing his solo forays up to 40 miles behind the lines, Bishop managed to claim three more victories on May 26, 27, and 31, when none of the other squadron members were even seeing aircraft with black crosses.[68] There had been no witnesses to these combats, either in the air or on the ground, and yet Scott endorsed all three

Opposite:
Billy Bishop's infamous dawn raid of June 2, 1917. The German aircraft depicted are Albatros DIIIs of Jasta 20. Bishop has just made a firing pass in Nieuport 17 B1566 over the airfield, scattering ground crew and aircraft in his wake. Unlike the original paint scheme and configuration of the Canadian National Aviation Museum's replica Bishop Nieuport, this painting accurately reflects B1566 as it appeared on this date. Note the blue propeller spinner and the identification letters/numerals on the wings and fuselage.

claims, to the chagrin of some of the other squadron members:

Such a move was unprecedented and it was to cause a great deal of discontent in the squadron mess. But Scott had his reasons. First of all, he had no cause to suspect Bishop of lying. Of the twenty-two victories claimed by his star pilot prior to the London leave, there were witnesses in the majority of cases. There is evidence, too, in German records confirming many of these earlier kills. Scott knew also that Bishop, with a roving commission, was free to fly forty or more miles behind enemy lines. He often covered four times as much territory as the other pilots, who flew together on escort duty or offensive patrol near the front lines. Billy's chances of finding — and surprising — a German were much better than those of his comrades.

But several pilots had doubts nevertheless. It was not uncommon in aerial combat for a man to submit accurate reports until he built up an impressive score and then, with an inflated opinion of his own ability, to begin over-claiming. Because his earlier, well-documented successes had made a favourable impression on the commander, such a man would have [his] exaggerated claims taken as gospel. This, some 60 Squadron flyers were now convinced, was exactly what Bishop was doing.

Whether they were legitimate conquests or simply flights of an overly active imagination, the three victories had been officially accepted and Bishop's score was, therefore, still climbing.[69]

Bishop was consumed with the idea of orchestrating a spectacular combat action, to ensure his everlasting greatness and recognition as a warrior. Ironically, Scott had secretly recommended Bishop for a Victoria Cross some weeks earlier, but the recommendation had been turned down by the War Office.[70] Bishop's upcoming airfield raid was a deliberately contrived, though undeniably courageous, event. As he wrote home on May 31: "I have a great plan in mind, a real hair-raising stunt which I am going to try one of these days."[71] This stunt was the airfield attack he and Ball seem to have discussed, and it synchronized with Trenchard's desire for pilots to rove at will and shoot at any

targets they discovered.[72] At a mess party on the night of June 1, Bishop debated the merits of such a mission the following morning with Grid Caldwell, Jack Scott, and William Fry, who was now Bishop's deputy flight commander.[73] This group of seasoned warriors thought it was too dangerous a scheme for one man to accomplish alone. Caldwell argued that with still wind conditions at dawn, German scouts, once aroused, could take off after him from any direction, severely limiting his chances of a successful escape. Bishop would not be dissuaded, and Scott told him to go ahead. "Billy made one last-minute pitch to talk his deputy flight leader, Willy Fry, into coming along on the mission. Unable to get a commitment out of the Englishman, he left the mess party early and asked his batman to wake him up at 3 a.m."[74] Greeted by a light drizzle at the appointed hour, Bishop again asked Fry to join him: "Early the following morning, before light, he came into my room and asked if I were going with him. I had a headache from the night's party and answered that I was not for it, turned over and went to sleep again."[75] Alone but still undeterred, Bishop bade his mechanic Walter Bourne goodbye and winged his way into the misty, grey dawn. It was precisely 3:57 a.m.

After overflying one of several enemy airfields in the vicinity of Cambrai, at which he observed no activity, Bishop proceeded southeast to a second airfield, which he had located by chance at 4:23 and identified as either Esnes or Awoignt. Here he observed seven aircraft (six Albatros DI or DII scouts and one two-seater). He also noted four sheds and a hangar resembling RFC hangars, along with a number of vehicles parked on a nearby roadside. Bishop strafed the aircraft, some of which were ground-idling their engines. One of them took off and he fired thirty rounds into it at close range, causing it to crash. A second aircraft took off, at which he fired a further thirty rounds from 150 yards range. This aircraft crashed into some trees near the aerodrome boundary. Two additional Albatros aircraft now took off in formation. Bishop engaged one of them at 1000 feet, finishing his first drum in the process. This aircraft crashed 300 yards from the aerodrome. The second aircraft of the pair pursued Bishop, and he fired a whole drum at it, causing it to break off its attack.

Bishop decided it would be prudent to leave the area, but there were four enemy scouts overhead

at 5000 feet, so he flew on a parallel course below them for some distance, heading south, and then broke off to the west. He had not been detected, but he was unsure of his exact location with respect to the front. During this portion of the return flight, he lowered his Lewis to install his last ammunition drum, but was unable to do so or to reposition the weapon back in its firing position on the wing. Frustrated, he then apparently undid the bracket that secured the gun to the Foster mounting and threw both the weapon and the drum overboard:

> He flew on and crossed the lines, but, still being lost, he landed in a field to establish his whereabouts. Having done so, he flew back to Filescamp Farm, firing off Very lights as he arrived, and landed at 0540. B1566 had 17 bullet holes in it, and the trailing edge of a lower mainplane was shot away in two bays.[76]

Bishop's mates were both awestruck and elated by his exploit. Sergeant-Major A.A. Nicod specifically noted the combat damage to Bishop's Nieuport: "His machine was badly damaged by anti-aircraft guns and machine gun fire."[77] Bishop had accomplished a significant act of valour, and a highly inspirational one, not just to 60 Squadron but to the entire Royal Flying Corps.[78] That afternoon, Scott arranged through his friend, Lord Dalmeny, to present Bishop to the 3rd Army Commander, General Allenby, to relate the essentials of his action.[79] Allenby and Trenchard were mightily impressed, and Scott now had all the ammunition he needed for Bishop's Victoria Cross. This recommendation was completely without precedent, for there were no witnesses. However, Rule Number 12 of the Warrant for the Order of the Victoria Cross states that, in the absence of the establishment of a claim on the spot, the monarch will confer the award, "but never without conclusive proof of the performance of the act of bravery for which the claim is made." This statement implies that a thorough investigation of the circumstances of the action would be required. When higher headquarters sought further supplemental information to the Victoria Cross recommendation on the raid, this was provided in a report to 13th Wing on June 30 by Grid Caldwell, the acting commanding officer of 60 Squadron.[80] After a full nine weeks of staffing and consideration by the War Office, the award was duly gazetted on August 11, 1917.

Meanwhile, Bishop had been far from idle. Still obsessed with surpassing Ball's record of forty-four claims, he continued flying and hacking down German aircraft at a fevered pace. Between June 8 and August 16, Bishop submitted a further twenty-two claims, bringing his total to forty-seven confirmed victories under the rules of the day.[81] Although still in command of C Flight and flying his fair share of formation patrols, he was probably not a diligent flight commander, consumed as he was by his quest to be the highest scorer in the RFC. Fry and others noted that he appeared increasingly aloof and austere, and, although popular, "I do not remember him having any particular friends."[82] Sholto Douglas felt that Bishop preferred to live his life in a hard and brittle world of his own making.[83] Roy Brown, another distinguished Canadian ace, also remembers Bishop's aloofness, a man who "kept his feelings corked."[84] The enormous stresses of combat and the repeated pressures Bishop was placing on himself were beginning to take a toll on his mental and physical health. As he wrote at the time:

> I am thoroughly downcast tonight. The Huns got Lloyd today, such a fine fellow too, and one of our best pilots. Sometimes all of this awful fighting in the air makes you wonder if you have a right to call yourself human. My honey, I am so sick of it all, the killing, the war. All I want is home and you.[85]

> I find myself shuddering at chances I didn't think about taking six weeks ago.[86]

> My bullets … shattered his face and skull. I can't get that picture out of my mind.[87]

Throughout June, Scott continued to endorse Bishop's claims as "decisive," even when there were no witnesses.[88]

Near the end of July, 60 Squadron re-equipped with the relatively potent SE5, and in the last three weeks of his first tour, Bishop scored eleven more times. These claims had a much higher witnessing rate, as had claims submitted earlier in the month when he was still flying the Nieuport. By August 16, Bishop had forty-seven confirmed claims to his credit, and was now firmly established as the leading British air hero. Trenchard decided he had done enough and removed him from combat. Given

Bishop's mental fatigue, it was a timely and fortuitous decision. In recognition of his latest string of victories, he eventually received a Bar to his Distinguished Service Order and a Mentioned in Dispatches.

Before he returned to Canada for an extended leave, he attended an impressive investiture ceremony at Buckingham Palace on August 30. There, for the first time in military history, His Majesty George V pinned on him the nation's three highest awards for gallantry: the Victoria Cross, the Distinguished Service Order, and the Military Cross. With a smile he said: "You *have* been making a nuisance of yourself out there, haven't you, Captain?"[89]

In Bishop, a war-weary Canada found just the tonic it needed. Having been bludgeoned with the mind-numbing daily slaughter of the Western Front for three long years, the nation was captivated by the exploits of the charismatic young air hero. Under the ever-watchful eye of the wartime censor and propaganda bureau, both organizations keen on taking whatever measures deemed necessary to induce recruitment, he helped pen his story in *Winged Warfare*. The publisher's preface to this exercise in hyperbole, which included a thrilling combat engagement with Baron von Richthofen that never occurred,[90] makes clear the intended purpose of this account: "His book will prove an inspiration to every young man already in the army 'wings' or who contemplates an army career." In fairness to Bishop, he was later embarrassed by this embellishment of combat events that had been exciting enough in their own right.[91] Spencer Horn, a distinguished colleague who served with Bishop on both his first and second fighter tours, later denigrated the book as "too much line-shooting" in a letter to 60 Squadron.[92] There can be no doubt that it further rankled his peers in RFC combat units.

While the press had a field day recounting his combat exploits, Bishop regaled many thousands on speaking tours of the nation. And on October 17 he married Margaret in Toronto at Timothy Eaton Memorial Church. He then embarked on an official tour of the United States. Ostensibly, his task was to help organize US aircraft production, but his principal job was to stimulate enlistment and support for the Allied war effort in the recently committed United States. Again, he was enormously successful, achieving tremendous rapport with his audiences. On his return, however, at a speech to the Canadian Club in Montreal, some inappropriate remarks about the woeful unpreparedness of American industry for war production landed him in trouble, and he was nearly court-martialed.[93] Instead, he was reprimanded, promoted to major, and sent back to England, Margaret in tow, to form a new fighter squadron.

Bishop had been clamouring for a return to combat and an opportunity to reclaim his title as the empire's unrivalled virtuoso of aerial combat. At the head of 85 Squadron, nicknamed the "Flying Foxes," his star shone very brightly during an abbreviated second fighter combat tour. The War Office had been inundated with over two hundred applications from pilots who wanted to join Bishop's squadron and have the opportunity to fly combat with him. This would hardly have been a likely turn of events had Bishop been considered an open fraud at the time.[94] At any rate, Bishop was given a reasonably free hand in the selection of his pilots, who would fly the latest variant of the SE5a into battle. It was a truly international unit, with several Americans (including future ace Elliott White Springs), two New Zealanders, six Canadians, two Australians, two Scots, one Irishman, and six Englishmen.

Posted to Petit Synthe, France, on May 22, 1918, Bishop gunned down a German two-seater five days later east of Passchendaele in Flanders. The very next day he resumed his trademark audacity by attacking a flight of nine Albatros DVs southwest of Cortemarck, near Ypres, and felling two of them.[95] Again, while still leading formation patrols, Bishop quickly reverted to his preferred "lone hawk" style of hunting,[96] which once more caused dissatisfaction on the unit. By June 4 he had added a further eight victories to his tally. Moving the squadron south to St. Omer on June 8, he destroyed a Pfalz DIII on June 15 east of Estaires, a two-seater and an Albatros the following day east of Armentieres, a triple victory on June 17, followed by a double success on June 18.[97] This frantic pace made Bishop anxious that he would soon be withdrawn from operational flying, as the Canadian government was increasingly concerned that its great national hero would be killed in battle. His fear was legitimate. On June 18 Bishop was ordered to leave France the following day. Never one to acquiesce quietly, he took off on the morning of the 19th for "one last look at the war" and, in fifteen minutes of furious combat, accounted for five enemy aircraft: four Pfalz scouts and a two-seater near Ploesgsteert.[98] His final total now stood at seventy-two victories, including two observation balloons. In just twelve days of actual

typically taciturn monarch quipped: "You now have the VC, DSO, MC and DFC after your name. If you do anything more to distinguish yourself, perhaps we should call you Archbishop!"[100]

Why has Bishop's Great War record generated such a storm of controversy, particularly in recent years? There are a number of reasons, none of

Pfalz DIII

combat during the tour, he had destroyed a further twenty-five enemy aircraft. This time his victories were much less contentious and more reliably witnessed.[99]

On his return to England, Bishop was promoted to lieutenant-colonel, awarded the new Distinguished Flying Cross for his recent successes, and named Officer Commanding-Designate of the Canadian Air Force Section of the General Staff, Headquarters Overseas Military Forces of Canada. The plan was to field a two-squadron fighting force in France as an indigenous Canadian Air Force, but the Armistice intervened before it came to pass. At year's end, Bishop was demobilized, but not before another visit with George V at Buckingham Palace. While pinning the DFC on Bishop's breast, the

them particularly mysterious. First, one must come to grips with his propensity for yarn spinning and recognize the paradox inherent in his writings. On the one hand, there is the terse, laconic nature of his combat reports, which formed the foundation of his victory claims and recommendations for awards. On the other, there is the unadulterated hyperbole of his social writings. They ranged from the harmless exaggeration in letters home, particularly to his fiancée, to material that was published under his name, such as *Winged Warfare,* and articles he penned for trade and adventure journals between the wars.[101] Although Bishop may not have written all these published words himself, he was a willing accomplice. He did nothing to deny or retract the fables that were concocted about his war exploits — a characteristic he shared with another great Canadian flyer of the war, his good friend Will Barker,[102] and other famous aces. William Avery Bishop loved to regale audiences and his family — a pastime to which he freely admitted. These stories should not be confused with his highly professional combat reports, often the antithesis of his social musings.

There is no doubt that Bishop preferred solo combat sojourns to formation teamwork, though he led his fair share of group efforts. However, some of his colleagues found his bloodlust and his overly ambitious pursuit of status tedious. Though capa-

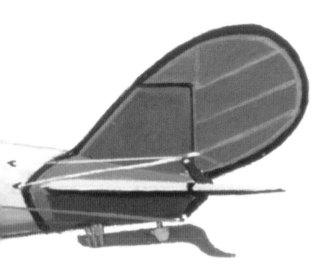

ble of being a jolly extrovert, he could also be moody, self-obsessed, and withdrawn. He was not a considerate flight commander, and was a squadron commander for only a brief spell. Nevertheless, he certainly set a fine example for courage and tenacity. Some journalists have portrayed Bishop as fearless, and even his most passionate detractors have never questioned his courage. However, fearless people do not experience combat stress, and there is ample evidence that Bishop so suffered. Perhaps he exhibited the highest form of courage by continuing to fly hazardous missions, by returning to combat even after he had been significantly stressed and could easily have sought safer duties, and by staunchly resisting rotation away from the front during the course of combat tours.

During the Great War, Bishop had a few detractors, but a legion of supporters. It was not until 1982, long after his death, that a National Film Board "docudrama," *The Kid Who Couldn't Miss*, strongly suggested that portions of Bishop's distinguished combat career had been fabricated. Singled out for special attention was the solo airfield raid of June 2, 1917, which garnered Bishop his Victoria Cross. The film implied that Bishop faked the entire

event, landed somewhere on his side of the lines, and shot up his own Nieuport with his Lewis gun to simulate enemy battle damage. Canadian historian Brereton Greenhous felt that the producer, Paul Cowan, was guilty of slipshod handling of historical facts, both through carelessness and in a quest for dramatic effect. "Artistically, the film is a minor triumph; historically, it is a sloppy, sleazy piece of work which raises a significant question: Was Bishop a liar and a cheat?"[103] Subsequently, the Senate of Canada charged a subcommittee with an examination of the accuracy and propriety of the NFB production. In the final analysis, its findings were inconclusive. While highly critical of Cowan's work, the subcommittee was frustrated by the lack of hard evidence to support Bishop's claims.

The principal detractors of Bishop in the film were First World War British fighter pilots who had not actually served with Bishop, but knew of him by repute. They were all of advanced age and they appeared to have been coached in their testimony when they were interviewed for the Imperial War Museum. Another detractor of Bishop, according to Cowan, was William Fry, Bishop's gallant deputy in 60 Squadron and a decorated and distinguished scout pilot in his own right. In his excellent autobiography, *Air of Battle*, published in 1974, Fry suggested that some of the bullet holes observed in Bishop's Nieuport on his return to Filescamp Farm after the airfield raid were in a close grouping, implying a shot from exceptionally close range. The remark in context may have been totally innocent.[104] Fry is also the only source to state that Bishop told him he landed on the Allied side of the lines to ask directions back to Filescamp Farm after the raid. In all other respects, Fry's words about Bishop are laudatory and, at worst, objective and detached. However, there must have been some bone of contention between Bishop and Fry in 1917, since Jack Scott apparently took Fry to task for making a scurrilous remark about Bishop's claims. When Fry refused to apologize, Scott posted him back to England. Therefore, Fry may well have harboured a long-standing grudge against Bishop. When Dan McCaffery contacted Fry for clarification, Fry was reticent. "He waited six months before replying to a letter and then would only say, 'I much regret being unable to help you.'"[105]

Other apparent detractors included Squadron Leader (Ret'd) Joe Warne, 60 Squadron's historian, and Grid Caldwell. Although Warne testified before the Senate as a denegrator of Bishop's Great War record, he was also highly critical of the NFB production. His own testimony with respect to Bishop contains inconsistencies, inaccuracies, and misleading assumptions. Caldwell's belated denouncement of Bishop is somewhat mysterious. A gallant and able airman who served with distinction in both world wars, it appears that he later became convinced, owing to a lack of substantiating German records, that the airfield raid, and other Bishop claims, were bogus.

Collectively, the doubts about the airfield raid centre on six points:

•Bishop could not have conducted the mission as he claimed to have done (with an airfield raid at Esnes or Awoignt) at the flight parameters stated, within the accepted endurance specifications of the Nieuport 17 aircraft.

•He admitted to landing behind Allied lines before returning to Filescamp Farm.

•Some of the battle damage to his Nieuport was closely grouped, with the concomitant insinuation that the aircraft may have been stationary when it was inflicted.

•Bishop's Lewis gun was missing when he returned from the raid.

•Damage to his aircraft was not as extensive as has often been expressed.

•German records make absolutely no mention of this event.

Philip Markham has demonstrated through meticulous technical research that Bishop would have had adequate fuel for the duration of his flight, provided he returned from his target at a medium altitude. Bishop's combat report stated that he used various altitudes, from 50 to 7000 feet, throughout the mission. Although the endurance of the Nieuport 17 has repeatedly been generalized to a figure of two hours, many combat aviators of the period, including Bishop, commonly logged flights of that duration. Markham states that the aircraft's endurance was as high as 2.4 hours under certain flight profiles.[106] The undisputed duration of this particular flight was 1 hour 43 minutes. If Bishop in fact made a brief stop on the Allied side of the lines to ask for directions, his overall endurance capability for this mission would have increased further.

Fry's *Air of Battle* is the only book that mentions Bishop's making an interim landing. It

seems, then, that Bishop did not feel the stop was of any particular consequence. He may indeed have made a brief stop for guidance, or because he was experiencing a post-traumatic stress incident and needed the stability of being on the ground for a few minutes. In Bishop's own words:

I now headed in the approximate direction of our lines, and flew in rather a dazed state toward them. I had not had any breakfast, and was feeling very queer at my stomach. The excitement, and the reaction afterward, had been a bit too much, as well as the cold morning air. It seemed, once or twice, that my head was going around and around, and that something must happen. For the only time in my life it entered my thoughts that I might lose my senses in a moment, and go insane. It was a horrible feeling, and I also had the terrible sensation that I would suffer from nausea any minute. I was not at all sure where I was, and furthermore did not care. The thrills and exultation I had at first felt had all died away, and nothing seemed to matter but this awful feeling of dizziness and the desire to get home and on the ground.[107]

The NFB suggestion that, while on the ground, Bishop shot up his aircraft with his Lewis gun defies logic for a number of reasons. First, the Nieuport did not have brakes, which meant that, to perform this act, he would have had to shut the engine down or enlist witnesses to hold the aircraft while he did the shooting.[108] If he shut the engine down, he would still have needed accomplices, since the starting procedure for a Nieuport required the help of someone to cycle the propeller. In addition, this raid occurred at a time when the Nieuport's structural integrity was causing a great deal of anxiety. The suggestion of deliberately weakening an already suspect aerodynamic structure in the course of a flight makes no sense. Finally, the damage to Bishop's aircraft centred around damage to the lower plane being shot away in two bays.[109] Such battle damage is consistent with the firing of a weapon from underneath the aircraft, either from the ground or from another aircraft in a flight dynamic, but not with a burst fired from a Lewis gun beside the aircraft.

Although Fry suggested that some of the battle damage was closely grouped, implying firing from a close range, he may have used the expression "bullet holes" loosely. He stated that this damage was in the elevator, or horizontal component, of the tailplane — again, an unlikely location for self-inflicted damage fired from beside the aircraft. The close grouping may not have been from bullet holes, but from shrapnel tears. Nicod later testified to both types of damage[110] and Bishop, according to his son, referred to the effects of shrapnel when he re-crossed the lines at 1000 feet on this mission.[111] Arthur Bishop's book was published in 1965, nearly a decade before Fry's, and well before the raid became the subject of a full-blown controversy.

In truth, any number of weapons could have damaged Bishop's aircraft. Even below 3000 feet altitude, Bishop could have received far more than machine-gun fire. In the area of the front, he could well have flown through low-trajectory shell bursts in his "dazed state." Had he strayed near an observation balloon launch site, he would have been exposed to Maxim guns, or fortress guns firing 1.5 inch solid shot.[112] The damage may have been caused by "flaming onions," or 37 mm cannon shells,[113] which were widely deployed at the front. Also, by 1917, Becker 19 mm cannons capable of firing small explosive shells were reaching the front, and it is known that 131 of these weapons were issued to the German anti-aircraft service for short-range air defence.[114]

It is true that Bishop's Lewis gun was missing from his aircraft when he returned to Filescamp Farm. Again, the only recorded explanation is found in the Fry book. According to Fry, Bishop said he had unfastened the screw-up release of the securing

Lewis gun mounted
on SE5a

collar and thrown the weapon overboard after he had been stymied in an attempt to install a fresh ammunition drum on the way home.[115] Bishop had let the gun down on its loading quadrant, but was unable to replace the drum or to move the gun back to the firing position on the wing. Stewart K. Taylor testified to the Senate subcommittee that changing a ninety-seven-round Lewis drum in the aircraft slipstream in a distracting combat situation was a very difficult task. Mannock, Bishop, and Ball had all reported complications in so doing. Taylor also testified, however, that "it would have been relatively simple for him to loosen the screw on the securing collar, let down the Lewis gun on the quadrant, and throw the 15-pound Lewis gun overboard."[116] The gun would have been not only useless but in his way — reasons enough to jettison the weapon.

The extent of the aircraft's damage is well documented. It is also known that Bishop flew it again later in the afternoon.[117] The damage was apparently superficial and confined to the fabric, so was easily repairable at the unit level. Bishop returned early in the morning, and the application and doping of fabric patches could have been completed in ample time for the afternoon flight. Bishop flew the aircraft with the patched planes for some time thereafter.

By default, then, the most controversial aspect of the June 2, 1917, raid is the absence of any acknowledgment of it in German records. However, there are reasons for this lack of German verification. In the past, certain historians have dismissed the raid because it had no documented impact on any of the resident German scout units in the area. They placed particular emphasis on Jasta 5 at Estourmel airfield, the place Bishop was thought to have attacked. However, until Stewart Taylor intervened, no one had paid any attention to transient units in the region at the time. He testified that, contrary to the long-held and widespread belief in the Estourmel theory, Bishop actually attacked a transiting scout unit at a temporary field near Esnes, approximately 4 miles south of Estourmel.[118] The unit was a kette, or flight, of Jasta 20 that had been based further south at Guise in the Somme region. However, German air units in Flanders needed bolstering in preparation for the British attack anticipated there in early June. Jasta 20 was notified

... that they had a week to fly north directly across the path of Esnes, up into Flanders to a

place called Middelburg where they were to operate. They had their last combat on the Somme Front on the 24th of May, 1917. A day later, they commenced to move by kette; in other words, in groups of three, four, five, six or seven. In this case, the weather closed in on the 28th and there was little flying. On the 29th, the weather was bad. Probably the first group of five machines got away on the 1st of June or perhaps the 31st of May. On the night of May 31, the weather was good.

The last group of German machines, seven Albatros and one LVG two-seater, left on the 1st of June. They flew as far as Esnes for refueling and landed on what was almost an emergency landing ground. They figured there would not be any Allied aircraft there because there were only three or four Allied squadrons opposite the Cambrai Front at that particular period, so they thought they were safe.[119]

Machines in transit would require servicing and support en route. Although there was no permanent airfield at Esnes until the following year, a temporary airfield, probably supported by a resident unit in the area,[120] would likely have included some form of portable hangars, which may well have been the hangars and sheds to which Bishop was referring in his reconnaissance report of the mission.[121] While Bishop correctly identified the scouts as Albatros and also singled out the two-seater, he probably mistook the subvariant of Albatros as DIs or DIIs instead of the more likely later DIII variants of the type then at the front. He also counted six single-seaters instead of the seven known to have been with Jasta 20. But these are minor discrepancies. The other Albatros may have been hidden from view at the time or in a tent hangar. In any case, many contemporaries have documented that Bishop's aircraft recognition was never his strong suit. Alternatively, the entry on the combat report may have simply been an error of hasty recording or of typography.[122] At any rate, when thundering over an enemy airfield at more than 100 miles per hour with danger all around, concentrating on an attack, the visual differences between a tent hangar and a permanent structure from this fleeting airborne perspective are insignificant. The same argument applies to the identification of specific subvariants of a known enemy aircraft type. Black crosses on wings were black crosses on wings, and Bishop would have considered all enemy aircraft he encountered to be fair game for his Lewis gun.

The paucity and unreliability of the German Air Force war records are discussed in Appendix C. With respect to the June 2, 1917, raid, Jasta 20, had it been fully moved to its new operating base, would have made the usual daily reports to the Kommandeur der Flieger, the officer in charge of all flying units assigned to a particular numbered German Army. However, Jasta 20 was still transiting from the 2nd German Army to the 4th German Army and was temporarily unattached. Under these dynamic conditions, it would have been unusual to have kept any records other than the Jasta 20 War Diary, which was lost to Allied bombing during the Second World War.[123] With the unit on the move, it is highly unlikely that the War Diary even accompanied this transiting kette. It was probably moved, along with other Jasta records, by ground transport with the unit's administrative echelon, and this incident may never have been written up under the circumstances. On August 17, 1985, Major E. Guth of the German Military Historical Department in Freiburg, Germany, confirmed via letter to Colonel (Ret'd) A.J. Bauer of the Billy Bishop Heritage that no official documents are available on this unit from this period.[124] In the past, much has been made of American historian Ed Ferko's notes on Jasta 20, a portion of the handwritten collection of the German historian Turnuss. In them, nothing was mentioned about the airfield raid.[125] In fact, the Ferko notes apparently fail to show much Jasta 20 activity of any sort between May 27 and July 11, 1917, a condition that appears suspect for a supposedly healthy, fully manned unit sent to reinforce what was then an active front.[126] It is possible, although unlikely, that Bishop's attack may have had a prolonged effect on the manning of this unit. It is also interesting to note that when Jasta 20's available records surface after the movement north, the names of three of the unit's pilots — Baurose, Geisler, and Heiss — all of whom had been on the strength of the unit on May 20, are missing from Jasta rosters.[127] However, an excellent recent work by Norman Franks, Frank Bailey, and Rick Duiven notes that Baurose was a member of the Jasta from April 1917 until February 6, 1918. A Geisler was

with the unit from November 27, 1916, to July 27, 1918. But the name Heiss does not appear in unit rosters. A member having the closest spelling is Heising, who was actually the Jasta commanding officer for a year from the autumn of 1916 until the autumn of 1917.[128] Although this circumstance does not make a resounding case for the meticulousness of German records, it may also be an indication that these men were wounded but not killed by Bishop during the raid, and that their wounds necessitated their temporary removal from the unit. It would have been logical for the Jasta commander to be the last to shuttle northward, and the deliberate lack of recording of non-fatal casualties would have been in keeping with accepted German practices of the time. Temporary removal from the unit for treatment of wounds and/or subsequent leave may well not have been recorded. It is also entirely possible that some of the aircraft shot up by Bishop were repairable or partially salvageable.

Did the Germans deliberately suppress reporting of the aerodrome raid at the time, only to brand it a hoax at a later date? If so, what would have been their rationale for doing so? Sadly, the long-term subscription of Bishop advocates over the years to the theory that Estourmel was the location of the attack has unnecessarily undermined his credibility. It quite simply did not occur there. However, there may well have been an Estourmel connection. Estourmel was at that time the home of Jasta 5, which was responsible for the air defence of a considerable portion of the Cambrai front, including the local area of Esnes and Estourmel. It is common knowledge that the temporary commander of Jasta 5 at the time was Leutnant Werner Voss, then Germany's second highest-ranking ace to Manfred von Richthofen and a formidable public relations asset in his own right.[129] It is also known that German authorities were often selective about what they chose to record, particularly information that could fall into the hands of the journalists and embarrass the German Air Force. Bishop's solo raid would inspire many more low-level airfield raids in the near future, some solo performances and others in formation. These raids would be mentioned, though not dwelled upon, in German unit records, for they eventually became commonplace. However, Bishop's sortie was the precursor to the others, and the Germans may well have been reluctant to document it at a higher level, for fear of tarnishing

Voss' pristine image with the German public. Once Bishop's Victoria Cross was announced nine weeks after the event, the Germans publicly discounted it as an Entente propaganda hoax — a natural response given that they may have chosen to suppress the event in the first instance.[130]

British records have served to cast further doubt on the raid, for a lot of them have been lost over the years. The Victoria Cross records are particularly disappointing. Philip Markham's extensive correspondence with senior officials at the British Ministry of Defence in the 1980s and 1990s yielded some information from the head of the Reviewing Section in the Public Record Office. The building containing many older files, including the First World War Victoria Cross papers, was bombed by the Germans during the Second World War and many of the files were destroyed. Any surviving Great War paperwork on awards was subsequently retained at the Public Record Office under Files WO-32 and WO-86, Code 50. These particular file boxes were rechecked, but no correspondence regarding Bishop's Victoria Cross was found. It is fascinating to speculate what exactly constituted the "conclusive proof" required for the award.

Although it appears that no definitive written evidence of the raid exists from the German side of the lines, a significant body of circumstantial evidence has surfaced over time. Early reports that an Allied balloonist had witnessed the entire event turned out to be false, but a narrative of the raid published as early as 1918 by *The Times* implied corroboration.[131] After the war, numerous authors made reference to secondary confirmations, both by Allied agents behind the lines and through the interrogation of recently captured German prisoners of war:

> After long weeks of careful investigation as to the authenticity of his report, the decoration was confirmed on August 11, 1917. Agents inside the German lines discovered that the two-seater had been seriously damaged, several of the single-seaters had been put out of action, and the fourth Albatros pilot had been lightly wounded.[132]

Bishop's exploit was confirmed, particularly since a Victoria Cross was involved. Captured airmen told what he had done. It had been the talk of the German flying forces.[133]

This daring exploit, which was confirmed in the days following by German pilots who were taken prisoner, won Bishop the greatest of all decorations for valour, the Victoria Cross.[134]

These snippets of circumstantial evidence were all published long before there was a swirling controversy over the raid. Other passages of support for Bishop have materialized, both before and after the release of *The Kid Who Couldn't Miss*. Some are particularly interesting, in that they imply acknowledgment of the raid by the Germans.

Some German authorities have questioned Billy Bishop's record, particularly in reference to his claim of having shot down three of their planes and damaged three others during his famous attack on a German airfield on June 2, 1917. They have long insisted that Bishop made only one quick pass at a number of planes on the ground, and that when their scouts went aloft to intercept him, he hurried home.[135]

The Germans questioned William Bishop's record of three enemy planes shot down and three damaged on a raid on a German airfield, stating that he left in such a hurry he had no way of knowing what he had destroyed and what he had merely fired on.[136]

In the wake of the NFB production, Dan McCaffery, after years of extensive research, introduced new source material concerning Bishop's raid. Although these references imply that the raid took place on Estourmel, the reader must bear in mind that Estourmel and Esnes were only 4 miles apart, with farmland in between. Therefore, it is not unreasonable to assume that the following source references refer to the Estourmel area, not the exact airfield location, and that the Esnes field was only temporary at the time of the raid. To begin, McCaffery quoted a recollection of former British airman Lieutenant Philip B. Townsend, an RE8 pilot with 12 Squadron in 1918. Writing to *Cross & Cockade* in 1985, Townsend reiterated that his squadron had moved to Estourmel aerodrome on October 12, 1918, where they were told that a British scout had attacked German aircraft one morning in 1917 "and had shot down three Huns."[137] On subsequent contact by McCaffery in 1986, Townsend said that this information had been "learnt from local French people, local farmers resident at the time of Townsend's posting there."[138] Based on this input, McCaffery suggested that this information confirmed that the raid had been on Estourmel. Townsend later recanted this unqualified interpretation in correspondence with Markham, stating that the information he had received at the time was hearsay only.[139] Still, this sequence of revelations is interesting, since it appears that farmers near Estourmel were aware of an attack on an airfield somewhere in the vicinity at the appropriate time.

In his book, McCaffery also relates a supportive confirmation of Bishop's exploit by his old friend George Stirrett. The Major distinguished himself greatly during the war, rising rapidly through the ranks and winning both the Distinguished Conduct Medal and the Military Cross. As a Captain, he accompanied a force of Allied soldiers who had just taken the crew of a German two-seater as prisoners. Stirrett's testimony is interesting, both for its circumstantial confirmation of the raid and for the incidental, though inaccurate, reference to Voss:

> Recalling the incident in a 1981 interview, he [Stirrett] said: "The observer spoke fairly good English and I talked to him quite awhile before he was taken away … Anyway, I had applied to get into the RFC earlier in the war had had been turned down but still had a real interest in flying. Billy Bishop was at this time quite famous and I bragged to the German that he was a friend of mine, that we'd served together in the cavalry and gone overseas together — the whole works. He told me Bishop was well-known to the German airmen and that his airfield attack had been the talk of the whole German air force. He said Bishop had shot down three planes and that two of the pilots had been badly shaken up. It created a real stir because the squadron that Bishop beat up was commanded by Werner Voss, who he said was considered by a lot of Germans to be their greatest pilot, even greater than Richthofen." Werner Voss, it should be noted, was Jasta Fuhrer of Staffel 5, which was stationed at Estourmel on the morning of June 2, 1917. Equally important to note is that Stirrett made his remarks a year before the Bishop controversy became public. He knew nothing about the doubts about the

Billy Bishop (centre) in a lighthearted moment while serving with 60 Squadron. "Grid" Caldwell is on the right.

ace's record and could not be accused of attempting to cover for an old friend.[140]

In closing the discussion with respect to circumstantial evidence, and adding still more credence to the confirmation of the raid through German prisoners of war, McCaffery had an interview with former German Rumpler pilot Otto Roosen in Bracebridge, Ontario, in 1993. This interview is interesting not only for the circumstantial support for confirmation it provides to Bishop's airfield raid, but also for the allusions to German record-keeping practices:

> I then asked him if he had heard of Bishop's VC raid. I made it very clear I was asking if he had heard about it *during* the First World War. He replied, "Oh yes, we all knew about it. Our pilots talked about it for weeks. I talked to pilots who were there, but I can no longer remember their names." I asked Roosen about the lack of confirmation in German records and he was openly contemptuous of the records. "Our leaders didn't want to admit that sort of thing," he said. "If they could salvage a compass from the cockpit they'd say the

plane was only damaged. It wouldn't go into the records as having been shot down."[141]

By its sheer volume, this mountain of circumstantial evidence acquires a certain legitimacy of its own in support of Bishop's claim, and there is no countering empirical evidence to prove it false. Though the extent of damage inflicted by Bishop can never be confirmed, the mere prosecution of the raid was an inspirational, highly courageous, and incredibly dangerous act. It served as a catalyst for others to emulate, and there lies its true value. In any case, Bishop's Victoria Cross would eventually be justified, and more, by his combat results, which legitimized the award for sustained rather than isolated acts of valour. The First World War German Aces Association also honoured Bishop as the only Allied ace ever to be inducted into their membership — an unlikely distinction if they thought he was a fraud.[142] To briefly summarize, Bishop's aircraft had the technical capability to conduct the mission as claimed. The battle damage to his Nieuport was logical and explainable. Bishop repeatedly asked for accompaniment on the raid, which is inconsistent with the planned commissioning of a fraudulent act. Apparently, specific British records with respect to the event, other than early documents generated by Bishop himself and by 60 Squadron, no longer exist. However, there is a plethora of circumstantial evidence to suggest that the raid occurred. Finally, barring minor discrepancies in Bishop's recollections, a known and consistent target for Bishop's attentions was at Esnes on the early morning of June 2, 1917.

Perhaps the greatest tragedy of the controversy is that it has cast doubt over Bishop's entire combat record. It is not surprising that only a portion of Bishop's victories were witnessed or confirmed by a third party, given that, as a lone warrior, he sought the enemy over their own ground, without friendly witnesses and the advantage of mutual support. Considering these circumstances, as well as the scarcity and unreliability of German records, Bishop's claims still enjoy a high degree of verification. Stewart Taylor was able to relate specific German crew names to twenty-two of Bishop's victories.[143] Dan McCaffery, with help from Taylor and British historians Joe Warne and Dennis Hylands to supplement his own study of available German records, was able to assign names to a similar number of claims and to document Allied witnesses for twenty-six of them, including six that occurred on his solo flights.[144] Of his seventy-two confirmed claims, thirty-eight can either be paired with specific German crew names or verified by witnesses. Perhaps one of the most unusual witnesses was Manfred von Richthofen himself. When Bishop shot down Vizefeldwebel Sebastian Festner of Richthofen's Jasta on April 8, 1917, he claimed it only in the driven-out-of-control category. Although Festner made it back to his base, his aircraft, Albatros DIII 223/16, was so extensively damaged that von Richthofen consigned it to the scrap heap.[145]

Bishop's combat reports, far from embellishing the truth, were renowned for their terse, laconic nature. He tended not to claim categorical success:

Indeed, his combat reports are often very modest. There are numerous statements such as: "I fired the remainder of my drum from long range at it, but cannot say whether I hit it or not." Or, "He dived away and I fired about thirty shots at him with no apparent results." Or, "I engaged them and one double-seater went down in a nose-dive but I think partly under control." In that last case, which occurred on April 8, 1917, Bishop received credit for a "driven down" victory.[146]

On April 22, 1917, for example, Bishop had four witnesses, including Jack Scott, to an action in which he claimed one enemy aircraft damaged and another as driven down out of control. On his own instigation, and based on what he had witnessed, Scott increased Bishop's damaged claim to the higher category of driven down.[147] Also, for those who would argue that Bishop's claims were being given *carte blanche* approval by the War Office, the Public Records Office at Kew holds numerous unconfirmed claims from his war combats, suggesting that his claims were subject to the same close scrutiny accorded to everyone else.[148]

Bishop's record must be compared with that of his contemporaries, and not analyzed in isolation. Of the three highest-scoring empire aces who availed themselves extensively of the roving commissions — Ball, Bishop, and McCudden — only McCudden has a higher claim verification record with respect to assignation of specific German crew names to each of his victories. Against Bishop's seventy-two confirmed claims with names assigned in twenty-two cases, Ball has twelve with names assigned on forty-four confirmed claims, and five of the named cases are indefinite.[149] McCudden's record boasts a superb thirty-five named cases on fifty-seven confirmed claims, with only five named cases being indefinite.[150] McCudden's preferred targets were enemy two-seaters operating over the Entente side of the lines, a choice that accounts for his particularly large score of nineteen conquests in the "captured" category, and also the unusually high confirmation rate. With respect to Ball and Bishop, their prey of choice was the single-seat scouts which operated almost exclusively on their own side of the lines, making claim verifications difficult. If a criterion were imposed of requiring claimed victories to be matched with the specific names of enemy personnel, many other empire aces would not measure up well. The great Irishman Edward "Mick" Mannock has names matched to only twenty-one of his sixty-one accepted claims, and in six of the cases the names are indefinite. This fact is pivotal, since Mannock is widely touted as having a very high corroboration rate, and as having fought almost exclusively as a patrol formation member, usually as the leader. George McElroy, with forty-six confirmed claims, would fare much worse. Only one name has been matched against all his victories, and even that one is indefinite.[151] Similarly, Anthony Beauchamp-Proctor would drop from fifty-four to just three, and even Grid Caldwell, a Bishop critic, would have his score fall from twenty-five to three. Ira Jones, another Bishop detractor, would be particularly hard hit, having his confirmed score plummet from thirty-seven to two.[152] To place all these statistics in the context of Bishop's record, Philip Markham said: "Bishop's claims throughout his career enjoy formidable verification — from his Combat Reports, from Squadron Records, from Official Communiqués, and from his letters home."[153]

Was William Avery Bishop a deliberately concocted propaganda weapon of the Allies? Certainly not at the outset. Given the RFC survival rate during Bloody April and the rest of his first tour, coupled with his particular penchant for aggressively seeking extreme danger, his longer-term chances of survival were extremely remote. But as his successes mounted, the propaganda opportunity was a happy marriage of Bishop's success, Jack Scott's ambition for his unit, and the changing propaganda policy of the RFC. After his first combat tour as a pilot, Bishop was a willing participant in the propaganda initiatives of the Canadian government. That he was so effective in this role was due to the credibility of his formidable fighting record, his natural charisma and charm, and a war-weary public's need to be assuaged through heroic example. He also re-entered combat for the second pilot tour of his own free will in order to win further fame and glory. Far from being prodded back into combat at the behest of the propaganda apparatus, the nation was actually afraid it was going to lose him, resulting in his premature withdrawal from the fighting front during his third tour of operations. Through it all, Bishop never slacked in his relentless drive to engage the enemy, right until his last day of combat.

In 1919 Wing Commander Ira Jones[154] and a group of stalwart Mannock supporters managed to convince RAF authorities that Mannock's wartime score was actually seventy-three confirmed victories,[155] one ahead of Bishop and substantially more than Mannock was officially being credited with at the time. This initiative was eventually accepted by the RAF, displacing Bishop from his perch as the empire's ace-of-aces. However, British expert Christopher Shores and his fellow writers, after the closest scrutiny, have not been able to rationalize a confirmed score of seventy-three for Mannock. The most they have been able to justify is a score of sixty-one confirmed claims under the rules of the day.

Billy Bishop was in many respects a product of his own success and, often through his own embellishments, a victim of his own success. However, he was a skilled and resourceful warrior, possessed of uncommon valour, who served his nation with great distinction. Canada should take great reflected pride in his accomplishments and be grateful for his tenacity and daring. He richly deserves that measure of respect and recognition. As S.F. Wise attests:

A very high proportion of Bishop's kills, so-called, were in fact verified as the result of corroborative testimony. The allegation that there is fraudulence in the Bishop record I find without foundation whatsoever, and I believe I can say that authoritatively, having examined the whole record.[156]

CHAPTER FIVE

PER ARDUA AD ASTRA

1918

"If ever there was a storm after a lull,
it was the German offensive of March."

– Donald R. MacLaren

The role of air power as an integral part of military operations coalesced during the last year of the war. Although large numbers of air engagements and greater use of fighters in ground attack operations characterized much of 1918, the air war still operated on a limited scale at the dawn of the new year. As Canadian ace Donald MacLaren elaborated:

Early in 1918 there occurred what might truly be called a lull before the storm. Every branch of the service felt it, and none more than the Air Force. It was almost as if an armistice had been declared in the air, for German machines were seldom seen, and when encountered invariably avoided combat. The enemy fighting squadrons (Jagdstaffel) were composed of Albatros and Pfalz scouts, and now and then a Fokker triplane would be seen.

The British squadrons were superior in equipment, as we had the Sopwith Camel, the Sopwith Dolphin, and the SE5, all single-seater fighting scouts, better than the German machines in every way. However, even when we met formations of the enemy with conditions favourable for them, they would not attack unless outnumbering us.

So, for some unaccountable reason, the first months of 1918 passed by with the German Air Force living up to the best traditions of the German Navy. An average report in those days read: "No enemy aircraft seen. Visibility fair. Anti-aircraft fire normal."

Lack of action is very hard on airmen, and we used up considerable nervous energy trying to decide what ailed the Hun. At times we heard that he lacked material to manufacture machines, at others that he was conserving resources for his big offensive.[1]

If nervous tension and concern for the future was a fair characterization of most combatant airmen in early 1918, those feelings ran rampant throughout the Allied camp — and with good cause. In Canada on December 17, 1917, Borden's Unionist government had barely received the majority it needed to govern a profoundly divided nation. On December 6, Halifax had been all but levelled in a massive harbour explosion that left 1630 dead and thousands injured. Winter blizzards added to their misery. Rising prices and disappointing harvests combined to produce grave shortages of food and fuel, which in turn forced some schools and factories to close. And there seemed to be no end to the official war death notices coming out of Ottawa.

The rest of the Allies, with the exception of the Americans, were faring even worse. Britain's manpower crisis was by now extreme. Deployments to Italy had further depleted resources, eighteen-year-olds were being conscripted, and the war industries were combed for every available man. Deep divisions over continuance of the conflict existed in war-weary France. Her land forces, bled white by mutinies and manpower shortages, were in no shape for anything but defensive actions. British forces had been obliged to extend their own lines southward by 28 miles to relieve exhausted French troops — an act that further weakened the Flanders front. In the east, a Russian armistice had been declared in December, followed by a triumphant peace accord for the Germans — the humiliating Treaty of Brest-Litovsk of March 1918. At last Germany would be free of war on two fronts. Although the Americans were now in the war on the Allied side, they were taking significantly longer than anticipated to field their much-needed army.

Opposite: RFC Jenny at Deseronto, Ontario

An engine change on a SE5a in the field

131

The four-bladed propeller variant of the SE5a, 41 Squadron

Basic Training. Opposite: At RFC Camps Mohawk and Rathbun at Deseronto, Ontario, cadets flying, and crashing; Jenny meets Orillia, Ontario (centre, left)

nearly 8 million in 1914, totalled 214,000 by mid-1918. In Germany alone, 800,000 people would die of malnutrition before the Armistice.[2] General von Ludendorff decided that the only way to win the war was through the massing of forces and the use of surprise in a single great offensive — and the sooner the better.

In Canada, although the nation was in the midst of a conscription crisis, young men were flocking in record numbers to join the flying services. The previous year had witnessed a vast expansion of British military air interest in Canada, including the official formation of RFC Canada, "an autonomous imperial organization assisted by the Canadian government,"[3] designed to tap into the receptive Canadian manpower pool. Its first major airfield had been lashed together by June at Camp Borden, 70 miles north of Toronto. Soon, other sites had been completed at Deseronto, 130 miles east of Toronto, and in Toronto itself. The chosen instrument of instruction was the Curtiss JN4, commonly known as the "Jenny," a two-seat biplane powered by a water-cooled V-8 engine. By the end of July, the Curtiss Company had produced more than 150 for RFC Canada.

Soon after the Americans entered the war in April 1917, reciprocal arrangements were made with the United States government to train American pilots in Canada during the summer, and empire pilots south of the border during the winter. By year's end, a complex of three airfields in the Dallas/Forth Worth area of Texas, known collectively as Camp Taliaferro, was up and running. Although, by 1918, post-wings flight training at the operational training units in Britain had become increasingly specialized, codified, and sophisticated, accidents were frequent in both Canada and the United States. Flying discipline was exceptionally lax, exacerbated by the fact that students were encouraged to stunt and show dash. Ken Guthrie, a Canadian pilot trainee in Texas during 1918, recalled some unique experiences associated with the Texas training operation:

This sergeant-pilot of mine, he said, "You've got to go up and do some loops." I said, "Aren't you going to show me how?" He said, "No. Shit. Nobody showed me. You go up and do it yourself." So I climbed up to the maximum height a Jenny could go, about 7000 feet, put the nose down, put the engine hard on,

Furthermore, unrestricted submarine warfare, Germany's answer to the Allied blockade, was inflicting a dreadful toll. In the first six months of 1917, German U-boats sent 3.75 million tons of shipping and nearly 4000 Allied sailors to the bottom of the North Atlantic.

On the positive side, the Allied maritime blockade of Germany had become an extremely effective weapon of war. Although the agricultural and mineral potential represented by the eastern conquests was staggering for Germany, these resources could not be harnessed for some time. Serious social and political dissent divided the nation, and riots and labour unrest abounded. Whole regions had been decimated and people were starving. Half the cattle in the Austrian Empire had been killed, and the swine population, which had stood at

pulled back on the control and around I went. However, I forgot to shut off the engine at the top of the loop and I went around about three times! Must have taken me about half an hour to recover, and I didn't do it again, not for awhile. It was the same thing with spinning. We were told about the dangers of a spin, but nobody showed us how to get out of one …

… We wore the old Royal Flying Corps cap, known as the Splitass Cap, with the white flash at the front. The mechanics let it be known to the young ladies of Fort Worth and Dallas that the flash meant we had a social disease.[4]

The young men of Canada reacted positively to this first major military aviation recruiting campaign in Canadian history. Initiated in May 1917, it enrolled nearly 2400 recruits by year's end. The total war contribution of RFC Canada and its successor organization, RAF Canada, was considerable. By war's end, nearly 9200 cadets had enlisted, of which 3135 completed pilot training and more than 2500 served overseas. Had the war continued until 1919, the organization would have yielded roughly one-fifth of the pilot and observer replenishment requirements for the Western and Italian fronts.[5]

In Europe, empire pilots ushered in 1918 with some new scouts and improved variants of others. For example, 19 Squadron traded in its dated Spad S VIIs for the significantly improved S XIII two-gun model. However, the unit soon re-equipped with the entirely new Sopwith Dolphin. This aircraft proved to be an excellent fighter, although the unusual back-stagger of the upper wing, a design characteristic it shared with the less than stellar DH5, caused initial prejudice among pilots who had not flown it. Formidably armed, it boasted virtually double the firepower of existing empire scouts by augmenting its pair of Vickers guns with two flexible Lewis guns, installed above the cockpit on a mounting designed for upward fire.[6]

Although the first three months of 1918 yielded only desultory air combat engagements for the most part, there was still some action. George Robert Howsam from Port Perry, Ontario, established himself as a skilled, effective warrior flying Camels out of Poperinghe with 70 Squadron. He first scored on December 28, after pouring nearly 400 rounds into an Albatros two-seater over Zarren:

He sent another two-seater down out of control on January 19, 1918, and on the 22nd he had a busy day, scoring two victories on his own and sharing in two more. He was a member of a No. 70 Squadron patrol which was attacked by seven Albatros scouts. A member of the patrol, and presumably leading it, was Captain Francis Quigley, another Canadian who achieved fame as one of the war's top-scoring fighter pilots. Howsam shot down one of the enemy and then teamed with Quigley to bring down another. Quigley fired at the German from the side while Howsam attacked from below, and the enemy went into a spin and then burst into flames. A few moments later the pair together attacked yet another of the enemy, which went down "until it became enveloped in a cloud of black

An excellent perspective of how the pilot's head protruded above the upper wing of the Dolphin. The pilot is Second Lieutenant Norman S. Swan of 79 Squadron.

Basic Training. Opposite, top: A Curtiss JN4 stunting over the aerodrome, and one forced down during a snowstorm. Centre: the fire brigade complete with their "truck." Bottom: beds out for sunning at the School of Aerial Gunnery, Camp Hicks, Texas.

A Sopwith Dolphin after engine start. An upper wing Lewis gun is plainly visible, along with one of the twin Vickers guns.

smoke." Later in the day, while on a bombing raid, Howsam attacked a German two-seater over Houthulst Forest. The enemy aircraft burst into flames and went down to crash after Howsam had fired 400 rounds at it.

Howsam ended the month with three more victories, scored on the 24th, 25th, and 29th. The first of these was an Albatros two-seater that he shot down and which crashed, and the second was an Albatros scout which had been attacking a British RE8. Howsam sent it down "completely out of control" after following it down for a thousand feet, firing all the while. The third was a machine of unidentified type, which crashed after being attacked.

On February 4 he was awarded the MC, and it appeared that the recommendation may have been written following his victory of January 25. When later gazetted, the citation read in part, "... He had destroyed five enemy machines and driven down others out of control, showing splendid courage and initiative on all occasions."[7]

Howsam would score three more times during early March, and finish the war with a total of thirteen confirmed victories. His squadron-mate Quigley was even more successful, adding twenty-four confirmed victories to his 1917 ledger during 1918.

Other Canadians were also scoring during this period of relative inactivity. Frederic Elliott Brown from Quebec served as a very able flight commander with 84 Squadron during February and March, flying SE5as. On February 16, 1918, he scored a "hat trick" by gunning down three enemy machines — a feat mentioned in the citation to his Military Cross and published in the *London Gazette*, dated April 22, 1918:

Whilst leading a patrol of five machines, on observing four hostile scouts diving on one of our formations, he at once engaged them, driving one of them down completely out of control, while his formation dispersed the others. Later, on sighting another hostile scout, he engaged it and forced it down spinning out of control. While returning to his aerodrome, he observed an enemy two-seater, and, although his engine was running badly and might have failed at any moment, he attacked it and drove it down in a vertical nose-dive. Previous to this he had driven down one other machine, which was seen to crash, and a third completely out of control. He is a most daring and skilful pilot.[8]

Brown scored six more times in March, for a wartime total of ten victories, and was awarded a Bar to his Military Cross before being injured in a landing crash on March 31.

Not only the single-seater crews were scoring during the period. Bristol pilot Robert Dodds' matter-of-fact diary entries belie his triple victory success on January 9, a feat he repeated on March 8.[9] It is noteworthy that his bath receives equal billing with his combat success:

Wed. Jan. 9, 1918

Partly fair. Up at 10.35 with Hart on photos. Engaged with 5 EAs got 3. Capt Fields brought down. Worked on machine in afternoon. Had bath and wrote letters.

Thur. Jan. 10, 1918

Partly fair. No flying in forenoon but went up on OP with McMichael in afternoon & got badly archied over Cambrai. Lecture at 6.00 by a Lieut who escaped from Germany. Wrote letters.[10]

Moving away from the Western Front, Canadians were amassing distinguished air combat records in other theatres during 1918. In the Middle East, 72 Squadron was stationed at Basra in Mesopotamia (present-day Iraq) with a potpourri of aircraft. Meanwhile, 150 Squadron was formed in Macedonia from scout flights of 17 and 47 Squadrons. It became the first air fighting unit in the area and was kitted out with a mixed bag of Bristol M1Cs, Nieuports, SE5as, and, later, Camels. In Palestine the Australian 67 Squadron had replaced its earlier types with Brisfits received from 111 Squadron, which in turn augmented its Nieuports with a number of SE5as. Both these latter units would see considerable action during 1918, as they gained command of the skies in the region.[11] Lieutenant A.G. Goulding of Holland, Manitoba, performed well with both 17 and 150 Squadrons in this unappreciated theatre of operations. Flying both Nieuports and SE5as, he hacked down nine Alliance aircraft, winning a Military Cross, a Distinguished Flying

Lieutenant A.G. Goulding (right) of Holland, Manitoba, with captured enemy airmen he helped shoot down on March 20, 1918

Opposite: In an attempt to mate the new 200 horsepower Hispano-Suiza engine with a heavily-armed stable gun platform providing optimum pilot visibility, the Sopwith Aircraft Company devised the unorthodox Dolphin. The design was not initially welcomed by service pilots, due to some teething problems with the engine and crash concerns in the event of a tip-over, since the pilot's head protruded through the top wing. But in the hands of Canadian ace Albert Desbrisay Carter and other skilled empire pilots, it became a precision weapon. He is seen here successfully shooting down an LVG C VI, March 24, 1918.

Cross, and the French Croix de Guerre in the process. At 150 Squadron, Goulding found himself in the company of other Canadians, including Captain G.M. Brawley of Toronto, Lieutenants H.M. Jennings of Hagersville, Ontario, J.P. Cavers of Toronto, and A.M. Pearson from Manitoba. Four more of his Canadian colleagues were awarded the Distinguished Flying Cross before hostilities concluded in the region. Still other Canadians were Captain Gerald Gordon Bell from Ottawa, Lieutenant Walter Ridley from British Columbia, Lieutenant Charles Bremneri Green from Oakville, Ontario, and Lieutenant Arthur Eyguem de Montaigne "Jacko" Jarvis of Toronto. Bell, the most successful of the group, ultimately accounted for sixteen of the enemy, and the piquantly named Jarvis, a further seven. Green was the confirmed victor in eleven combats. A typical action for these battle-tested veterans occurred on June 1, 1918, two days after Goulding shared his seventh victory, when two enemy scouts fell to the guns of Green and Bell, fighting alone against a dozen Alliance aircraft. According to Bell's combat report:

When escorting a bomb raid on Cestovo, Captain Bell and Lieutenant Green on SE5as were attacked by twelve hostile machines over Casandule. A lengthy combat ensued. An E.A. (Siemens Schuckert) Immelmanned in front of my machine. I fired at point blank range. He burst into flames. Two E.A. then dived on my tail. I turned sharply to my right and observed Lieutenant Green diving on one of them which turned over on his back and went down out of control. We were attacked continuously but managed to keep E.A. off until bombers regained our lines. My engine then cut out and as Vickers gun was jammed we fought a defensive fight towards our lines. [12]

Of the many "side show" theatres removed from the Western Front, none generated as much intense aerial activity as Italy. Air combat over the Italian front produced a rollercoaster of emotions and stress equal to the air war over the Western Front. Duelling to the death in an azure sky above the pristine Italian Alps provided a terrible backdrop of beauty, none more so than when consigning an enemy to a grisly death by fire. Yet the euphoric celebration of victory demanded its own release, even when tempered with the conflicting

emotion of taking a human life. H. Brooke Bell, a ten-victory ace who won both the Military Cross and the Italian Bronze Medal for Military Valour, explained:

Soon after this I got my first "flamer." He was a lone Albatros DIII painted in spiral stripes like a barber pole. We were well over the line and cut him off trying to get home. It is a wonderful and terrible sight to see a machine go down burning like a torch. At the time, I cheered as though I had won a game of something, but afterwards started to think of the fellow who was killed and of his family…

… When I got back after shooting this one down, I thought I would do a few stunts around the aerodrome, just to show the boys how I felt. There was a strict rule against low stunting but this I felt was rather an occasion. I noticed a group of officers standing near one of the sheds, but paid no particular attention to them. Away I went around and round playing the fool like a young idiot. When I landed, and was taking off my flying clothes I received a message that the C.O. wanted to see me. I sent word back that I would be there as soon as I had my shoes on. The message came back to come at once. I rushed out of the shed with no collar or tie on, unshaved, and my shoes not laced, to find that Lord Plumer, General Officer Commanding Italy was there inspecting the aerodrome. I felt about six inches tall as I saluted him and the C.O. I was told off in no uncertain terms and thoroughly frightened but then the old gentleman smiled and shook hands, congratulated me and said he didn't blame me for doing it. [13]

The emotions generated by air combat during the Great War were also manifested in unusual ways, and from unexpected quarters. Again, Brooke Bell:

On a beautiful morning early in May, three of us were patrolling above the mountains and saw far below us, two Huns chasing an Italian. We dived immediately and found they were two Albatros DIIIs. I doubt if they ever saw us, so intent were they on shooting down the Italian. We swung in behind them and shot them down without a fight. The Italian followed us home waving wildly. He landed

on our aerodrome and insisted on thanking us for saving his life.[14]

In Italy, the unparalleled king of audacity remained Bill Barker. Having served in this theatre before, when the Austro-Hungarians launched their final major offensive in June, and later, Barker's exploits were the stuff of legends. One such event occurred in June when he, supposedly accompanied by Lieutenant Gerald Alfred Birks of Montreal and Lieutenant Clifford Mackay McEwen from Griswold, Manitoba, dropped a challenge on Godega airfield:

> Major W.G. Barker and the Officers under his Command present their compliments to Captain Bronmoski, 41 Recon. Portobouffole, Ritter von Fiala, 51 Pursuit, Garjarine, Captain Navratil, 3rd Company and the Pilots under their command and request the pleasure and honour of meeting in the air. In order to save Captain Bronmoski, Ritter von Fiala, and Captain Navratil, and gentlemen of his party the inconvenience of searching for them, Major Barker and his Officers will bomb Godigo [sic] aerodrome at 10:00 a.m. daily, weather permitting, for the ensuing two weeks.[15]

Major William George Barker, VC, in front of his Camel, while serving as Commanding Officer of 139 Squadron in Italy

There is no record that the Austrians responded in any manner to this challenge. Perhaps more to the point, there is no conclusive evidence to suggest this challenge was ever actually issued, though it would not have been out of character with Barker's well-documented audacity. In fact, McEwen was serving with 28 Squadron at the time,

and Birks was en route to Canada. This story, perhaps at least partially apocryphal, has become "an enduring legend."[16]

Nonetheless, serving as a flight commander with 28 and 66 Squadrons, and ultimately as the commanding officer of 139 Squadron from mid-July, Barker would notch thirty-nine more victories in Italy before repatriating to Britain in September. He would also win a second Bar to his Military Cross, the Distinguished Service Order and Bar, three Mentioned in Dispatches, the Italian Silver Medal for Military Valour, and the French Croix de Guerre. Number 139 Squadron was a Bristol Fighter unit that Barker was allowed to lead in his famous Camel, B6313. A bold and caring leader who took great pains to bring along his inexperienced charges, Barker lusted for all forms of aerial combat. In a postcard to a friend in Dauphin, dated June 26, it is clear that though proud of his record and his decorations, he was self-effacing about all the recognition:

> Pardon me for being so long in answering. I have just got 7 days leave and am visiting Rome, Naples, Florence, Genoa & Milan. It came as a very welcome surprise. Yesterday morning at 6 am I met 9 Huns all alone and in the fight that ensued I got down their leader, an Austrian "ace" with 21 victories to his credit and then got away myself. On my return, the Colonel gave me 7 days leave. Bye the bye, did I tell you that on the 27.5.18 I was awarded the French Croix de Guerre with Gold Star & now have just been notified that I was Mentioned in Dispatches in the King's Birthday Honours. I really don't know what it is all about. My total Bag of Hun planes destroyed now is 34. I will write later Marion.[17]

The "Austrian 'ace' with 21 victories to his credit" to whom Barker referred has proven impossible to identify. Barker probably meant Godwin Brumowski, and his combat report mentioned duelling with a red Albatros, similar to the colour scheme adopted by Brumowski. However, the Austrian ace had been sent on leave that morning, though someone else may have been flying his aircraft.[18] Other persistent, often contradictory, rumours and legends have sprung up around Barker. One of the most enduring is that he flew Edward,

Will Barker flying a Bristol F2b (D8063) at Villaverla, Italy, in September, 1918. According to Barker's biographer, Edward, Prince of Wales, is manning the rear Lewis gun on this occassion.

Prince of Wales, over the front lines in September 1918 and was reprimanded for doing so. His biographer contends that the flight took place on September 16 in Bristol Brisfit D8063 and that Barker *may* have flown His Royal Highness over the lines, though neither man would acknowledge the fact. Barker was certainly not reprimanded for this action. Stanley Stanger, a thirteen-victory ace and winner of both the Military Cross and the Distinguished Flying Cross, was in-theatre at the time and had a significantly different recollection of the event, though it is not clear if he was present at the airfield when it occurred:

I have heard a lot of stories about Barker which I know to be exaggerated or untrue. But that is not his fault. My letters and notes may give you information more exactly than what I can remember. But I do know for sure that Barker did not cross the lines with the Prince of Wales. He made one trip only in a converted Italian single seater Caproni pusher aircraft. It was merely a short sightseeing trip for a look at the lines and well on the safe side of anti-aircraft fire. There was no escort and none was needed. Barker was not reprimanded. The exploit was not considered an exploit. It was of small passing interest at the time.[19]

At any rate, Barker's greatest fight still lay ahead of him, and he was far from being the only accomplished Canadian fighter pilot flying in Italy. At least fifteen Canadian pilots became aces fighting in this theatre, including Brooke Bell, Stanley Stanger, Gerald Birks, Richard Dawes, Joseph Hallonquist, Earl Hand, William Hilborn, Harold Hudson, Mansell James, William MacDonald, and Tom "Voss" Williams. Also, Clifford M. "Black Mike" McEwen, so-named for his ability to tan darkly, won a Military Cross, a Distinguished Flying Cross and Bar, and the Italian Bronze Medal for Valour while

Lieutenant Clifford M. McEwen (second from left) with a Camel and Italian colleagues

in Italy. A skilful and fearless officer, McEwen scored twenty-seven times during his nine-month tour. The citation for the Bar to his DFC, gazetted on December 3, 1918, speaks volumes about his fighting spirit:

A brilliant and courageous pilot, who has personally destroyed twenty enemy machines. Exhibiting entire disregard of personal danger, he never hesitates to engage the enemy, however superior in numbers, and never fails to inflict serious casualties. His fine fighting spirit and skilful leadership inspired all who served with him. [20]

This documented score did not capture McEwen's final tally, nor did the system recognize one of his victories until much later. On February 18 McEwen, Barker, and the rest of C Flight from 28 Squadron were on an offensive patrol at 15,000 feet above the town of Rustigno. In the words of McEwen's combat report:

My engine began to run badly. I left the patrol and flew back towards the lines, heading southeast. My engine picked up and on re-crossing the lines to rejoin the patrol, I spotted an E.A. below me. I got in several bursts and the E.A. did not offer to avoid me and went down out of control. As my goggles frosted up I could only follow him down to 4000 feet. I last saw him out of control over Rustigno.[21]

Since the frosted goggles had prevented McEwen from witnessing the enemy aircraft's impact, he was officially credited with only an out-of-control victory. Years later, this claim was upgraded to "destroyed" when the tangled remains of the appropriate aircraft were found in the proper vicinity. [22]

From the end of June 1918 until mid-October, the Central Powers held on in Italy, though it was clearly only a matter of time until they were defeated. The crux of the Allied offensive was to cross the Piave River in late October and contain the Austrian 6th Army while doing so. The British 10th Army and the Italian 8th Army would then strike north and cut off Austrian forces on the Venetian Plain from those in the mountains. Empire airmen were to obtain mastery of the air, and to maintain it throughout the ensuing land battle. They did, and by the end of October the Austro-Hungarian Empire was in total disarray, with minimal military resistance. On November 4 an armistice was declared in the region.

The potential for terrifying flight incidents, due in no manner to enemy action, was just as great on the Italian as on the Western Front. Brooke Bell explained:

I was ordered to take my flight over with 4 bombs each and drop them on a certain road back of the line. For the first time I had a pre-sentiment of trouble and was quite nervous. The trouble started before I got off the ground, when my rudder control jammed. I cut my engine, and was lucky to stop before I hit the trees at the end of the aerodrome. Mechanics rushed out and repaired this and away I went to catch up with the others. Just as I did so, however, I felt the controls stiffening up and found that the message bag had fallen out of its pocket and its long tail of bunting had wrapped itself round and round the control wires in the fuselage. It was too far away for me to reach so I had to undo my safety belt and crawl back into the fuselage and free the controls. While I did this the machine became out of control and was spinning down. I was able though to get back to my seat in time to pull it out of the spin and started climbing again in order to clear the mountains. [23]

Meanwhile, in Central Europe, the war was about to enter its final throes. Donald MacLaren elaborated:

Then, one day, Intelligence reported that the great German offensive would be launched on the 21st of March, and his first attack would be at Quéant. We knew that our lull was over at last, and that we should soon meet the Hun at his strongest in the air, as would our armies on the earth. From that time up to his great attack his machines began to appear in ever-increasing numbers.

When it came, the tremendous onslaught shook our whole line and caused the greatest anxiety everywhere; but the airmen were in their glory, and fought from dawn to dusk. If ever there was a storm after a lull, it was the German offensive of March. [24]

Although the Allies knew it was coming, the German offensive, code-named Michael, caught the British by surprise. General Gough's 5th Army, severely weakened by the Battles of Passchendaele, was

Donald Roderick MacLaren, fifty-four-victory ace, cuts a jaunty figure in the cockpit of a Sopwith Snipe, 1918

Fred McCall, a thirty-five-victory ace from Vernon, BC, with canine friends

the chosen focal point. Innovative German tactics, which included smoke screens, massive artillery support, poison gas, and assault divisions of elite Stosstruppen or stormtroopers, were assisted by dense ground mists. The highly disciplined stormtroopers simply ignored British strongholds and pushed rapidly and deeply into Allied territory. In three days the Germans had retaken all their territorial losses from the Somme of two years before. But Michael soon lost its momentum. The assaulting German forces were famished and exhausted, and they suffered terrible casualties in spite of their significant land gains. Nearly a quarter-million of their shock troops were felled in battle — a staggering loss for the Central Powers.

Ludendorff's spring offensive had air components too. Many German corps units were converted to Schlacht duties — the provision of close air support to ground forces. All told, the number of Jastas was increased to eighty, though many of them were understrength and equipped with aircraft past their prime. Other sections of the front were stripped to provide 326 German scouts in the attack sector. Although Allied air strength across the entire front was much greater, the British could muster only 261 scouts in opposition in the immediate area of the March 21 offensive.[25] At the start of Ludendorff's desperate bid for victory, all available empire units

Lieutenant William Shields, a twenty-four-victory ace from Lipton, Saskatchewan, in front of austere quarters, which were typical for airmen on the move

were thrown into the defence, with almost all the scouting units flying a majority of ground attack sorties at the outset. Reinforcements soon arrived from both sides, and the amount and frequency of air combat increased sharply as large opposing formations of fighters met and clashed, each seeking to provide protection to its ground support units. For the Allies, March 25 was the day of greatest crisis. Squadrons were shelled out of their airfields by the advancing Germans, and confusion reigned as several units were forced to retreat. Many records were lost, and this period remains one of the worst documented of the war for empire airmen. Several new aces emerged during this time and, from March until the Armistice, dozens claimed more than twenty victories, yet remain in near-total obscurity. They received even less publicity than their predecessors had the year before. Many young

Canadians, including Donald MacLaren, Hank Burden, Al Carter, Bill Claxton, and Bill Shields, blossomed during this period. Albert Desbrisay Carter of Pointe de Bute, NB, flew both Spads and Dolphins with 19 Squadron during 1917 and 1918, amassing twenty-nine victories and winning two Distinguished Service Orders in the process. One of the most bizarre incidents of the air war occurred to one of his 19 Squadron Canadian colleagues, John Dartnell DePencier of New Westminster, BC, during the spring of 1918. After a morning scrap flying Dolphins, this eight-victory ace landed with a hole in his stomach which both the doctors and his colleagues thought was a mark made by a spent bullet. It was only after lunch, when DePencier discovered blood on his bed, that a second medical examination revealed that a bullet had gone right through him without causing any serious damage. DePencier deserved some recognition for stoicism; instead, he was given seven days' leave in England to recover.

One of the greatest Canadian air combat exploits of the war was fought not by a scout pilot, but by a corps pilot flying a cumbersome Armstrong Whitworth FK8 "Big Ack" observation aircraft. Second Lieutenant Alan "Babe" McLeod of Stonwall, Manitoba, was a fearless, enthusiastic eighteen-year-old when he joined 2 Squadron at Hesdigneul at the end of November 1917. He made an immediate impression:

The boyish Canadian pilot lost no opportunity to show off his big aircraft's fighting qualities to any enemy pilot who dared to come near or who let himself be caught, and when the regular Corps duties became boresome McLeod even undertook the work of a scout, "strafing" the streets of a town, or diving down to shoot up an "Archie" battery which had been disturbing the registration of artillery fire. On one occasion he and his observer (Lieutenant Comber) took on eight enemy pilots and gave them the fight of their lives.

The most amazing of all his exploits, however, was an attack on an enemy observation balloon near Bauvin, which he and Lieutenant Key sent down in flames, and then topped it off by crashing one of three Albatros scouts which attacked them. For that bold deed the Ack-W crew were Mentioned in Dispatches. Within a few weeks of his arrival the boy of eighteen had become the general favourite of

Willaim Shields
and Arthur Goby,
41 Squadron,
Western Front,
1918

Second Lieutenant
Alan "Babe" McLeod

sent another Fokker tumbling earthwards and forced two more to withdraw. Kirschstein persisted and registered a savage burst, which wounded both the pilot and the observer and set the fuel tank ablaze. But McLeod would not give up. He set his aircraft in a gentle dive, crawled out of the cockpit now rendered untenable by extreme heat, stood on the port wing, and deftly sideslipped to blow the flames away from himself and his observer. Hammond, feeling the cockpit floor giving way beneath him, clambered up to his gun sight and, bracing himself against the cockpit sides, shot down yet another triplane that had ventured too close. At

the whole squadron, and in daring and flying skill had proved himself the equal of any of his older and more experienced comrades.[26]

On March 27 McLeod and his observer of the day, Lieutenant A.K. Hammond, were assigned to bomb enemy troops in the Bray-sur-Somme area. Flying below clouds in poor weather, they were just about to release their bombs when they encountered a Fokker triplane in the target area. McLeod temporarily postponed his bomb run and aggressively positioned the big FK8 to afford Hammond a killing shot. The observer made good and the Fokker was driven down out of control. This brief action attracted a flight of seven other triplanes, which dove through a gap in the clouds to attack the audacious McLeod. The enemy flight leader was Leutnant Hans Kirschstein from Jasta 10 of von Richthofen's JG I, an eventual twenty-seven-victory ace and Ordre pour le Mérite winner. McLeod and Hammond fought with great skill and daring, McLeod throwing the Big Ack about as if it were the lightest of scouts. Hammond kept up spirited fire, which

this juncture, Kirschstein engaged the doughty crew one more time and riddled the aircraft with bullets. By now, the observer had been wounded six times and the pilot, five. Their fate appeared sealed. However, McLeod was able to flatten out of the dive just before impact, cushioning the crash landing in a shell hole in No Man's Land. Amid the blazing wreckage and exploding ammunition, McLeod dragged the now-helpless Hammond to relative safety — only to be wounded once again by a British bullet. McLeod passed out from loss of blood, but was soon rescued by British troops in the vicinity. The fearless young pilot from Stonwall became the youngest airman ever to win the Victoria Cross — Canada's second aerial Victoria Cross of the Great War. Hammond, who also survived, won a richly deserved Bar to his previously awarded Military Cross.[27]

On April 1, 1918, a momentous event occurred that was hardly noticed, given the tempo of battle at the time. On that day the RFC and the RNAS merged to form a single indigenous third service, the Royal Air Force. The former RNAS squadrons all adopted the 200 series of squadron numbers: Naval 3 became 203 Squadron, Naval 9 became 209 Squadron, and so on. For uniformity, the distinctive

The Armstrong Whitworth FK8, similar to the one in which Alan McLeod won his Victoria Cross

The engagement on March 27, 1918, that resulted in a Victoria Cross being awarded to Second Lieutenant Alan A. "Babe" McLeod. He is on the wing root of FK8 B5773, holding the aircraft in a sideslip to avoid the flames pouring from its engine while his gunner uses his Lewis gun to hold the attacking Fokker triplanes at bay.

officer ranks of the RNAS became standardized to the army ranks used by the RFC. A unique RAF rank structure was not adopted until after the end of the war. Ray Collishaw, now at the helm of 203 Squadron as a major, recalled the union and some of the new operational trends, though some service bias may be inherent in his account:

By the time the RAF was formed on April 1st 1918, a measure of British fighter numerical superiority had been attained and the British army commanders then demanded that the

major portion of the fighter force had to be employed in low flying attacks on hostile troop positions … The six Naval fighter squadrons operating with the British Army in France emerged from the air war of attrition with the respect and admiration of their RFC comrades. There was a sharp distinction between the RFC system of employing fighter pilots in France and the conduct of events in the Naval squadrons. Whereas RFC pilots were individually and regularly sent back to England for rest from active service after 8 months duty, the Naval squadrons were (collectively) withdrawn from an active front to a relatively quiet front when a rest was needed. The general result was that the RFC fighter squadrons were often manned by novices, while the pilots on the Naval squadrons remained constantly in France for years. Thus, the Naval squadron pilots normally possessed a far higher standard of flying ability and war-like experience.

… A distinctive difference between a Naval squadron and an RFC fighter squadron lay in the Naval officers' custom of performing regular aerobatics over the aerodrome. The Naval pilots had had years of practice in "stunting" and they loved the game. In the RFC, "stunting" was rather frowned upon, probably because of casualties due to the lack of many hours of flying experience. The Naval pilots' love of stunting was doubtless an important contributory factor to success in combat.[28]

Collishaw racked up a further nineteen air combat victories during 1918, securing a second-place tie position with Edward "Mick" Mannock on the list of highest-scoring empire aces of the conflict.

Henceforth, the dangerous world of air-to-ground tactical support became regularized to an extent never before imagined, let alone conducted, by empire scout pilots. Although the Camel squadrons were most frequently tasked with this onerous and terrifying duty, the other scout types were not immune. Ground strafing got little credit, "although it was the most dangerous, nerve-racking, and perhaps the most valuable work that scouts did."[29] Assaults on trenches were the most trying, owing to the extreme concentration of enemy machine guns. It was far safer to attack ground targets well back of the lines. Decoration citations of the day reflect this duality of role for the scout pilots, as can be seen in two examples pertaining to Canadian aces:

For conspicuous gallantry and devotion to duty. On one occasion he attacked and shot down an enemy plane which had been engaged at firing on our infantry. He then led his patrol over the enemy's lines, dived down to an altitude of 100 feet, and attacked large numbers of hostile infantry with machine-gun fire, causing the utmost panic amongst them and inflicting heavy casualties. His continuous gallantry and initiative have been most conspicuous.[30] [Lieutenant William Duncan]

This officer has shown great bravery and devotion to duty both in destroying enemy aircraft — ten of which he has accounted for — and in silencing anti-tank guns. On 27th Sept., flying at altitudes between 200 and 1500 feet, he engaged and silenced many anti-tank guns, thereby rendering valuable service. He at the same time completed a detailed and accurate reconnaissance of the area, locating the position of our troops.[31] [Captain William Hubbard]

Along with random and isolated attacks on ground targets, empire scout pilots in 1918 could look forward to increasing participation in raids on enemy installations. These raids involved extensive and coordinated force packaging. Sometimes it worked and sometimes it did not, even on the same target, as Canadian aces Harold Molyneux and Henry Burden, respectively, explained:

The most outstanding special mission I can recall was the bombing raid on Epinoy. We had 40 aircraft in the raid and No. 56 carried the bombs (13-lb. Cooper bombs) which we dropped just above the targets (hangars, petrol dump, H.Q., barracks, etc.) We then machine gunned the aerodrome and set 16 German aircraft on fire in front of the hangar. We were only there about 15 minutes but completely wrecked the depot, which was a large one. Bristol Fighters did the escorting, also Sopwith Camels, while we, the SE5s, dropped our small bombs (4 on rack under fuselage) at point blank range.[32]

Tuesday, 30 July 1918
Started for Epinoy Aerodrome to bomb it. 57 of our machines, incl. 6 Bristol Fighters. 12 SEs from 60 led by Bert Doyle. 18 Camels from #3 who led the show and made a mess of it and 12 of us. Got over the aerodrome and No. 3 leader got cold feet and washed out the whole show. Everyone simply fed to the teeth. Groused around all morning.

Siemens-Schuckert DIII

> Got up at dawn and got up to 1000 feet
> and washed out the patrol. Altogether a day
> of washouts. [33]

From the spring of 1918 onwards, two new German scouts began appearing in the skies over the Western Front. One was the Siemens-Schuckert DIII — a very fast biplane that also demonstrated excellent manoeuvrability and climb characteristics. However, the aircraft was plagued with early engine problems that needed to be corrected. The DIIIa variant featured a cutaway lower engine cowling, which greatly improved powerplant cooling. As a type, it was very popular with home defence squadrons, but it was used only in small numbers over the Western Front and in other theatres of war. The DIV variant was even faster, and although it was generally considered to be superior to any other single-seater then in action, its October 1918 operational arrival in very small numbers was too late to influence the war. The other new type was the Fokker DVII, arguably the best fighter produced by either side in quantity during the Great War. The brainchild of Fokker's chief designer Rheinhold Platz (as was the Dr.1 triplane), its definitive variant was powered by a 185 horsepower BMW in-line engine that pushed it to speeds of over 120 mph at 20,000 feet. So formidable was this aircraft that it was singled out by name to be handed over to the Allies after the Armistice. Rugged and manoeuvrable, the first examples of the type were sent to von Richthofen's JG I in April. Ultimately, it was flown by many German aces in 1918 who capitalized on its excellent flying characteristics in running up their victory scores. MacLaren recalls his initial exposure to this formidable adversary:

> A new type of German fighting-machine appeared, the Fokker Biplane scout. It was much the best machine the Huns had ever had, and as they appeared in great numbers we began to have a lively time of it. They patrolled in formations of from fifteen to thirty machines. On bright days they would fly as high as possible, and on dull days one would meet them on the fringe of the mist. After one or two brushes with them, it could be seen that the German flying corps had regained the offensive spirit, and were fighting with a ferocity that they had never equaled in the past. It was their last bid for supremacy, and, provided they were in large numbers, they fought furiously — but always on their own side of the line.

> The first Fokker I had seen had shown himself two months previous to this, and we had enjoyed some good sport at the time. He was

The Fokker DVII scout

the leader of the White-Tail Squadron (although his own machine was entirely black), and one day, while flying alone, I spotted him, evidently on the same quest as myself, out for a small and quiet scrap. At ten thousand feet we met, but when I made towards him he turned across my front. I had not seen a Fokker before, so I turned to have a good look at him, climbing at the same time. He seemed enormous in size, and looked very grim in his dull black with white crosses. The colour of his machine was, I suppose, his expression of German psychology.

When he saw that I was alone he swung away from me, but I put my nose down and started to close up with him. He looked back at me once, and then went straight down; but I followed. When we flattened out of our dive I found I was being fired at from the ground, and also that his speed was superior to mine. I let loose a few rounds from my guns, but, try as I would, I could not get closer to him; so, giving it up, I climbed again. I had not gone far when, to my amazement, he began climbing after me. Evidently this was a Hun of some kidney!

In a few minutes we were at it again, but when I approached him he would dive towards the ground before a burst could be got on him; and when I climbed to a few thousand feet, up he came too. After this had happened several times, and each of us had missed the other by inches, I thought I should like to show my appreciation of his sportsmanship by flying alongside and waving. I was on the point of doing this, when the memory of what some of their chaps had done altered my decision, so I went after him again, and this time he flew straight for home and never looked back.

It was the last time I saw a Fokker alone, and, to the best of my knowledge, the last time that a German airman showed that he loved the game and was ready to take on any passing adventurer for the zest of a fight. [34]

In May the Canadian Corps, which had miraculously been spared the brunt of Operation Michael, was pulled out of the line in preparation for the upcoming Allied counter-offensive. Under

Sidcot flying suit

Canada's own innovative and dynamic Sir Arthur Currie, a legitimate Canadian Army was being created. In London Sir Edward Kemp, the Minister of the Overseas Forces of Canada, was determined that the army would remain under Canadian control — a point the British grudgingly accepted. Canada was, in short, a full ally and no longer a colony. Although the Canadian Corps would deliberately never achieve army status, its contribution was no less significant. By the end of July, the Allies were ready. The period encompassing early August until the Armistice in November has become known as "Canada's Hundred Days," for, during these arduous months, the Canadian Corps was in the vanguard of the drive to Mons. On August 8, attacking in the utmost secrecy, with no preparatory bombardment and using deception tactics, the Canadians and the Australians broke open the German front at Amiens. Moving rapidly, making extensive use of tanks, and bypassing areas of steadfast resistance wherever possible, the dynamic of combat was swinging in favour of the Allies. On August 21 they fought the Battle of Bapaume, followed five days later by the Battle of the Scarpe. On the 28th the final battle on the Somme commenced. Naturally, Allied airpower was extensively involved with this counter-offensive. Captain William S. Stephenson of Winnipeg, a twelve-victory ace who had previously won a Military Cross for "conspicuous gallantry and devotion to duty," further distinguished himself through his exploits as a Camel pilot with 73 Squadron. The citation to his Distinguished Flying Cross elaborates on the continued dual role of scout pilots over the Western Front:

This officer has shown conspicuous gallantry and skill in attacking enemy troops and transports from low altitudes, causing heavy casualties. His reports also have contained valuable and accurate information. He has further proved himself a keen antagonist in the air, having during recent operations accounted for six enemy aeroplanes. [35]

The German army was by now on the defensive and showing signs of disintegration. In the air, the Allies were temporarily having things their own way as well. "Hank" Burden, a sixteen-victory ace from the last months of the war, who won both the Distinguished Service Order and the Distinguished Flying Cross (and was the brother-in-law of Billy Bishop), had a great pair of operational days flying SE5as with 56 Squadron during the period:

Saturday, August 10, 1918

Got up at 8:30 tired stiff and sore. Went on patrol with "C" Flight. The first flight show we have had. Chased a 2 seater D.F.W. to 100 feet E of Mault but couldn't get below him. At 6000 feet over Bray we met 6 Fokker Biplanes flying East under us about 500 feet. They didn't see us and we attacked. I got 2 crashed, climbed to 12,000, got into the sun and dived on 15 Fokkers. I got another in small bits. Sambo came back at noon with one in flames and one crashed. Bill Boger is missing. Also Flintoff & Allen. Slept till tea time then went out with Sambo and B & C flights. Played

A man called Intrepid. Captain William S. Stephenson beside his rather time-worn Camel in 1918.

around a balloon that had broken loose and hadn't the gumption to shoot it down. About 20 Fokkers flew East under us at 13,000. I attacked from the sun. Sambo Irwin joined in. I got 2 crashed and got considerably shot up by the last one who fired at me, head on. Sambo got one. Paul Winslow & Stenning. Making 10 for the Squadron in a day — and 5 for me. Telegram tonight from GHQ to say I have been awarded the Distinguished Flying Cross. [36]

Monday, August 12, 1918

Dawn show at 5 AM with Stenning, Molyneux & Elmslie. Stenning & Elmslie left so Molyneux and I went over Bapaume where I dropped a message asking for news of Bill (Boger). Chased 5 Fokkers East over Nestle. At 3:30 Sambo, Borncamp, Blair, Herney & Holleran on top — with me, Molyneux, Ellis,

Captain Hank Burden (right), a sixteen-victory SE5a ace and Billy Bishop's brother-in-law, in front of a Brisfit

Clermont & Elmslie below. Before we got to the line there was only myself, Sambo, Blair, Herney, Ellis & Molyneux left. We went over to within 4 miles of St. Quentin then West. Dived on a L.V.G. and nearly got caught by 4 Fokkers. Climbed west again & then went East & South. Got behind 5 Fokkers headed for the lines and caught them coming out of a cloud. Sambo got 2, Ellis and Molyneux one each and I got 3. About 20 more Fokkers joined in but we kept on top and then when they got too many for us we came home. That makes 20 Huns for the Squadron in 4 days. [37]

Still, a fighter pilot's life during the Great War did have its lighter moments. As Burden reported less than a week after his diary entries quoted above:

Saturday, 17 August 1918

Didn't do a show. Went to Aix-le-Chateau in the Squadron car with Maj. Gilchrist & saw Brigade sports. Then to 2nd Canadian General Hospital at Le Treport where we saw Miss Wilson, Bill Boger's aunt. From there we went to Ault 5 miles up the coast. Met Madame Richard, her mother, 2 sisters & 2 brothers and had dinner with them. They are fabulously wealthy. Pop being a Belgian Banker, but dead now. The old home is in the hands of the Huns. Awfully charming people. Mme. Richard is almost pretty but certainly very charming. Was educated in England. Her kid brother is at Eton now. On a dare C.O. & I took M.R. (Madame Richard) to Dieppe in the Squadron car and got there at 11 … Had supper there and got back at 3:30 dead to the world. One of the most amusing days I have ever spent in France. [38]

This period of action was relatively euphoric for Allied airmen compared with what lay ahead. After decisive but costly victories on the Scarpe River at the Drocourt-Quéant Line, the Germans had retreated behind the Canal du Nord by September 3. Here, the exhausted Canadian and British survivors paused for breath. In spite of Canadian losses of 5622 dead and wounded in taking the line, their infantry had prevailed against the toughest German troops and defensive fortifications on the Western Front.

Crew of a Bristol F2b
preparing for a mission

In the air, things were different. The inherent risks associated with conducting an all-out offensive campaign, coupled with the emphasis on dangerous ground attack missions, made "Black September" the worst month of the war for the Allies. And it occurred just six weeks before the Armistice. Raymond Collishaw explained that many of the empire's experienced air veterans from Bloody April 1917 were no longer engaged in combat. The Germans, in contrast, had dozens of veterans who had vast air-fighting experience and a will to pass that experience on to their novice airmen. Unlike April 1917, where the RAF's losses had been concentrated within the fighter and reconnaissance squadrons, by September 1918 they had shifted to the fighter-bombers and the day bombers. Also, the German fighter force had nearly doubled its number of Jastas (eighty) by 1918, and the quality of its equipment had vastly improved with the arrival of new types, such as the Fokker DVII and a new Pfalz scout, the DXII. Twelve of the leading Jastas were grouped into three Jagdgeschwaders, and they inflicted casualties out of all proportion to their strength — a mere 15 percent of the German fighter force. The concentration of scout aircraft that the

German Air Force had begun the previous year had by now become truly regularized. In all, nearly 560 Allied aircraft were lost during September 1918, including 373 British types, 100 French, and 87 American warplanes.[39] Nearly 830 Allied airmen were killed or captured that month, including roughly 600 empire aircrew. German losses, although difficult to determine accurately, were much less — probably between 107 and 214 aircraft and a concomitant number of aircrew.[40]

This greater German emphasis on massing their fighter aircraft demanded a response in kind by the Allies. MacLaren explained:

To meet the German tactics we now began to fly in squadron formation — that is, three flights of five machines each, generally flying one flight above the other, the lowest flight leading. In this way we were better able to cope with the Hun as regards numbers.

One fine, bright morning we took off as a squadron for the first time on this front, and, in conjunction with an S.E. squadron, started towards Roye to see what we could see. We crossed the line at twelve thousand feet with the SE5s well above us, covering every manoeuver. We went a good way over the lines, and were swinging up towards Péronne when a large formation of Fokkers became visible, flying towards us from the east. They were slightly above us, and by the way they flew, it looked very much as if they meant business. Right over the top of us they came in good formation, thinking, of course, that there was no one else in the sky but themselves and us. They turned and swooped down on us, but as they did so the SE5s were on them.

I had turned to meet them as they attacked us, and they seemed to be in utter confusion. Some of them began to spin, others were doing extraordinary half-rolls, and over to my right was a deal of smoke-tracer about, and looking to its source, I got a shock.

It was my friend of the black Fokker making quick flat turns and firing in every direction. This time I determined that the air wasn't vast enough for both of us, and I gave him a heavy burst. He did not wait, but, up to his old tricks, put his nose down and made straight east. I had just started off after him, when I noticed a white-tailed Fokker to my right, about my own level, and about one hundred yards away. He did not seem to know what was happening, so I opened out, going under him, then pulled up, giving him a good burst from underneath at very short range. He turned over, made one large curve, and burst into flames.

But my grim enemy had managed to get clear away again. He was an undoubted adept at extricating himself from hot corners.[41]

Along with operating in greater numbers, empire scout pilot leaders began to tailor the composition of their patrolling forces, using different types in their best flight envelopes. For example, a Camel unit would often position itself at the lowest altitudes, which would in turn be covered by a force of SE5as, or, occasionally, a mixed force of SE5as and Dolphins. If all three types were available for a force package, the Dolphins, which enjoyed a high operational ceiling, often provided cover from altitudes in excess of 18,000 feet. By August and September, empire Dolphin pilots, including a number of Canadians, were scoring heavily against the Germans.[42]

More new fighter types were making appearances on both sides. The superb Fokker DVIIs were now being supplemented by the excellent Pfalz DXII. Essentially a refined Pfalz DIII, it probably suffered unfairly against the propaganda and production priority given to the Fokker, but in some respects it was a superior machine.[43] One unusual German type, which would see only limited service at the front during the last few months of the war, was the high-wing monoplane Fokker DVIII. In many ways, this aircraft was better than the Fokker DVII. Although the German Army was rapidly losing the land battle, the German Air Force was by no means a whipped service. In the final analysis, the Germans were outdone in the

A Fokker DVIII monoplane after its capture. Canadian ace (and future air marshal) Captain G.O. Johnson is in the cockpit.

air owing to the sheer weight of numbers of the opposing Allied Air Order of Battle, as well as the fact that they ran out of fuel to power their aircraft. These factors in turn led to cuts in training standards and the combat losses of many inexperienced pilots. Still, several new high-scoring aces emerged from the German camp during the war's closing months, and none shone more brightly than Ernst Udet. The losses he and others were able to inflict on the Allies during the closing months of the war were far more than had occurred at any previous period of the air conflict.

In the RAF, a new indigenous decoration for bravery — the Distinguished Flying Cross — had been introduced to replace the RFC's Military Cross

and the RNAS's Distinguished Service Cross. Many Canadians won this new award, and, like most airmen of the period, they tended to be modest and self-effacing as to why they were awarded. When asked why he had received the medal, one wag cryptically responded, "for gettin' Huns."[44] Con Farrell from Regina, Saskatchewan, explained: "I was informed at one time that the reason I got the DFC was because I took a lorry and two other officers into the French city of Amiens when it was being shelled and helped ourselves to cases of champagne, liqueurs, wines, etc. all for free from 'Jimmy's Bar' and got it back to 24 Sqn. Mess where we naturally had a few 'Wing Dings' on the French."[45] In fact, the actual citation to Farrell's award belies his own lighthearted response and provides another example of scout pilot diversification and the operational tempo of the period:

This officer rendered conspicuous service on the 8th August in attacking enemy troops and transport with machine-gun fire and bombs. Having silenced a machine gun, he attacked some transport, driving off the personnel. Later on he attacked a dump and carried out a reconnaissance in an area where our Cavalry were reported to be held up, rendering a most valuable report of the situation. Eventually, in a combat with about forty scouts, he was shot down. He has destroyed or taken a leading part in the destruction of seven enemy machines.[46]

Yet another example of this late-war tempo can be found in the Distinguished Flying Cross citation to William McKenzie Thomson of Toronto, a Brisfit pilot who had also won a Military Cross for his previous exploits. With twenty-six eventually confirmed victories, Thomson was the third-highest scoring Canadian two-seater pilot:

This officer has destroyed thirteen enemy machines invariably displaying courage, determination, and skill. Disparity in numbers never daunts him. On a recent occasion, in company with eight other machines, his formation was attacked by twenty-five scouts. He shot one down. On another occasion his formation of ten machines engaged between twenty and thirty Fokkers; in the combat that ensued this officer shot down one out of the four that were destroyed.[47]

By mid-September, there was fighting all up and down the front. The Americans had begun a major drive in the St. Mihiel salient, and Byng's men had combined to push successfully eastward. The Canadians would next have to take the Canal du Nord, and they had most of September to prepare themselves for this task. On the 28th, heralded by an overcast and dreary dawn, the opening barrage began. The last great push of the war was on, but many bloody battles remained to be fought for the Allies in general and for the Canadians in particular. From August 8 until the end of September, the Canadian Corps under Arthur Currie suffered 30,000 casualties. The British, Canadians, and

Australians were all exhausted, but Haig's armies were still in better shape than those of Général Pétain and the Americans, recently decimated in the Argonne Forest. Von Ludendorff's hard-fought withdrawal had inflicted a costly toll on the Allies. However, Cambrai was finally retaken by the Canadian Corps on October 12 and, with that breakthrough, the Allied mood became victorious.

During the closing weeks of the war, a superb new scout from the Sopwith stables began reaching the front — the fast, manoeuvrable, rugged, and

A Sopwith Snipe

reliable Snipe. The embodiment of all Sopwith's scout-design experience to date, this fighter boasted excellent cockpit visibility and innovative concessions to pilot comfort and efficiency, including oxygen and electric heating. In one of these aircraft, a Canadian fought what has generally been regarded as one of the greatest individual air combat engagements of the war.

"Will" Barker, as he was known to his family and closest friends, had returned to England from the Italian front at the end of September, festooned

with medals, supposedly to become commander of the School of Air Fighting after a period of leave. But he craved more action, and, like Bishop, he wanted to add to his score. With an adroit mixture of determination and charm, he fast-talked his way into a ten-day roving commission on the Western Front.[48] He claimed that he needed a refresher combat experience in-theatre to become familiar with the present style of air fighting there, if he was going to perform with the best situational awareness and operational credibility in his new

159

assignment. When he arrived for temporary duty with 201 Squadron at LaTarguette on October 17, Barker was not warmly received. For one thing, he was a relative unknown in this theatre, and he had not shared the misery of the March offensive and Black September. For another, he had his own personal Snipe, E8102, painted with five white bands around the fuselage, as had been done to his Camel in Italy. In contrast, 201 Squadron still flew the inferior Camel. Stymied by miserable flying weather in the region, Barker took part in three offensive patrols with this unit between October 21 and 23. Flying high above the Camels as a wild card, Barker hawked their formations, but targets of opportunity never presented themselves. For the last three days of his abbreviated tour, the weather totally grounded him. On the 26th he received orders to return his Snipe to No. 1 Aircraft Supply Depot and to report forthwith for duty in London. Frustrated and exhausted, Barker decided to make one last survey of the lines en route to the depot the following morning.

At 12,000 feet, in a brilliant blue sky over the Fôret de Mormal at 8:25 a.m., Barker spotted a white Rumpler C two-seater reconnoitering the lines from well above him at 21,000 feet. After several climbing turns to gain advantage, Barker put telling bursts into the German aircraft. As the Rumpler broke up in the air, one of its crew members emerged in a blossoming parachute. Barker stared transfixed by this scene, a near-fatal mistake, for he in turn was hammered by a Fokker DVII, the first he had ever encountered, and he was severely wounded in the right thigh. Fainting from the pain, Barker somehow threw the Snipe into a spin, only to recover consciousness some 2000 feet lower in the midst of a total force of approximately fifteen DVIIs! For the next several minutes, Barker was everywhere in the sky. Flying with consummate skill, yet believing he was doomed, he gave even more than he got. He fired at two of the Fokkers inconclusively, but set a third one on fire from 10 yards' range. Wounded a second time, now in the left thigh, Barker again fainted and again spun downwards, regaining consciousness at 15,000 feet amid a portion of the enemy formation. Barker gunned down a Fokker in flames, but one of this group peppered his Snipe and shattered his left elbow. Passing out once more, he entered a third spin and recovered in a further

group of the enemy scouts flying at 12,000 feet. With his Snipe now riddled and smoking, Barker selected yet another Fokker for attention and blasted it to bits, though his aircraft suffered more damage as he flew through the wreckage of this latest victim. Still in dire peril, Barker seized on a brief exit corridor, dived westward, and streaked towards the British lines, adroitly dodging more of the enemy in the process. Crossing the lines at scant feet, he crash-landed into the barbed-wire entanglements protecting a British observation balloon site.

One of the many British and Canadian soldiers who witnessed this epic fight had been Lieutenant-Colonel (later General) A.G.L. "Andy" McNaughton, then commander of the Canadian Corps of Heavy Artillery, who called it a "stimulating event." Some time later, he wrote that the cheers that echoed across the front for the little British fighter were "never matched … not on any other occasion."[49] The balloonists of 29 Kite Balloon Section raced to the downed Snipe and promptly extricated the unconscious young pilot, now awash in his own arterial blood.[50] Billy Barker's last war flight was over and, although he did not know it at the time, he had just won the Victoria Cross.[51]

Back on land, the Canadian Corps had driven relentlessly forward through Valenciennes and Mont Houy. By November 10, in hot pursuit of the now rapidly retreating Germans, elements of the corps finished the war in Mons. News of the Armistice reached the Canadians there at 7:00 a.m. on November 11, 1918, but it still took hours to spread the word on both sides that all fighting was to cease at precisely 11:00 a.m. At 10:55 a.m. a German sniper caught sight of Private George Price of the 28th Northwest Battalion and fired a round into his chest.[52] He died minutes later, the only Canadian to be killed on Armistice Day and the last of 59,544 fatalities in the Canadian Expeditionary Force alone. The War to End All Wars was officially over. From Ottawa, Washington, and Canberra to Rome, Paris, and London, teeming millions celebrated with uninhibited joy and relief. Meanwhile, in a British Hospital in Rouen, France, William George Barker, dazed and exceptionally weak, lay fighting for his young life against wound infections in his torn and battered body.

Opposite:Will Barker's Victoria Cross fight, October 27, 1918. The Fokker DVIIs are depicted in the colours of Jasta Boelcke 2 (lozenge pattern fuselage with white and black tails) and Jasta 26 (black & white striped fuselages). Barker is in Sopwith Snipe 7.F1, E8102, one of the early production aircraft that featured the smaller tail fin. The aircraft sports his personal markings of five white vertical bands on the rear fuselage. The Foret de Mormal can be clearly seen below.

CHAPTER SIX

ARTHUR ROY BROWN

and

MANFRED VON RICHTHOFEN

*"If he had been my dearest friend,
I could not have felt greater sorrow."*

– ROY BROWN

Arthur Roy Brown was born in 1893 in Carleton Place, one of a seemingly disproportionate number of Canadian scout aces during the Great War to come from that scenic southern Ontario town.[1] An intelligent, outgoing lad who was also an excellent hockey and basketball player, he developed an early passion for flying. At his father's expense, he enrolled at the Wright Brothers' school at Dayton, Ohio, and obtained Aero Club of America Pilot's Certificate Number 361 on November 13, 1915.[2] He joined the Royal Naval Air Service in Canada and completed additional flight training with that service at RNAS Chingford, England, in the spring of 1916. Although he broke part of a vertebra in his spine in an April training crash, his recovery was rapid, perhaps spurred on by being reduced to half-pay while on sick leave.[3] By early 1917 he had completed all the required courses of instruction and had been given an active posting on scouts.

After some shifting among 9, 11, and 4 Squadrons RNAS, he was eventually posted back to Naval 9, where he scored his second air victory on September 3, 1917. By November he was an ace and had been awarded the Distinguished Service Cross. In February 1918 he was promoted and made a flight commander. His confidential report from the period states that he was "a very good flight leader and fearless pilot, with good ability to command."[4] A kind, compassionate, and honourable man, Brown did everything within his power to shepherd his novice charges through their earliest combat experiences as safely as possible. He was well known for offsetting himself from engagements after he had led the initial attacks so he could come to the aid of novices in distress. Like many Great War pilots, he preferred to think of success in air combat as the vanquishing of a machine, not of the occupants. He worried about his charges and colleagues, and suffered when they were lost.

During the German March offensive of 1918, Allied casualties were very high. Brown repeatedly flew at least two missions a day on average, and tried at every opportunity to provide extra training for the youngsters fresh out of the schools and now under his command. The strain of sustained combat began to show. Raymond Collishaw noted on one early April visit that Brown looked

Roy Brown in 1918

exhausted: he had lost 25 pounds, his hair was prematurely greying, and his eyes were bloodshot and sunken. Not only was the food bad, but Brown had eaten contaminated rabbit that severely upset his gastro-intestinal tract.[5] Despite Collishaw's entreaties, Brown doggedly refused to quit combat flying. On top of everything else, Naval 9's base at Bertangles was a cheerless place. "When they landed they had no diversions, no hot water, just tents in a muddy field. Every morning the field was shrouded in a thick fog. The spring was dreary, with cold rain and wind."[6]

Although there had been a brief lull in the German advance in the Amiens sector, it was clear that the enemy was gearing up for another attempt to capture the city. On April 21 the unit, now renamed 209 Squadron, was assigned patrol duties in its Camels at 12,000 feet over the Australian-held portion of the front between Albert and Harbonnières, above the Somme River valley. The force was divided into three flights of five aircraft each, with Roy Brown's "A" Flight in the lead. One of the four lieutenants Brown was shepherding that day was a former school chum from Edmonton, Second Lieutenant Wilfred "Wop" May, a Squadron tyro who was on his third combat patrol. Brown had warned May to stay clear of any air combat that might ensue, to adopt an "observe and learn" posture, and to separate rapidly towards Bertangles should he be threatened. Ironically, Manfred von Richthofen would provide parallel instructions to his novice cousin Wolfram, who would be a member of his flight on this fateful day. Other members of Brown's flight

Second Lieutenant Wilfred Reid May, von Richthofen's intended 81st victim

were Lieutenant W.J. Mackenzie, Lieutenant L.F. Lomas, and Lieutenant F.J.W. Mellersh. "B" Flight was led by Captain Oliver C. "Boots" LeBoutillier, an American, while "C" Flight was headed by Lieutenant O.W. Redgate. Brown's five Bentley-powered Camels lifted off from Bertangles at 9:35 a.m., followed by "B" Flight and "C" Flight at 9:40 a.m. and 9:45 a.m., respectively, all on separate patrols in the same general area.

At Cappy, approximately 35 kilometres east of Bertangles, the pilots of Jagdgeschwader I were ebullient. The spring day held the early promise of clearing skies, and Manfred von Richthofen himself was in an effervescent, if not mischievous mood. Now at the zenith of his fighting career, he had achieved his 79th and 80th aerial victories the day before. He had been promised a short period of leave at the Voss hunting lodge in the picturesque Schwarzwald region of southern Germany. Although the German nation was in dire straits, the situation on the battlefield was far from hopeless, and a continuation of the stalled Spring offensive was expected soon in the Flanders region. Von Richthofen's unit was awaiting orders to launch an attack against Entente air efforts in their designated sector of the front. Meanwhile, von Richthofen socialized with his aircrew. At one point, he playfully upended the supports from a stretcher that was occupied by one of his junior pilots, who was trying to have a quiet nap. A few moments later, Moritz, von Richthofen's handsome brindle Great Dane, tentatively approached his master for assistance and comfort. An enormous aircraft wheel chock had been tied to the unfortunate hound's tail in a gesture of playful retribution.

At approximately 10:30 a.m., word came that British aircraft were approaching JG I's operational sector. Two Ketten of Fokker triplanes were launched, the first led by von Richthofen in Fokker Dr.1 425/17, a scarlet machine with a white rudder. Other members of his Kette were Leutnant Wolfram von Richthofen, Oberleutnant Karjus, Leutnant Wolff, and Vizefeldwebel Scholtz. The second Kette of four members was led by Leutnant Weiss. At approximately 10:45 a.m., von Richthofen and Weiss detached from the formation and attacked two RE8 observation two-seaters of Number 3 Australian Flying Corps (AFC) Squadron at 7500 feet over Hamel.[7] A staunch and effective defence by the seasoned and forewarned Australian

crews resulted in the red triplane abruptly diving away from the engagement, not to return. The second triplane was visibly damaged by accurate RE8 defensive fire, and it also separated from the fight. Based on this albeit inconclusive result, and the later reality of von Richthofen's demise, 3AFC Squadron soon claimed responsibility for downing the Red Baron. The claim was quickly discounted as being too early for von Richthofen's final engagement. [8]

After his unresolved scrap with the RE8s, von Richthofen rejoined his formation and continued the hunt for more quarry. He would not have long to wait. He spotted Brown's flight approaching Hamel from the south, with LeBoutillier's "B" Flight in the same general airspace. The Baron led his small force in an attack. A free-for-all rapidly developed, in which Lieutenant Mackenzie was wounded and forced to return to base. May initially did as he was told, but eventually, tempted to the extreme, he rolled in on his German counterpart, Wolfram von Richthofen. After an inconclusive engagement, May, with his guns now apparently jammed, decided to head for the sanctuary of the Allied lines. His rapid exit from the fight was witnessed by Brown and by the Baron, who sensed a quick kill.

Manfred von Richthofen (centre) and members of Jagdgeschwader I. Moritz is on the extreme left.

167

Fokker triplanes of von Richthofen's Jagdgeschwader I at Cappy aerodrome, April, 1918

Opposite: The Red Baron's last flight, April 28, 1918. Captain Roy Brown hurls his Sopwith Camel at great speed directly at von Richthofen's red Fokker triplane Dr.I 425/17, which is taking evasive action. Of note are the triplane's late-war markings (still in transition on this aircraft) and the Baron's amber goggles, which are thought to have caused a reduction in his peripheral vision. The depiction of the hill and surrounding area has been pieced together from contemporary descriptions and aerial photographs.

What happened in the next few minutes has been extensively mired over the years in a morass of faulty and conflicting recollections, wishful thinking, shoddy bureaucratic reporting and procedures, and irresponsible journalism. Fortunately, in 1997 Norman Franks and Alan Bennett published *The Red Baron's Last Flight*, the definitive chronology of the last few minutes of Manfred von Richthofen's short but illustrious life. Although the basic evidence in the case has always been present, it has taken these two scholars to reconstruct the demise of the Baron with objectivity and impartial clarity.

To summarize, May was soon speeding west at an extremely low level along the Somme River valley, with von Richthofen in hot pursuit. May was acutely aware of the danger, but ignorant of the exact identity of his pursuer: "I was crippled because both my guns were jammed. Richthofen dived and went for me. He usually stayed in his own lines but he got so mad at me that he followed me over into our lines and chased me for 20 miles. At the end I was flying right down above the ground and couldn't go any lower. I didn't know it was Richthofen at the time or I should have died of shock."[9] Brown's main concern was to save the fledgling May, and, given von Richthofen's relative proximity to the novice, time was of the essence.

Using the potential energy of his height advantage as well as a certain amount of geometric flight path prediction, Brown commenced a steep 45 degree dive at very high speed towards May's and von Richthofen's relative positions.

This dive, witnessed by Oliver LeBoutillier,[10] was a courageous act in its own right. Brown wound the Camel up to approximately 190 miles per hour in this last-ditch offensive manoeuvre. The Camel had some notoriously vicious flight characteristics when flown at the extreme edges of its flight envelope, even for an experienced pilot on type such as Brown. Under ideal circumstances, Brown would have closed to approximately 50 yards range, to employ a conventional co-speed shot with his gun sight stabilized on the target, but that might have been too late for May. Instead, he elected to fire a long, high-closure-rate burst, the accuracy of which would be diminished by the rapid overtake (roughly 80 miles per hour), the looming terrain below, and the marginal handling characteristics of the Camel — which included excessive vibration at the speeds involved. In the words of Brown's own combat report, he "got a long burst into him and he went down vertical and was observed to crash by Lieut. Mellersh and Lieut. May."[11]

This succinct statement requires elaboration. In later years, Brown repeatedly and publicly stated that he had fired from above, behind, and to the *left* of von Richthofen.[12] One of the most tangible pieces of evidence reflecting this fact lies in the words of the plaque accompanying von Richthofen's pilot's seat, which Brown donated to the Royal Canadian Military Institute in Toronto in 1920. The words on the plaque were dictated by Brown[13] and read in part: "Captain Brown was flying after Richthofen, and behind him on his left rear, brought him down by the shot mentioned."[14] Given the time of day and year, the date and the geographical location of the engagement, the sun would have been relatively low in the southeast portion of the sky at roughly 26 degrees of elevation from the horizon.[15] Thus, both for surprise and for a flight-path interception, Brown's firing position with the sun at his back would logically have been from the left, or southeast, of the Baron's triplane. It would have been only a slight variation from a pure pursuit position. Given the relative positions of all concerned in trail or line astern, however, Brown fired a long burst of a recorded five-to-seven seconds from an absolute maximum effective range of 300 yards, closing down to approximately 50 yards. At this point, relatively violent action was required to avoid a mid-air collision, and Brown reefed his Camel up and away to the left as best he could, considering the limited manoeuvrability and skittishness of the Camel at high speed. In the process, he went belly up to the other two aircraft and temporarily lost visual contact with both May and von Richthofen because of the masking effect of his own wings.

There is no concrete evidence to suggest that Brown scored any hits on this pass. LeBoutillier, who witnessed the entire engagement, later said that he saw Brown's tracer rounds strike the triplane, although he did not specify exactly where.[16] At this point von Richthofen, again witnessed by LeBoutillier, reacted strangely, since it is clear from his subsequent actions that he must have been aware of Brown and the threat he posed. Instead of honouring the threat by breaking into it, or to the left, he initially performed a hard climbing break turn to the right. Perhaps he feared a mid-air collision with Brown, or perhaps he was concerned about breaking into the sun at low level with abruptly rising terrain ahead. At any rate, the right

break was fortuitous for everyone except von Richthofen: until the Baron quickly reversed course to the left, it bought May some vital separation, and also displaced Richthofen further north, where he was in a considerably more vulnerable position from the guns of the Australian Corps situated ahead and below.

By this point, von Richthofen had developed serious gun jam problems. Several ground witnesses have since remarked on the sporadic, limited firing he conducted and also on the apparent gun-clearing gestures he performed with his hands and body. Extensive ground examination later revealed that both his machine guns were essentially disabled at the end of this flight.[17] It is not clear what caused Richthofen to break off his attack — the gun problem, the realization that he was getting closer to formidable ground defences,[18] or the fact that May had gained sufficient separation to put him out of immediate danger. However, he did so. After a few seconds' further pursuit of May, which brought him over the Morlancourt Ridge and roughly abeam the Corbie-Méricourt-l'Abbé road, he abruptly reversed course in a climbing right-hand turn, directly into the strong easterly winds. The force of these winds significantly reduced his ground speed and accentuated his vulnerability to ground fire. Roughly one minute after Brown broke off his firing pass, the Fokker was seen to wallow around the sky, before making an abrupt and rough forced landing in a sugar-beet field beside a brickworks at Sainte Colette. Roy Brown, meanwhile, whose hard left turn off the attack had taken him about a mile south to the town of Corbie, had reversed course to the right and attempted to visually reacquire May and von Richthofen. Nearly a minute later he spotted von Richthofen's triplane on the ground, almost immediately below where he had left him. May and Mellersh both observed the triplane going down vertically and the subsequent heavy landing.

Back at the sugar-beet field, Gunner Ernest Twycross of the Royal Garrison Artillery was the first person at the landing site. His son later testified that von Richthofen, who was covered in blood, gasped a short phrase that sounded like "Alles kaput"[19] and then expired. RAF examiners noted that the Baron had had the presence of mind in his last airborne seconds to close the fuel valve,

open the vent valve of the pressurized fuel tank, and switch off the magneto, thereby minimizing the risk of fire during his forced landing. Manfred von Richthofen, himself the victor of so many combats, now numbered among the legion of the vanquished.

Who killed von Richthofen? For the most part he killed himself, for he violated several of his own cardinal tenets of air warfare in going after May without a supporting cast, and on the enemy side of the lines, while simultaneously flying a predictable flight path. Two official postmortem examinations, as well as one subsequent confirmation inspection by a senior medical officer, were done on von Richthofen's remains. Both Brown and one of the 3 Australian Flying Corps RE8 crews claimed von Richthofen as a victory, as did several soldiers of the Australian Corps. The RE8 crew's claim was quickly ruled out based on the time constraints.

Richthofen's physical condition in death was seriously misleading. Although his face was lacerated and there was a great deal of blood on his head, torso, and upper legs, much of it had come from his mouth, owing to his extensive chest trauma. The bullet had not necessarily pierced his heart.[20] On

closer examination, the round that killed von Richthofen had entered the right side of his chest "about the level of the ninth rib … just in front of the posterior axillary line. The bullet appears to have passed obliquely backwards through the chest, striking the spinal column, from which it glanced in a forward direction and issued on the left side of the chest at a level about two inches higher than its entrance on the right and about in the anterior axillary line."[21] This trajectory is significant, as, given these entry and exit wounds, there is no way that Roy Brown could have fired the fatal shot. Furthermore, the elapsed time from when Brown ceased firing until Richthofen ended up in the beet field was in the order of 90 seconds.

Brown had reasonable grounds to think he had been responsible for the Baron's death. First, the other early claimants, such as the RE8 crew, had fired largely frontal shots or were otherwise eliminated. Further, the initial information on the Baron's wounds seemed to suggest "a large multiple bullet entry hole in von Richthofen's left breast with the apparent choice of exit locations low down in the abdominal area on his right."[22] This description fuelled the RAF's belief that Brown was the de facto victor, and they proclaimed him

The remains of Richthofen's famous triplane after it had been thoroughly vandalized by souvenir hunters as such. To Brown's credit, by the time he saw the triplane, which had been extensively damaged in the forced landing, from a ground perspective, the red fabric covering had been ravaged by souvenir hunters, possibly obliterating the evidence of some battle damage. However, while there may have been some battle, not crash-generated, damage to one of the interplane struts, earlier witnesses who saw the aircraft before it was pillaged testified that it appeared remarkably free of firearms damage. The only obvious bullet hole was on the right-hand side of the fuselage, below the cockpit rim.[23] No bullet holes were observed on the left-hand side of the fuselage, on the rear fuselage decking behind the cockpit, or through the pilot's seat. Also, the amount of time involved and the actions performed by von Richthofen from the moment when Brown ceased firing until Gunner Twycross witnessed the Baron's death defy medical credibility. However, given that Brown had not seen von Richthofen's full flight path after his attack, and also the relative nearness of the crash site, it is easy to understand how the senior officers of the RAF were able to convince both Brown and themselves that Brown was responsible for the Baron's death.

Franks and Bennett have determined that the most likely vanquisher of Manfred von Richthofen was Sergeant C.B. Popkin of the 24th Australian Machine Gun Company, from a position north of the Somme on a slope that would have had a clear view of von Richthofen's final turn reversal. In fact, Popkin fired his Vickers gun twice at von Richthofen, once with no apparent effect from relatively short range when the Baron was still headed westbound, followed by a long-range burst at the Fokker's right-hand side from a later-estimated 800-850 yards after the turn reversal to eastbound.[24]

The Royal Air Force and the Australian Army each continued to claim that their personnel had been responsible for von Richthofen's death. Brown's squadron mates took great reflected pride in his accomplishment: "I am sure you will be pleased to hear that the renowned Baron von Richthofen was bested by one of our chaps a few days ago. The victor is a Canadian boy who belongs to this squadron. It makes me feel proud to think that I took part in the scrap, although I had nothing to do with the bringing down of the

Baron. All the credit goes to Brownie. I hope you won't think I am 'swanking' in telling you this, but I imagine you like to hear a little about our work. I hope I may be able to tell you about the whole scrap some day."[25] In fact, 209 Squadron's official crest, until the squadron officially disbanded on December 31, 1968, depicted a red eagle, falling.

It appears that Brown, May, and others from 209 Squadron were not privy to the exact nature of the entry and exit wounds until many years after the event. In the meantime, Brown repeatedly claimed that he had taken the shot from the left-hand side. In 1927 American journalist Floyd Gibbons wrote articles and then a book entitled *The Red Knight of Germany*. Unaware that Brown had ever declared he had shot at Richthofen from the left-hand side, and at a loss to reconcile the now known trajectory of the wounds, Gibbons stated that Brown had fired from the right side. "A subsequent article written for the American *Liberty* magazine, entitled 'My Fight with Richthofen,' very loosely based upon an interview with Brown, borrowed heavily from Gibbon's book and thus each one appeared to confirm the other. Brown was falsely cited as the author."[26] Furthermore, "Gibbons legacy to mankind is that from 1928 onwards most drawings and paintings show Brown attacking from the right, and this has become the popular belief or misconception."[27] The myth of the right-hand attack was born, and it has been perpetuated by many distinguished historians over the years.[28] Brown became very close-mouthed on the subject, refusing to enter debate or provide further clarification right up to the end of his life in 1944.

Nonetheless, Roy Brown, aside from von Richthofen himself, was the pivotal character in this drama. There is no doubt that his courageous and dangerous high-speed attack forced a reaction from the Baron that probably saved May's life and drove von Richthofen deeper into the firing zone of the guns of the Australian Corps. Although Brown subsequently received a Bar to his Distinguished Service Cross for this event, he took no joy from what he had done. The words of this gentle man, written after he viewed the body of the dead German airman, are telling:

The sight of Richthofen as I walked closer gave me a start. He appeared so small to me, so delicate. He looked so friendly. Blond, silk-soft hair, like that of a child, fell from the broad, high forehead. His face, particularly peaceful, had an expression of gentleness and goodness, of refinement. Suddenly I felt miserable, desperately unhappy, as if I had committed an injustice … If I could I would gladly have brought him back to life, but that is somewhat different than shooting a gun. I could no longer look him in the face. I went away. I did not feel like a victor. There was a lump in my throat. If he had been my dearest friend, I could not have felt greater sorrow.[29]

EPILOGUE

*"There won't be any after-the-war
for a fighter pilot."*

– RAOUL LUFBERY

For Raoul Lufbery, the great expatriate American ace of the French Air Service, those fatalistic words would be prophetic. So also for many Canadian fighter pilots, although others would enjoy rich and varied futures. In the immediate aftermath of the Great War, however, Fate struck another cruel blow in the form of disease. The Spanish Flu of 1918-19 probably had its origins in India. As vaccines were not available, this plague stampeded across Europe in the spring and summer of 1918, then returned in even more virulent form that autumn. It killed some 21 million people worldwide, more than the war, including roughly 50,000 Canadians.[1] Many servicemen were afflicted on both sides of the lines, and, unlike most influenzas, it demonstrated a perverse attraction to the young and the hearty. In both suddenness and incidence of attack, it was worse than the great epidemics of cholera and smallpox that struck during the early nineteenth century.

Although the disease was not caused by the war, extensive wartime movement of personnel helped to spread it. Soldiers on both sides were targeted, and it struck down healthy and wounded, rich and poor alike. Individuals would be incapacitated with a high fever, and dead within a few days. There was no cure, nor any preventive measures. Spread to Canada by returning war veterans, it made its way to even the most remote communities in the nation. Quebec and Labrador were the hardest-hit regions, and some villages were completely exterminated by this pandemic. Nor were the bravest, the most resolute, spared. Captain Francis Granger Quigley, victor of thirty-three combats during 1917 and 1918, had been wounded and had returned to Canada to convalesce. After a brief tour as a flight instructor at Armour Heights in Toronto, he asked to be returned to overseas duties. However, he caught the flu on the troop ship carrying him back to Britain and died in a Liverpool hospital on October 20, 1918.

After months of recuperation, Alan Arnett "Babe" McLeod had recovered enough to receive his simple cross of bronze from his king in early September. Returning home, he was hailed as the dominion's youngest winner of the Victoria Cross and as the youngest VC of the air war. All this attention left him totally unaffected. He was still the modest, fun-loving youth to whom his colleagues at 2 Squadron had been so attracted. Although in a weakened state from his wounds, he was well on the road to recovery when he also fell victim to influenza. He succumbed quickly, passing away in Winnipeg just five days before the Armistice.

Others would die accidentally either just before or shortly after the war's final shots. Sterne Edwards represented one-third of the trio of childhood pals from Carleton Place, Ontario, who had volunteered to serve in the RNAS. Like his two kindred spirits, Murray Galbraith and Roy Brown, he had become an ace and had also won the Distinguished Service Cross and Bar. After 430 flight hours on active service at the front, war's end saw him instructing in Sopwith Pups at RAF Tadcaster in England. The day after the Armistice, Edwards failed to recover from a spin and he crashed into the airfield perimeter. He lingered until November 22, losing a leg by amputation during the process, and then quietly passed away in the early morning hours. While relations between men from Britain and the dominions were frequently strained, there were at least as many occasions where a tremendous amount of mutual respect and goodwill existed. Edwards' British commanding officer, who liked the personable and experienced Canadian, wrote a candid and moving letter of condolence to Edwards' mother: "The men simply worshipped him and would do anything for him, and at the same time, he ruled them with a rod of iron, but gently. In Sterne I not only lost my best officer, but my best friend."[2] Murray Galbraith chose to remain in the service after the war, but was killed in an automobile accident at Camp Borden on March 29, 1921. Of the three, only Brown lived on for several years after the Great War.

In Britain during the summer of 1918, a Canadian Air Force was finally being established on a similar basis to that of the Australians. It would consist of a training base, RAF Upper Heyford in Oxfordshire, and two operational RAF squadrons, manned entirely by Canadians. Number 1 Squadron, Canadian Air Force, was initially equipped with Sopwith Dolphins. Number 2 Squadron was kitted with de Havilland DH9as, but the war ended before either unit was operationally ready. Transferred to Shoreham-by-Sea in March 1919 and manned by a stellar cast of Canadian airmen with exceptional war records, the units enjoyed temporary relative stability, but technical problems soon grounded the Dolphins. Although re-equipped with SE5as and Snipes, the fledgling service could hold

Opposite:
A Sopwith Snipe

Major Andy McKeever with a captured Fokker DVII. Note the 1 (CAF) Squadron emblem on the fuselage.

out only until January 1920, at which time it was quietly disbanded.

On December 1, 1918, Lieutenant W.J. Sampson of Vancouver was killed while ferrying a Dolphin to Upper Heyford. On May 8, 1919, Captain C.W. Warman of Norfolk, Virginia, a twelve-victory ace who was apparently considered a "honourary Canadian" by the Canadian Air Force, was killed while low flying at Chingford. Then, on May 22 the embryonic service lost one of its most distinguished members when Major Albert Desbrisay Carter perished while flying a captured Fokker DVII. Its wings collapsed and it went straight down in a nose-dive from 7000 feet.[3] Hawkeye McKeever, king of the two-seaters, had been chosen as 1 Squadron's first commanding officer and given exceptionally able

flight commanders in Donald MacLaren, Carl Falkenberg, and George Johnson. Early in 1919 McKeever returned to his hometown of Listowel, Ontario. However, on September 3, while en route to New York to assume a new position as manager of Minneola airport, he was injured in an automobile accident and died on Christmas Day, 1919.

Others survived the most harrowing experiences during the war only to die in freak accidents at a later date. John DePencier, the son of the Bishop of New Westminster, BC, who had a bullet pass through him while flying Dolphins in 1918, was serving with the Army of Occupation in Germany after the Armistice. By the spring of 1920 his 12 Squadron RAF was the sole empire squadron remaining in Germany. On May 17 this excellent fighter pilot was killed while flying as a passenger in a Bristol Fighter at Lindenthal near Cologne.

Although a great deal of planning and coordination had been expended in getting the men from the dominions overseas and into the fight, little thought was given to those waiting at home. The grieving widow of one Canadian airman killed while training in England discovered that the marking of grave sites was left to friends and family, and was not an acknowledged responsibility of the British government at this time:

You asked if the authorities erect wooden crosses for the boys killed; regret to say that they don't here in England, but all the boys of our squadron who have been killed are having crosses placed on their graves by their fellow comrades. We took up a subscription for this purpose and received enough money to erect a cross for each one. [The padre said] Roy's grave would have its cross in a day or two … I have talked with our padre in regard to having a fitting stone put up & he told me if you could write him, why he would be only too pleased to look after this for you. [4]

Nor was the British government sensitized to getting dominion men reunited with their families as expeditiously as possible once hostilities had ceased. Ken Guthrie recalls:

I bought my own fare home. That's how I got home. Word came out that all Canadians were to be repatriated at their own expense. The irony was that you joined the Imperials. They took you over and they could bloomin' well bring you back. But the Royal Air Force said, "Well, we're not going to send you back tomorrow. We'll send you back when we feel like sending you back." Period. My brother had been in the ground battles, Vimy Ridge and all that. They sent him down to Camp Whitby and he spent months there. He didn't get back until September 1919 … I came back at my own expense in January 1919. Fifty-six bucks from London to Liverpool to Halifax to Ottawa for transportation. Fifty-six dollars. Boy, you can't even move a taxi for that kind of money now. [5]

All the fighting associated with the Great War did not end on Armistice Day 1918. Between 1919

Canadian pilots of 1 (CAF) Squadron at Shoreham in 1919; Andy McKeever is seated centre, while Donald MacLaren is seated left, beside George Johnson

Top: Lieutenant
John MacLennan

and 1920 many Allied airmen volunteered to fly in Russia on the side of the Czarists, or White Russians, against the Bolsheviks, or Reds. A number of Canadians were involved in this intervention, including Major Raymond Collishaw, DSO, DSC, DFC. Although he mainly flew with bomber forces, Collishaw managed to score one more victory over an Albatros during his Russian service. He was awarded a number of Czarist decorations, along

Lieutenant John
MacLennan's
repatriation
certificate.
Note the date
stamp.

with being made an Officer of the Order of the British Empire (OBE). After serious reversals late in 1919, by the spring of 1920 all counter-revolutionary forces had either been withdrawn from Russia or had been vanquished. Collishaw remained in the RAF and, during 1940, commanded all RAF units in the Western Desert as an air commodore. Under his capable leadership, this command conducted a courageous campaign of reconnaissance and ground support for its own forces, as well as active air operations against Italian forces in the region. While Collishaw's forces had some spectacular successes, including the bombardment of the ports of Tobruk and Bardia, their greatest achieve-

ment was creating a defensive mentality among the Italians.

After service in Britain commanding 14 Fighter Group as an Air Vice-Marshal, and a further decoration in the form of an appointment as a Commander of the Order of the Bath (CB), Collishaw returned to Canada to retire in 1943. He would later become a successful businessman and historical writer. In his later years, he had the following to say about his Great War service:

I feel that my days of command in North Africa, when we had to depend upon superior strategy, deception and fighting spirit, faced with a numerically-superior enemy, represented by far my best effort. Yet if I am known at all to my fellow Canadians it is through more carefree days, when, as a fighter pilot with the limited responsibilities of a flight commander of a squadron in France, I had the good fortune to shoot down a number of the enemy without in turn being killed.[6]

Will Barker recovered to a certain degree from his grievous war injuries, but those wounds tortured him for the rest of his all-too-short life and may well have factored in his death. On March 1, 1919, he received a record six decorations at Buckingham Palace from his King, including the Victoria Cross. He was now the most decorated warrior in Canadian history. Later that year he returned to Canada and formed a short-lived flying business with his friend, Billy Bishop. However, they were soon forced to sell their small fleet of aircraft to cover their debts. In 1922 he joined the newly formed Canadian Air Force, resigning four years later to help develop a tobacco business in Norfolk County, Ontario. Unfortunately, this venture also failed. In January 1930 he became president of Fairchild Aircraft Limited's fledgling Canadian operation, headquartered at Longueuil in Quebec. On March 12, while Barker was demonstrating the company's newest two-seater training aircraft to Department of National Defence representatives at Rockcliffe airport in Ottawa, the aircraft stalled and crashed nose-first onto the frozen river beside the field, killing him instantly. Although it was impossible to determine what caused the crash, the need for a rapid throttle adjustment to assist in the aircraft's stall recovery appears to have been an issue. Barker's British surgeon, Robert Dolbey,

in a letter of condolence dated March 15, 1930, made a chilling observation with respect to the great ace's physical limitations:

> After the War, I operated on his elbow joint, after which – though it was no fault of mine, but an inevitable result of the destruction of the bone, he was never able to have any power in his arm, unless he had a retentive apparatus, so that Barker, from that time onwards, flew entirely with one arm.
>
> He was one of the finest young men that I ever met and I think his death is a terrible loss, not only to Canada, but to the whole of the British Empire.[7]

Rumours of suicidal depression or alcoholic impairment would dog Barker's last flight, but his definitive biographer dismisses these factors as unsubstantiated conjecture.[8] It is true that anxiety about his future, his failed business ventures, and his extreme physical discomfort had depressed and frustrated him, led him to drink, and seriously disrupted his marriage. Like so many returning veterans, he had been shamefully treated, not only by Britain but by Canada as well, with respect to proper

A postwar shot of Billy Bishop and Will Barker in front of one of their privately-owned Fokker DVIIs. Barker's left arm hangs limp.

treatment of his wounds, fair financial compensation for his suffering, and a caring rehabilitation into society. However, the Fairchild appointment had redressed a lot of the ills, and he viewed the future with a spirited optimism and determination to succeed. In all likelihood, Barker died because his physical limitations did not permit him to recover the out-of-control aircraft in a proper and timely manner. Barker was just as much a casualty of the Great War as the tens of thousands of his Canadian brethren who would sleep forever in Europe.

Billy Bishop, who had formed that unsuccessful flying partnership with Barker in 1919, moved to England with his wife at the end of 1921. There he prospered, marketing the foreign rights to a new process for selling iron pipe, but the stock market crash of 1929 wiped out his paper fortune. Returning to Canada in 1931, he assumed the position of vice-president of McColl-Frontenac (later Texaco) Oil and settled with his young family in Montreal.

In 1938 Bishop was made an honorary air marshal in the Royal Canadian Air Force, and by January 1940 he had become its director of recruiting. But Bishop became far more than just a recruiter. He became a morale booster extraordinaire and a tireless promoter of the RCAF, the nation, and the cause of freedom at home and abroad. He also made forceful, articulate entreaties for peace and for international cooperation in developing the airways of the world for commercial purposes, and documented those views in a second highly successful book, *Winged Peace*. Much of his vision was brought to fruition in the United Nations International Civil Aviation Organization (ICAO), established in 1947.

Four years of relentless campaigning had exhausted him, and in 1944 Bishop asked to be retired from active duty. The King's Birthday Honours List that year made him a Companion of the Most Honourable Order of the Bath (CB). Although pleased, Bishop complained that the ribbon broke up his "fighting row," sitting as it did between his VC and DSO ribbons! He again volunteered for service in the RCAF during the Korean War, but the Canadian government politely declined his offer. Retiring to Palm Springs, Florida, he died peacefully in his sleep during the early morning hours before dawn on September 11, 1956. In August 1994 Canadian Forces Air Command and Canada Post honoured this great airman with a stamp bearing his likeness.

Many of the Great War's Canadian aces would serve with prominence and distinction in the RCAF. Lloyd Breadner, eventually the most senior of them all, became the Chief of the Air Staff in 1940 with the rank of air chief marshal. Wilf Curtis also held the same post as an air marshal in 1947, as did Robert Leckie in the years just preceding Curtis' final appointment. Mike McEwen became an inspirational combat leader during the Second World War. As an Air Vice-Marshal in February 1944, he was appointed Air Officer Commanding (AOC) of the Canadian 6 Group of Bomber Command. Although he advocated arduous training and stern discipline, he was no armchair commander. He fearlessly led from the front, accompanying his crews on the toughest missions, even against the explicit orders of Air Marshal Harris, the AOC of Bomber Command. His presence on missions was soon taken for granted by his crews, and he became a symbol for good luck. If the man with the moustache was on board, his men felt that things would be fine. They were drawn to this gallant airman who wanted to share their danger, and who could not sleep while his men were flying raids.[9]

Others contributed to the war effort in other positions. Alan Duncan Bell-Irving and Hank Burden both served as senior officers in the Home Establishment. Bell-Irving established a Canadian altitude record of 34,900 feet in a Hawker Hurricane while he was commander of the Trenton Air Station. Bill Stephenson directed all British wartime counter-intelligence and espionage work in the Western Hemisphere, which was fully recorded in his biography and the subsequent movie, *A Man Called Intrepid*. He was knighted for his wartime services, and decorated by the Americans with the US Presidential Medal for Merit. Later, he became a Companion of the Order of Canada. John Maclennan, a Camel pilot who had flown ground attack missions with distinction in 1918, flew actively as a crewman in Beaufighters on night fighter operations out of England.

Roy Brown suffered profoundly for his role in von Richthofen's demise. Gravely injured in a flying accident towards the end of the war, he took years to recover. The trade magazines and pulp action journals of the 1920s and 1930s hounded him relentlessly to tell his story, but he refused to discuss von Richthofen, either in public or in private. For a time, he ran a small commercial airline operating between Noranda, Quebec, and Haileybury, Ontario. At the outbreak of the Second World War, he attempted to rejoin the RCAF, but was rejected on medical grounds. He became an advisory editor to *Canadian Aviation,* a magazine for which he had done some previous writing. In 1943 he made an unsuccessful bid for public office, but died on March 9, 1944, in Stouffville, Ontario, of a heart attack.

Many of the returning Canadian Great War aces continued to seek adventure through aviation, and in many cases they flew in the northern wilds. Wop May, so very nearly Manfred von Richthofen's eighty-first victim, finished the war as a captain with thirteen victories and a Distinguished Flying Cross. In 1929 May and Vic Horner, both from Edmonton, wrote aviation history when they saved the settlement of Little Red River by carrying out an extremely hazardous mercy flight. Flying through a blinding blizzard to nearby Fort Vermillion in -30 degree temperatures, the intrepid duo brought in enough life-saving serum to quell a deadly diphtheria epidemic. For this mission May was awarded the coveted McKee Trophy, given for the advancement of aviation, and later that year he made the first non-stop flight from Edmonton to Winnipeg. He had also been made an Officer of the Order of the British Empire in 1934. Later, he served as chief test pilot for Canadian Airways and, during the Second World War, ran three air observer schools for the British Commonwealth Air Training Plan.

Other pilots also had colourful pioneering aviation careers. A.E. "Steve" Godfrey made the first trans-Canada seaplane flight from Montreal to Vancouver in 1926, and, in 1928, flew the first airmail across the nation. Ernie Hoy made the inauguration airmail flight across the Rockies in a Curtis JN4 on August 7, 1919. C.H. "Punch" Dickins, while not a scout pilot, had brought down several of the enemy while flying DH4 and DH9 bombers in 1918, winning a Distinguished Flying Cross in the process. The 1928 winner of the McKee Trophy, Dickins was instrumental in opening up mail routes in the vast Northwest Territories. Like May, he was also recognized with an OBE, and later the Order of Canada.

Not all the Great War aces pursued pioneering ways, though their lives were no less productive. Fred McCall and Donald MacLaren both remained in aviation, but had successful careers as executives. Others became captains of industry or distinguished

Clifford M. "Black Mike" McEwen in full-dress splendor after the war

educators, solicitors, and journalists. Harry Symons, a six-victory Camel ace, won the prestigious Stephen Leacock Memorial Medal for Humour in 1947. Bill Duncan, victor in eleven combats and winner of the Military Cross and Bar, went on to a notable career in the National Hockey League, both as a player and as the first coach of the Toronto Maple Leafs.

They are all gone now, save one,[10] those stalwarts of the Somme and the skies above Flanders. They fought gallantly from the Channel coast to the Middle East as the knights of the air, giving Canada many proud moments along the way and providing exceptional inspiration to those who followed in their footsteps. Canada can take great reflected pride in the stellar achievements of this small band of brothers who fought so well, so far away, so very long ago. May they never be forgotten.

APPENDIXES

APPENDIX A
The Canadian Scout/Fighter
Pilot Aces of the Great War

This compendium lists the 171 known Canadian scout/fighter pilots who achieved ace status (five or more air-to-air victories) under the empire rules of determination. These men were either Canadian by birth or through immigration to or settlement in Canada before the commencement of hostilities. The rank given is the last known wartime rank attained. The sources for this listing, presented alphabetically, are an amalgam drawn from Christopher Shores, Norman Franks, and Russell Guest, *Above the Trenches*: *A Complete Record of the Fighter Aces and Units of the British Empire Air Forces, 1915-1920* (1990) and its *Supplement* (1996).

Pilot	Score	Pilot	Score
1. Captain William Melville Alexander	23	36. Captain John Bonnicher Crompton	5
2. Flight Lieutenant George Benson Anderson	5	37. Captain Lumsden Cummings	5
3. Flight Commander Frederick Carr Armstrong	13	38. Flight Commander Wilfred Austin Curtis	13
4. Captain Alfred Clayburn Atkey	38	39. Lieutenant Ernest Francis Hartley Davis	7
5. Flight Commander Fred Everest Banbury	11	40. Lieutenant Hiram Frank Davison	11
6. Major William George Barker	50	41. Captain Richard Jeffries Dawes	9
7. Captain Louis Drummond Bawlf	5	42. Captain Roger Amedee Del'Haye	9
8. Captain Gerald Gordon Bell	16	43. Captain John Dartnell DePencier	8
9. Captain Hilliard Brooke Bell	10	44. Captain George Clapham Dixon	9
10. Captain Alan Duncan Bell-Irving	7	45. Captain Robert E. Dodds	10
11. Lieutenant Gerald Alfred Birks	12	46. Captain Jack Elmer Drummond	6
12. Lieutenant-Colonel William Avery Bishop	72	47. Major Chester Stairs Duffus	5
13. Captain William Otway Boger	5	48. Captain William James Arthur Duncan	11
14. Lieutenant Edward Borgfeldt Booth	5	49. Lieutenant Edward Carter Eaton	5
15. Major Lloyd Samuel Breadner	10	50. Captain Stearne Tighe Edwards	17
16. Lieutenant Cecil Guelph Brock	6	51. Flight Sub-Lieutenant Sydney Emerson Ellis	5
17. Captain Arthur Roy Brown	10	52. Captain Arthur Bradfield Fairclough	19
18. Captain Frederic Elliott Brown	10	53. Captain Carl Frederick Falkenberg	17
19. Lieutenant William Henry Brown	9	54. Flight Commander Joseph Stewart Temple Fall	36
20. Captain George William Bulmer	10	55. Captain Conway McAlister Grey Farrell	7
21. Captain Henry John Burden	16	56. Captain Maxwell Hutcheon Findlay	14
22. Captain Lynn Campbell	7	57. Captain Austin Lloyd Fleming	8
23. Major Albert Desbrisay Carter	29	58. Captain James Henry Forman	9
24. Major Alfred William Carter	17	59. Lieutenant George Buchanan Foster	7
25. Flight Commander Arnold Jaques Chadwick	11	60. Lieutenant Herbert Howard Snowdon Fowler	6
26. Captain Henry Gordon Clappison	6	61. Captain Daniel Murray Bayne Galbraith	6
27. Captain William Gordon Claxton	37	62. Lieutenant George William Gladstone Gauld	5
28. Captain Arthur Claydon	7	63. Lieutenant William John Gillespie	5
29. Captain Carleton Main Clement	14	64. Captain James Alpheus Glen	15
30. Lieutenant Harris G. Clements	6	65. Captain Albert Earl Godfrey	14
31. Lieutenant-Colonel Raymond Collishaw	61	66. Captain Frank Clifford Gorringe	14
32. Lieutenant Harry Neville Compton	5	67. Captain Acheson Gosford Goulding	9
33. Lieutenant Kenneth Burns Conn	20	68. Flight Lieutenant Edward Rochfort Grange	5
34. Lieutenant Earl Frederick Crabb	6	69. Lieutenant Charles Duncan Bremner Green	11
35. Lieutenant William Benson Craig	8	70. Captain John Edmond Greene	15

71.	Captain John Playford Hales	5		122.	Captain John Harry McNeaney	5
72.	Captain Joseph Eskel Hallonquist	5		123.	Lieutenant Russell Fern McRae	5
73.	Captain Earl McNabb Hand	5		124.	Captain Earl Stanley Meek	6
74.	Captain William Leeming Harrison	12		125.	Captain Norman Craig Millman	6
75.	Lieutenant-Colonel Harold Evans Hartney	7		126.	Lieutenant Harold Arthur Sydney Molyneaux	5
76.	Lieutenant Richard Alexander Hewat	6		127.	Captain Guy Borthwick Moore	10
77.	Captain Charles Robert Reeves Hickey	21		128.	Captain Ernest Theophilus Morrow	7
78.	Captain William Carroll Hilborn	7		129.	Captain Harold Edgar Mott	5
79.	Captain Reginald Theodore Carlos Hoidge	28		130.	Colonel Redford Henry Mulock	5
80.	Captain George Robert Howsam	13		131.	Flight Lieutenant Gerald Ewart Nash	6
81.	Captain Ernest Charles Hoy	13		132.	Captain Harold Anthony Oaks	11
82.	Captain William Henry Hubbard	12		133.	Flight Lieutenant John Albert Page	7
83.	Lieutenant Harold Byron Hudson	13		134.	Lieutenant Stanley Asa Puffer	7
84.	Major Victor Henry Huston	6		135.	Captain Francis Grainger Quigley	33
85.	Captain Gordon Budd Irving	12		136.	Lieutenant Henry Coyle Rath	12
86.	Captain William Roy Irwin	11		137.	Lieutenant Lewis Hector Ray	7
87.	Captain Mansell Richard James	11		138.	Flight Sub-Lieutenant Ellis Vair Reid	19
88.	Lieutenant Arthur Eyguem De Montainge Jarvis	7		139.	Captain Cyril Burfield Ridley	11
89.	Captain William Stanley Jenkins	12		140.	Captain William Wendell Rogers	9
90.	Captain George Owen Johnson	11		141.	Captain Stanley Wallace Rosevear	25
91.	Lieutenant Harold Waddell Joslyn	7		142.	Captain William Jackson Rutherford	8
92.	Captain Kenneth William Junor	8		143.	Captain Ernest James Salter	9
93.	Captain Ronald McNeill Keirstead	13		144.	Flight Commander John Edward Sharman	8
94.	Second Lieutenant Ernest Tilton Sumpter Kelly	6		145.	Captain William Ernest Shields	24
95.	Captain Arthur Gerald Knight	8		146.	Major Alexander MacDonald Shook	12
96.	Lieutenant Alfred Koch	10		147.	Lieutenant Emerson Arthur Lincoln Fisher Smith	7
97.	Captain Alfred Alexander Leitch	7		148.	Lieutenant John Henry Smith	8
98.	Lieutenant Robert Hazen Little	5		149.	Flight Sub-Lieutenant Langley Frank Willard Smith	8
99.	Captain Emile John Lussier	11		150.	Captain Frank Ormond Soden	27
100.	Lieutenant Ross Morrison MacDonald	5		151.	Captain Jack Victor Sorsoleil	14
101.	Lieutenant William Myron MacDonald	8		152.	Lieutenant Anthony George Allen Spence	9
102.	Captain George Chisholme Mackay	18		153.	Captain Stanley Stanger	13
103.	Major Donald Roderick MacLaren	54		154.	Captain William Samuel Stephenson	12
104.	Lieutenant Malcom Plaw MacLeod	7		155.	Captain Harry Lutz Symons	6
105.	Lieutenant John Finlay Noel MacRae	5		156.	Lieutenant Frank Harold Taylor	10
106.	Captain Reginald Milburn Makepeace	17		157.	Lieutenant Merril Samuel Taylor	7
107.	Lieutenant Reginald George Malcolm	8		158.	Captain Edmund Roger Tempest	17
108.	Flight Sub-Lieutenant John Joseph Malone	10		159.	Captain William McKenzie Thomson	26
109.	Second Lieutenant Patrick Scarsfield Manley	5		160.	Flight Lieutenant George Leonard Trapp	6
110.	Captain John Gerald Manuel	13		161.	Captain Hazel LeRoy Wallace	14
111.	Captain Roy Manzer	12		162.	Lieutenant Henry Ellis Watson	6
112.	Lieutenant George Ivan Douglas Marks	8		163.	Lieutenant Kenneth Bowman Watson	9
113.	Captain Wilfred Reid May	13		164.	Lieutenant George Arthur Welsh	5
114.	Captain Frederick Robert Gordon McCall	35		165.	Captain Arthur Treloar Whealy	27
115.	Lieutenant Roy Kirkwood McConnell	7		166.	Captain James Butler White	12
116.	Captain Roderick McDonald	8		167.	Captain Joseph Leonard Maries White	22
117.	Lieutenant Clifford Mackay McEwen	27		168.	Lieutenant Robert Kenneth Whitney	5
118.	Captain David Mackay McGoun	9		169.	Captain Thomas Frederic Williams	14
119.	Captain Douglas Urchart McGregor	12		170.	Lieutenant Claude Melnot Wilson	8
120.	Captain Alfred Edwin McKay	10		171.	Major Harry Alison Wood	5
121.	Lieutenant-Colonel Andrew Edward McKeever	31				

APPENDIX B
Lexicon of Idioms
Used by RFC/RNAS/RAF Personnel
During the Great War

As is the case with any technically oriented and highly specialized profession, the Great War airmen from the British Empire developed a unique language. With no attempt to be all-inclusive, here are some examples of their picturesque speech.

War politics were a frequent topic of conversation in messes at the time. *The Grab* was a cynical reference to the international quest for profit from the war. A *Jingo* was a person who practised jingoistic patriotism – something that the British, but not generally the "colonials," could feel about the war. Great Britain was referred to as the *home establishment, the interior,* or *Blighty*. To be *PBI* meant to be *posted back to the interior*, or returned to Britain. *Nissens* were a ubiquitous form of pre-fabricated hut used for myriad purposes, most frequently accommodation. Junior officers were most commonly housed in them at four to a hut. Two relatively senior officers, such as flight commanders, might share one hut, while a squadron commander often had his own private room or small hut to himself.

Many variations of physical illness were common during the Great War. *War strain*, otherwise known as *Flying Sickness D*, was tuberculosis – the most common long-term physical ailment to come out of the airmen's war. *PUO*, or *pyrexia of unknown origin*, was a common form of non-specific influenza. On the psychological side, being afraid was known as *having, or getting, the wind up*.

Cigarettes were *gaspers*. *Brass hats* was the universal sobriquet for senior staff officers, frequently the source of much contempt and derision. Germans were known collectively as *the Hun* or *Fritz,* and all Allied airmen were known as *merchants* of one sort or another, depending on their aircraft type or flying specialty. For example, there were *Camel merchants, Bristol Fighter merchants,* and *Bombing merchants*.

Archie was the generic term applied to all enemy anti-aircraft artillery. German flak normally burst in black smudges, whereas Allied flak bursts were usually white. To be hit by enemy flak was to be *Archied*. When this weapon burst close, according to V.R. Yeates, it "sounded like a jinn (supernatural spirit) with an iron throat coughing," an enormous bellowing cough with a secondary clanging note. *Flaming onions* were phosphorous patches of smoke generated by 37 mm anti-aircraft shells. A *Sidcot* was a contemporary flying suit, named after the manufacturer, and the *Effell* was an airfield's windsock or wind-direction indicator. Aircraft were *Grids* or *Busses*.

German aircraft were collectively known as *HAs* (hostile aircraft) or *EAs* (enemy aircraft) and specifically as *Albatri,* the plural of Albatros, or *tripehounds,* a term applied to all triplanes, whether friendly or enemy. Aircraft wings were *main planes* (top wings) or *lower planes*, and the *tailplane* was the horizontal stabilizer. *Buckingham* was an explosive incendiary machine gun shell, most commonly used against enemy observation balloons. The *pitot* was the term applied to the airspeed, while the *aldis* was an aircraft's gunsight. Aircraft possessing rapid rates of climb and descent could *climb like lifts* and *dive like bricks*. Anything exceptionally fine was *splitarse,* and therefore an excellent aircraft was *a very splitarse bus.*

APPENDIX C
A Note on Sources

On the question of victory scores, I have used *Above the Trenches*, the 1990 account by Christopher Shores, Norman Franks, and Russell Guest, and its 1996 *Supplement*, as the definitive authority, since no finer work is available on the tabulation of claims submitted and approved by the British War Office during the war, under the rules of claim acceptance at the time. Acceptance rules and the various categories of claims, along with similar rules governing claims by the other combatant nations, are covered in some detail. Endnotes are used throughout the text to credit specific quotations and to amplify points in the manuscript. Since virtually all the principals involved in these events have now passed away, other sources have been relied upon, including those of the Directorate of History of the Department of National Defence, the National Archives of Canada, and the Archives of the National Aviation Museum in Ottawa and the Royal Canadian Air Force Museum in Trenton. A large number of references have been culled for details, ranging from primary sources dating back to the war, including log book, journal, and diary entries and letters home, to recent offerings by reputable historians. Facts long accepted have not been credited in the notes, though specific statistics that may be open to question are cited, since the reader may wish to explore these sources independently.

The chapter on Bishop is especially well documented. Although these sources have their merits, many also have their limitations. For example, Bishop's son Arthur, who wrote a biography of his famous father and who has been a prolific author about Canadian military history, has been a rich source of anecdotal information. However, in a social context Billy Bishop was fond of embellishing real events, and some of the stories he passed on simply did not happen, at least not in the manner described. This is not meant to denigrate the value of Arthur Bishop's contributions, for in many ways his recollections and perceptions of his father are unique and highly informative.

It has been a formidable challenge to cite what viewpoints are felt to be appropriate and to seek alternatives to others. For those judgments, I accept full responsibility. Dan McCaffery, a distinguished journalist and historian, dwells in a similar camp with respect to his 1988 publication, *Billy Bishop – Canadian Hero*. He has in the past been criticized for this study,[1] and he freely admits to having made several factual errors during the book's development many years ago. The most obvious is the *carte blanche* acceptance of a Bishop–von Richthofen fight; an event that did not occur. Unfortunately, a very large body of writers has inadvertently perpetuated this myth, including Arthur Bishop. The problem originates with Billy Bishop's fabrication of the event in his biography *Winged Warfare*, written in 1917, and further embellished upon for various trade and adventure journals of the 1920s and 1930s. Many learned individuals have chosen to accept the tale, without challenge, until the present day.

On a related topic, even the RAF's distinguished official historian of the period, H.A. Jones, was completely taken in by fictional accountings of Manfred von Richthofen's last flight, and incorporated them into the RAF's official *History of the Great War* in 1932.[2] The essential point here is that the innocent perpetuation of some long-standing, unchallenged falsehoods should not negate the validity nor destroy the credibility of much larger bodies of work. As is the case with Arthur Bishop, McCaffery's extensive research and frequently unique, highly valuable offerings need to be treated with respect and accorded serious consideration. For example, his research into matching German losses with Bishop's numerous victory claims is the result of years of study of available records and collaborations with eminent air historians, such as Stewart K. Taylor in Canada and British historians Dennis Hylands and Joe Warne.[3]

Many other reputable and distinguished historians have been referenced in the development of this manuscript. Philip Markham was a gifted Canadian air historian and engineer whose insightful articles have repeatedly graced the pages of the prestigious First World War journal *Over the Front*.[4] However, even he was led to a significantly erroneous conclusion with respect to the death of Manfred von Richthofen owing to the acceptance of a long-perpetuated myth concerning the event. Stewart K. Taylor was, for a long period of time, the official historian of the World War 1 Flyers fraternity and a member of the *Over the Front* editorial board. A winner of the Thornton Hooper Award for Excellence in Aviation History, he is presently compiling a two-volume anthology of all the known Canadian airmen who flew over the Western Front, in Italy, and in Macedonia during the war.[5] Sydney F. Wise is the Dean of the Faculty of Graduate Studies and Research as well as a professor of history at Ottawa's Carleton University. He is a respected scholar and has authored *Canadian Airman and the First World War*, the first volume of the Official History of the Royal Canadian Air Force, which represents ten years of scholarship in its creation.

One particular source of wartime information needs to be placed in perspective. Historically, there has been a slavish reliance on German records for the claims verification of Allied air victories. This dependence has developed, in part, because of the relative casualness of the British claim system, but also because the Royal Flying Corps, the Royal Naval Air Service, and, later, the amalgamated Royal Air Force scouts operated more than 90 percent of the time behind German lines,[6] making crash verifications exceptionally difficult. For German air units operating in static conditions, the reporting of losses was, at least in theory, highly regimented. The flying sections, such as the fighter units, had to maintain daily activity records known as their Kriegstagebuch (KTB) or war diaries. American air historian A.E. Ferko has noted that some of these records survived the two world wars, but the vast majority did not.[7] Many of the KTBs were lost during the German retreat of 1918, while many others were destroyed during the Allied bombing of Dresden in the twilight hours of the Second World War.[8] Still, each Kommandeur der Flieger (Kofl), or officer in charge of all flying units assigned to a particular numbered German Army, was required to receive accurate status reports from each unit under his command every day, since casualties would have to be promptly replaced by the Armee Flug Park (AFPs), or aircraft supply depots, and the Flieger Ersatz Abteilung (FEAs), the aviation crew replacement units. However, this system was extensively employed for units in garrison or static conditions, but not for those in transit. Stewart K. Taylor provided additional testimony to the Canadian Senate with respect to German records:

Strangely, a lot of the German records were not accurate. They were not detailed. We always think of the Germans keeping very good records. They did not. They especially did not keep records of pilots injured, nervous breakdowns, battle damage, other than those who were killed outright – the reason being that the German commanders looked good to their superiors if they could show that they were inflicting damage on allied machines with a minimum of loss to themselves.[9]

Shores, Franks, and Guest have suggested that while German personnel fatality casualty lists are relatively correct and comprehensive, the same may not be said with respect to *matériel* losses. They imply that it is difficult for historians to verify all the claims against German aircraft, since even so-called official sources cite no losses where there is not the slightest doubt that losses did occur, even including aircraft that were downed and accounted for on the Allied side of the lines. They also state that there is strong evidence that, if no personnel losses occurred, no materiel loss record was registered, even if an aircraft was actually destroyed or consigned to the scrap heap.[10] Further, the surviving war diaries frequently do not include "the exact time that their airmen were wounded, where exactly this occurred, or in many cases, the nature of the wound or injury. The actual Jasta War Diaries examined by this writer [Stewart K. Taylor] do not always take into account the result of a combat in which the enemy pilot was forced to land, often damaging his aircraft in the process."[11] In the Imperial German Air Service, wounded airmen were often retained at their combat units and given a temporary ground job. "None of this would ever be entered in the Jasta or Flieger-Abteilung War Diary unless the pilot or observer was temporarily incapacitated. Often, damaged enemy aircraft were repaired at the squadron. If so, the high command of the Imperial German Air Service would never be made privy to this information."[12]

Between 1933 and 1936 Reichmarschall Hermann Göring allowed a select number of German historians limited access to the files[13] of the Reichsluftfahrtministerium to make longhand notes from some of the surviving First World War aviation files. Much has been made of these longhand excerpts, particularly those that originated from a German historian named Turneuss. However, it must be emphasized that these notes are incomplete and sketchy records at best,[14] and certainly do not constitute a credible and detailed record of events for the period and units under specific consideration.

If the lack of German documents was not frustrating enough for First World War air historians, this situation is exacerbated by the fact that many Allied records have also been destroyed or lost over time,[15] including significant background documents that were lost when the Public Records Office, then at Somerset House in London, was bombed by the Germans during the Second World War. Others were lost in a massive theft from the present Kew facility in recent years.[16] Thus, air historians of the Great War are dealing with a dearth of documentation from both sides of the conflict.

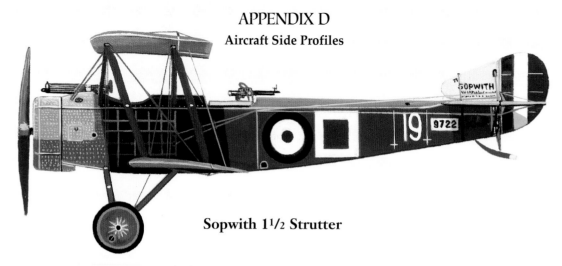

Sopwith 1¹/₂ Strutter

The Sopwith 1¹/₂ Strutter gained its name from the unusual layout of its struts and
rigging. It was the sometime mount of many young Canadian flyers, including
Ray Collishaw. The aircraft depicted is from No. 3 Naval Wing.

Bristol F2b

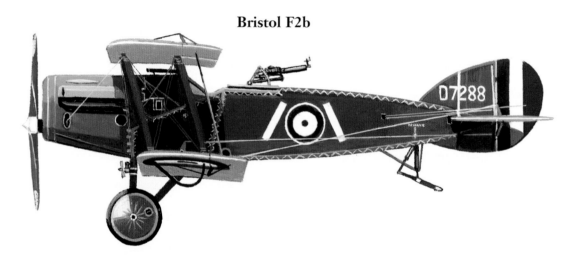

This Bristol F2b is shown in the colours of 11 Squadron. It was the usual mount
of Captain Andy McKeever and was the aircraft in which he fought his most famous
action. The markings are based on available sources and may be incomplete.

Spad VII

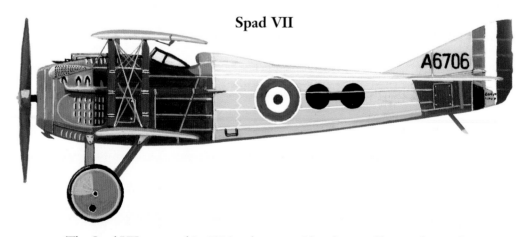

The Spad VII appeared in 1916 and was considered a very "hot performer."
Due to the lack of stagger in the wings it had a high landing speed, but it was
a sturdy aircraft and a stable gun platform. The aircraft depicted is from
19 Squadron and features their "dumbbell" motif on the fuselage.

Pfalz DIII

The Pfalz DIII featured the same plywood monocoque construction
techniques used in the Albatros scouts and it was a nimble and sturdy fighter.
The aircraft depicted is Pfalz DIIIa 4203/17 of Jasta 30, which was one of
the few outfits to use the Pfalz in the final year of the war.

Siemens-Schuckert DIII

This late-war fighter represented the pinnacle of First World War fighter design. It was very maneuverable,
sturdy, had a high rate of climb, was well armed, and, due to its lack of flying wires and aerodynamically
clean styling, it was fast. The DIII depicted is that of Ernst Udet, Germany's second-highest scoring ace.
It features his distinctive red paint scheme and his sweetheart's Christian name on the fuselage.

Fokker Eindekker

Although the diminutive Fokker Eindekker initially cut a swath through
the ranks of the RFC, it was in fact a slow and unwieldy mount. Its success was largely due to its
forward firing machine gun and the audacity and innovation of the early German aces that flew it.
The aircraft depicted is EIII 419/15.

ENDNOTES

PROLOGUE

1 Jay Winter and Blaine Baggett, *The Great War and the Shaping of the 20th Century* (London: Penguin, 1996), 362.

2 The 1911 Canadian population census was 7,206,643, while the 1921 census was 8,787,949. *The Canadian Encyclopedia*, 2nd ed. (Edmonton: Hurtig, 1988), 1720.

3 Desmond Morton and J.L. Granatstein, *Marching to Armageddon: Canadians and the Great War, 1914-1919* (Toronto: Lester & Orpen Dennys, 1989), 250, 279.

4 When all sources are compiled, including at least 1484 fatal casualties from the Dominion of Newfoundland, it would appear that 68,139 "Canadians" gave their lives in combat during the Great War. Nearly half the Newfoundland casualties have no known grave. Patricia Giesler, *Valour Remembered: Canada and the First World War* (Ottawa: Department of Veterans Affairs, 1995), 24-26.

5 Morton and Granatstein, *Marching to Armageddon*, 83.

6 Sydney F. Wise, *Canadian Airmen and the First World War: The Official History of the Royal Canadian Air Force*, Vol. 1 (Toronto: University of Toronto Press, 1980), 649.

7 Christopher Shores, Norman Franks, and Russell Guest, *Above the Trenches: A Complete Record of the Fighter Aces and Units of the British Empire Air Forces, 1915-1920* (London: Grub Street, 1990), 49-392, and *Supplement* (1996), 1-7, 16.

CHAPTER ONE: GENESIS, 1914-1915

1 Italy would initially profess neutrality in this war, and then intervene on the Entente side in 1915.

2 Patricia Giesler, *Valour Remembered: Canada and the First World War* (Ottawa: Department of Veterans Affairs, 1995), 2.

3 However, fighting outside the umbrella of the Canadian Expeditionary Force and on direct attachment to the British Army, the Canadian Princess Patricia's Canadian Light Infantry (PPCLI) would see action with Britain's 27th Division in Flanders as early as December 1914.

4 S.F. Wise, *Canadian Airmen and the First World War: The Official History of the Royal Canadian Air Force*, Vol. 1 (Toronto: University of Toronto Press, 1980), 126.

5 Ibid., 130.

6 Ibid., 133.

7 Ibid., 331.

8 Eventually most of the Entente nations, including Czarist Russia, Belgium, Italy, and later the United States, would employ some form of roundel or cockade markings in their national colours. Austria-Hungary initially used a roundel, but when it was readily confused with Italian markings, Austria-Hungary switched to using the Maltese Cross for the duration of the war.

9 These aircraft would include their first true fighter, the Fokker E series monoplane of 1915, and also the Fokker Dr.1 triplane of 1917.

10 Lee Kennett, *The First Air War, 1914-1918* (New York: The Free Press, 1991), 67.

11 Ibid.

12 Quenault doubted the dependability of his strip-feed firing system, which, at any rate, had to be changed after every twenty-five rounds fired.

13 Bryan Cooper and John Batchelor, *Fighter* (New York: Ballantine, 1973), 8.

14 Edward Jablonski, *The Knighted Skies* (New York: G.P. Putnam's, 1964), 35.

15 The device was actually patented by Franz Schneider, chief designer of the German LVG Company, in 1913 and was further developed by engineers Leimberger and Leubbe. Cooper and Batchelor, *Fighter*, 10, and Jablonski, *The Knighted Skies*, 40.

16 In fact, the Allies did not capture one until April 1916, nine months after its combat debut. In the meantime, they developed and fielded their own interrupter gear independently.

17 The term *ace* had actually been coined by the French to recognize prowess in air combat. It was first applied in a broad sense to Roland Garros for his accomplishments, but was soon more specifically applied to airmen who had achieved five or more aerial victories.

18 Wise, *Canadian Airmen and the First World War*, 20.

19 Ibid., 21.

20 Ibid., 30.

21 Ibid., 35.

22 "Thirty Wealthy Canadian Men Taught Aeroplane," *Sunday News*, Dayton, Ohio, October 31, 1915.

23 This American connection would continue, even after the RFC created its own training establishment in Canada in 1917.

24 Wise, *Canadian Airmen and the First World War*, 643.

25 Major McKelvey Bell, in a letter home to Canada, 1915, from Canada, Department of National Defence, Mulock DHist Biog File, Creagen Collection.

26 Kerby would also become the only Canadian to shoot down two giant Gotha bombers over Britain. These combats occurred during August 1917. Arthur Bishop, *Courage in the Air* (Toronto: McGraw-Hill Ryerson, 1992), 53.

27 Wise, *Canadian Airmen and the First World War*, 357.

28 Ibid.,353.

29 *Canada*, November 13, 1915, 182, from Caws DHist Biog File, Creagen Collection.

30 The Bell-Irvings were very much a fighting family. Five of Malcom's brothers and two of his sisters served overseas. Two of the brothers and a first cousin served in the RFC. All the airmen were decorated and they all survived the war.

31 R.D. Bell-Irving, letter to R.V. Dodds of the RCAF Historical Section, April 17, 1962, from M.M. Bell-Irving DHist Biog File, Creagen Collection.

32 Wise, *Canadian Airmen and the First World War,* 346.

33 *London Gazette*, January 22, 1916.

34 Wise, *Canadian Airmen and the First World War*, 348.

35 In September 1915 alone the RFC conducted more than 4700 hours of flight operations over the Western Front. Ibid., 357

CHAPTER TWO: ASCENDANCY WON — AND LOST, 1916

1 Christopher Shores, Norman Franks, and Russell Guest, *Above the Trenches: A Complete Record of the Fighter Aces and Units of the British Empire Air Forces, 1915-1920* (London: Grub Street, 1990), 145.

2 Sir Douglas Haig, in S.F. Wise, *Canadian Airmen and the First World War: The Official History of the Royal Canadian Air Force,* Vol. 1 (Toronto: University of Toronto Press, 1980), 359.

3 Ibid.

4 The initial cadre of 20 Squadron contained two Canadian airmen: Lieutenants W.K. Campbell of Mitchell, Ontario, and T. Jones of Toronto. Ibid., 361.

5 Canada, Department of National Defence, A.E. Godfrey DHist Biog File, Creagen Collection.

6 Shores, Franks, and Guest, *Above the Trenches,* 13.

7 A.E. Godfrey DHist Biog File, Creagen Collection.

8 Wise, *Canadian Airmen,* 361.

9 Severely wounded in June 1916 after scoring a total of twelve aerial victories, Navarre survived the war, but was killed while attempting to fly though the Arc de Triomphe in 1919. Edward Jablonski, *The Knighted Skies* (New York: G.P. Putnam's, 1964) 92.

10 Wise, *Canadian Airmen,* 362.

11 Elizabeth O'Kiely, *Gentleman Air Ace* (Madeira Park, BC: Harbour, 1992), 101.

12 Postwar analysis suggests that Immelman's death was probably attributable to the fact that his synchronization gear had failed, virtually severing his propeller, which led to the structural disintegration of his Eindekker. Jablonski, *The Knighted Skies,* 81.

13 Shores, Franks, and Guest, *Above the Trenches*, 15.

14 Bryan Cooper and John Batchelor, *Fighter* (New York: Ballantine, 1973), 34.

15 Bernard Fitzsimons, ed., *Warplanes of World War I* (London: Phoebus, 1973), 87.

16 Lee Kennett, *The First Air War, 1914-1918* (New York: The Free Press, 1991), 73-76.

17 No. 22 Squadron Air Combat Report, August 23, 1916, Air1/2248/209/43/12, pt.1.

18 Shores, Franks, and Guest, *Above the Trenches*, 15.

19 O'Keily, *Gentleman Air Ace*, 102.

20 Arthur Bishop, conversation with author, December 17, 1998, and Arthur Bishop, *Courage in the Air* (Whitby, Ont.: McGraw-Hill Ryerson, 1992), 11.

21 Shores, Franks, and Guest, *Above the Trenches*, 16.

22 Wise, *Canadian Airmen*, 364.

23 Air 1/997/204/5/239; Trenchard to GHQ, April 8, 1917, and Air 1/477/AI I15/312/225.

24 Wise, *Canadian Airmen*, 380.

25 Ibid., 392.

26 In contrast, earlier models of the Nieuport 17 had only a Lewis gun mounted atop the upper plane. Later variants had one synchronized forward-firing Vickers gun – and occasionally two such guns.

27 The Albatros' operational longevity precedes an interesting parallel with Willi Messerschmitt's extensive Bf-109 series of fighter aircraft during the Second World War.

28 The Albatros DI had a wing loading of 8 lbs/ft^2, compared with 5.5 lbs/ft^2 for the DH2 and 5.7 lbs/ft^2 for the FE2b. The Albatros DII was lighter than the DI and had a greater wing area, producing a wing loading of 7.4 lbs/ft^2. Wise, *Canadian Airmen,* 384.

29 The DIII design gave way to the definitive Albatros DV, which commenced service delivery in May 1917 and remained

in continuous production until the Armistice.

30 When Immelmann was killed in action on June 18, his death was a tremendous blow to the morale of both the German Air Service and the German public at large. The authorities dreaded the loss of their other national air hero, Oswald Boelcke, and promptly grounded him, sending him on goodwill tours of the Eastern Front. When the air force reorganized that autumn under Oberstleutnant Thomsen into seven specialized Jastas, Boelcke was recalled to the west to command one of them.

31 More often than not, Boelcke was successful on these outings.

32 Shores, Franks, and Guest, *Above the Trenches*, 227.

33 Knight DHist Biog File, Creagen Collection.

34 Shores, Franks, and Guest, *Above the Trenches*, 150, and Bishop, *Courage in the Air*, 36.

35 McKay later became a successful Spad pilot with 23 Squadron in 1917, and was credited with an additional six victories. Shores, Franks, and Guest, *Above the Trenches*, 275.

36 Wise, *Canadian Airmen*, 380.

37 Bishop, *Courage in the Air*, 39.

38 Wise, *Canadian Airmen*, 391.

39 Brigade Op Order No. 24, September 19, 1916, Air/1221/204/5/2634/27, in DHist SGRI, 196, set 61.

40 O'Kiely, *Gentleman Air Ace*, 121.

41 Wise, *Canadian Airmen*, 161. The previous policy of letter designations for squadrons within numbered Naval wings was now changing to numbered squadrons as well. A Squadron at Furnes became 1 Naval Squadron flying N.17s and Bristol Scout Cs. At Dunkirk, the similarly equipped C Squadron became 3 Naval Squadron. In like manner, 5 Wing A Squadron at Coudekerque became 4 Naval Squadron flying Strutters, and 6 Naval formed at Dover and moved to Petite Synthe in December was equipped with Nieuports. 8 Naval was initially formed at St. Pol, but had moved to the Front at Vert Galand by October. Shores, Franks, and Guest, *Above the Trenches*, 16.

42 Wise, *Canadian Airmen*, 167.

43 Shores, Franks, and Guest, *Above the Trenches*, 16.

44 John Gordon, *Of Men and Planes*, Vol. 1 (Ottawa: Love Printing, 1966), 16.

45 W.J. Tempest, letter to R.V. Dodds of RCAF Historical Section, November 2, 1963, from Tempest DHist Biog File, Creagen Collection.

46 Jablonski, *The Knighted Skies*, 13.

47 Gordon, *Of Men and Planes*, 2. Captain E.R. Tempest also had a distinguished career as a Great War fighter pilot. By war's end, he had been credited with seventeen victories and awarded both an MC and a DSO. Both survived the war. Wulstan Tempest eventually became a major and returned to Canada after the war. Shores, Franks, and Guest, *Above the Trenches*, 359.

48 At this time, transfers from the Canadian Expeditionary Force to the RFC were unrestricted and would remain so until October 1916, when the losses incurred at the Battle of Flers-Courcelette forced a temporary freeze on transfers to both of the flying services until reinforcements could restore the CEF manning levels to established strengths. Wise, *Canadian Airmen*, 365.

49 W.G. Barker, in *The Trailmakers Boys Annual*, 1921 (Toronto: Musson, 1921), 2: 56.

50 *Raymond Collishaw, World War I Fighter Ace*, at <http://www.accessweb.com/users/mconstab/ colishaw.htm>, 2.

51 This victory has never been confirmed in any category of destruction.

52 The figures are thirty-two killed, twenty-one wounded, and twelve captured. Wise, *Canadian Airmen*, 392

CHAPTER THREE: TRAGEDIES AND TRIUMPHS, 1917

1 S.F. Wise, *Canadian Airmen and the First World War: The Official History of the Royal Canadian Air Force*, Vol. 1 (Toronto: University of Toronto Press, 1980), 393-94.

2 Raymond Collishaw, letter to R.V. Dodds, RCAF Air Historical Branch, June 1962, from Creagen Collection.

3 H.J. Nowarra and Kimbrough S. Brown, V*on Richthofen and the Flying Circus* (Lechworth: Harleyford, 1958), 36.

4 Raymond Collishaw, letter to Mr. Alexander, December 9, 1962, from Canada, Department of National Defence, Collishaw DHist File.

5 All of McKeever's victories were achieved during the latter half of 1917, and all but two were Albatros DV Scouts – arguably, the toughest quarry of the period. Christopher Shores, Norman Franks, and Russell Guest, *Above the Trenches: A Complete Record of the Fighter Aces and Units of the British Empire Air Forces, 1915-1920* (London: Grub Street, 1990), 276.

6 Bryan Cooper and John Batchelor, *Fighter*, (New York: Ballantine, 1973), 42.

7 H.A.S. Molyneux, letter to W/C R.V. Manning, RCAF Air Historical Branch, June 24, 1962, in Molyneux DHist Biog File, Creagen Collection.

8 Shores, Franks, and Guest, *Above the Trenches*, 17.

9 Altogether, 3598 Canadian soldiers were killed at Vimy Ridge, while a further 7004 were wounded in action. Desmond Morton and J.L. Granatstein, *Marching to Armageddon: Canadians and the Great War, 1914-1919* (Toronto: Lester & Orpen Dennys, 1989), 143.

[10] Norman Franks, Russell Guest, and Frank Bailey, *Bloody April … Black September* (London: Grub Street, 1995), 111.

[11] Mulock DHist Biog File, Creagen Collection.

[12] V.M. Yeates, *Winged Victory* (London: Jonathan Cape, 1934), 136.

[13] Cooper and Batchelor, *Fighter,* 43.

[14] Part of the "morale-building" process consisted of convicting 23,385 mutineers by courts-martial, of whom 412 were sentenced to death. Ultimately, fifty-five were shot, but hundreds more were sent to penal colonies. In fairness, Pétain corrected many grievances, and would henceforth ensure that French soldiers were not blindly committed to battle in hopeless situations. Morton and Granatstein, *Marching to Armageddon,* 147.

[15] Wise, *Canadian Airmen,* 425.

[16] Yeates, *Winged Victory*, 23-26.

[17] John M. Maclennan, in an unidentified newspaper article circa 1942, from Lowell Butters' letter to author, June 25. 1999.

[18] Cooper and Batchelor, *Fighter*, 43.

[19] Lee Kennett, *The First World War, 1914-1918* (New York: The Free Press, 1991), 78.

[20] Norman S. Gilchrist, "An Analysis of the Causes of Breakdown in Flying," *British Medical Journal* 2 (October 12, 1918): 401, in Allan D. English, "Naval Aviators and 'Flying Stresses,' 1914-1918," paper given to the fourth Annual Air Force Historical Conference, Sherwater, June 1998, 1.

[21] Cecil Lewis, in Kennett, *The First World War,* 148.

[22] A.W. Carter, letter to H.A. Halliday, RCAF Air Historical Section, November 27, 1964, from Carter DHist Biog File, Creagen Collection.

[23] Allan D. English, *The Cream of the Crop* (Montreal and Kingston: McGill-Queen's University Press, 1996), 23.

[24] Wise, *Canadian Airmen,* 412.

[25] Kennett, *The First World War,* 142-43.

[26] Ibid., 167.

[27] Donald R. MacLaren, in *Chamber's Journal*, 7th Series, 9, 438 (April 19, 1919): 308.

[28] For example, the loss rates for French pilots officially considered aces and for German holders of the Ordre pour le Mérite were approximately 25 percent. The Austrian aces suffered 28 percent loss, and the Italian aces a full 30 percent. These figures are at least double the loss rate of the non-aces from their respective nations. Kennett, *The First World War,* 170.

[29] Yeates, *Winged Victory,* 156, 203.

[30] R.E. Dodds Diary, from Dodds DHist Biog File, Creagen Collection.

[31] Yeates, *Winged Victory*, 156.

[32] Ibid., 146.

[33] H.B. Bell, "War Experiences of H. Brooke Bell," from Bell DHist Biog File, Creagen Collection.

[34] Breadner DHist File, 74/707 File No. 30.

[35] Wise, *Canadian Airmen,* 647.

[36] Kennett, *The First World War,* 166.

[37] F.C. Farrington, from McCall DHist Biog File, Creagen Collection.

[38] F.R. McGuire, from McKeever DHist Biog File, Creagen Collection.

[39] Yeates, *Winged Victory,* 95.

[40] Willy Lomez, Great War pilot, in J. Clifford Chadderton, *Hanging a Legend: The NFB's Shameful Attempt to Discredit Billy Bishop, VC* (Ottawa: The War Amputations of Canada, 1986), 207.

[41] Manfred von Richthofen, ibid.

[42] Air Board Declaration, 1915, Ralph Barker, *The Royal Flying Corps in France* (London: Constable, 1995), 83-85.

[43] Ibid., 88.

[44] English, "Naval Aviators and Flying Stress, 1914-1918," 6.

[45] Ibid., 14.

[46] English, *The Cream of the Crop*, 65.

[47] Barrett Tillman, "Keeping Score," *Flight Journal* 4, 3 (1999): 66-69.

[48] Shores, Franks, and Guest, *Above the Trenches,* 6.

[49] Kennett, *The First World War,* 164.

[50] Franks, Guest, and Bailey, *Bloody April,* 200.

[51] Tillman, "Keeping Score," 69.

[52] Kennett, *The First World War,*163.

[53] Jablonski, *The Knighted Skies* (New York: G.P. Putman's, 1964), 73.

[54] Kennett, *The First World War,* 165.

[55] Jablonski, *The Knighted Skies,* 84.

[56] Arthur Gould Lee, *Open Cockpit* (London: Jarrolds, 1969), 150.

[57] Ibid., 151

58 James Byford McCudden, *Flying Fury*, 1918, 201-2, from Hoidge DHist Biog File, Creagen Collection.

59 J.S.T. Fall Combat Report, May 23, 1917, from Fall DHist Biog File, Creagen Collection.

60 Arthur Bishop, *Courage in the Air* (Whitby, Ont.: McGraw-Hill Ryerson, 1992), 61.

61 John Gordon, *Of Men and Planes* (Ottawa: Love Printing, 1966), 1: 72.

62 Shores, Franks, and Guest, *Above the Trenches*, 85.

63 Rosevear DHist Biog File, Creagen Collection.

64 A.E. Godfrey DHist Biog File, Creagen Collection.

65 Gordon, *Of Men and Planes*, 92.

66 F.R. McGuire, from McKeever DHist Biog File, Creagen Collection.

67 H.E. Creagen, February 1965, from Alexander DHist Biog File, Creagen Collection.

68 Raymond Collishaw, letter to Mr. Alexander, from Collishaw DHist File.

69 Creagen, from Alexander DHist Biog File, Creagen Collection.

70 Raymond Collishaw, from unidentified personal recollections, from Collishaw DHist File, 53.71

71 Excerpts from official reports, Collishaw/Alexander DHist Biog Files, Creagen Collection.

72 Gordon, *Of Men and Planes*, 99.

73 Wise, *Canadian Airmen*, 632.

74 Bill Gunston, *The Encyclopedia of the World's Combat Aircraft* (London: Hamlyn, 1976), 33.

75 In fact, Barker would shoot down the first *three* enemy aircraft for the RFC in theatre. Shores, Franks, and Guest, *Above the Trenches*, 63.

76 Barker DHist Biog File, Creagen Collection.

77 VC, DSO (Bar), MC (2 Bars), MiD (3), French Croix de Guerre, Italian Silver Medal for Bravery (2). Wayne D. Ralph, *Barker, VC* (London: Grub Street, 1997), vii.

78 28 Squadron Air Combat Report December 3, 1917, extracted from AH204/213/15, in Wise, *Canadian Airmen*, 457.

79 J. Mitchell, "Portraits for Posterity – Major W.G. Barker, VC, DSO, MC," *Popular Flying*, June 1935, 148.

80 Shores, Franks, and Guest, *Above the Trenches*, 63.

81 During this battle for Passchendaele, 15,654 Canadian casualties were incurred. Morton and Granatstein, *Marching to Armageddon*, 169.

82 Ibid., 204

CHAPTER FOUR: THE INCOMPARABLE BILLY BISHOP

1 Maurice Baring, a renowned British poet and diplomat, served as a war correspondent on the Western Front and as a private secretary to Lord Trenchard at RFC Headquarters in France. The chapter lead quotation, taken from his wartime journals, pertains to Bishop's dawn raid on a German aerodrome on June 2, 1917. Maurice Baring, *Flying Corps Headquarters, 1914-1918* (London: William Blackwood and Sons, 1968), 225.

2 William D. Mathieson, *Billy Bishop, VC* (Markham: Fitzhenry and Whiteside, 1989), 6.

3 *William Avery "Billy" Bishop: World War I Fighter Ace*, at <http://www.accessweb.com/users/mconstab/bbishop/htm>, 1.

4 Mathieson, *Billy Bishop*, 7.

5 Arthur Bishop, *The Courage of the Early Morning* (Toronto: McClelland & Stewart, 1981), 18.

6 J. Ross McKenzie, *The Real Case of No. 943: William Avery Bishop* (Kingston: Royal Military College of Canada, 1990). During this period of time, RMC had a three-year program, and the three classes were known in ascending order of seniority as the Third Class, Second Class, and the First Class.

7 At the time, the Battalion of Gentlemen Cadets was divided into four companies, commanded by appointed senior cadets in the following ranks: battalion sergeant-major, company sergeant-major, sergeant, corporal, and lance-corporal. Ibid., 4.

8 RMC Standing Orders, amended to December 1911, para 120, ibid., 10.

9 Bishop, *The Courage of the Early Morning*, 19.

10 McKenzie, *The Real Case of No. 943*, 11.

11 Ibid.

12 Mathieson, *Billy Bishop*, 9-13.

13 Ibid.

14 *William Avery "Billy" Bishop*, 2.

15 Mathieson, *Billy Bishop*, 13.

16 William A. Bishop, *Winged Warfare* (New York: Doran, 1918), 18.

17 Arthur Bishop, letter to author, November 1, 1999.

18 Bishop, *The Courage of the Early Morning*, 4.

19 H. Clifford Chadderton, *Hanging a Legend: The NFB's Shameful Attempt to Discredit Billy Bishop, VC* (Ottawa: The War Amputations of Canada, 1986), 206.

20 Ibid.,152.

21 Mathieson, *Billy Bishop*, 19.

22 Arthur Gould Lee, *No Parachute: A Fighter Pilot in World War I* (London: Jarrolds, 1968), 122.

23 Dan McCaffery, *Billy Bishop: Canadian Hero* (Toronto: James Lorimer, 1988), 55.

24 David Baker, *"Billy" Bishop: The Man and the Aircraft He Flew* (London: Outline Press, 1990), 37.

25 W.M. Fry, *Air of Battle* (London: William Kimber, 1974), 116.

26 Edward Jablonski, *The Knighted Skies* (New York: G.P. Putnam's, 1964), 96.

27 A.J.L. Scott, *Sixty Squadron RAF, 1916-1919* (London: Greenhill, 1990), 45.

28 Baker, *"Billy" Bishop*, 58-61.

29 Joe Warne, "60 Squadron: A Dedicated History, Part 2," *Cross & Cockade* 2, 2 (1980): 59.

30 Chadderton, *Hanging a Legend*, 188.

31 McCaffery, *Billy Bishop*, 58.

32 Chadderton, *Hanging a Legend,* 152.

33 Scott, *Sixty Squadron RAF,* 40-41.

34 Warne, "60 Squadron," 55.

35 Ibid., 56.

36 McCaffery, *Billy Bishop,* 91.

37 Jack Rutherford, a wartime squadron mate, once told Arthur Bishop: "Your father had the damnedest eyesight of anyone I ever knew. He could spot aircraft miles away when no-one else could see them." Arthur Bishop, letter to author, November 1, 1999.

38 Lee Kennett, *The First Air War, 1914-1918* (New York: The Free Press, 1991), 78.

39 Ralph Barker, *The Royal Flying Corps in France* (London: Constable, 1995), 43.

40 Bishop, *The Courage of the Early Morning,* 162.

41 Sydney F. Wise, *Canadian Airmen and the First World War: The Official History of the Royal Canadian Air Force,* Vol. 1 (Toronto: University of Toronto Press, 1980), 406.

42 Chadderton, *Hanging a Legend,* 157.

43 Specifically, nine 60 Squadron pilots were killed in action (KIA), three died of wounds (DOW), four more were wounded in action (WIA), of which two were made prisoners of war (POW). A further four were unhurt, but became POWs. Norman Franks, Russell Guest, and Frank Bailey, *Bloody April … Black September* (London: Grub Street, 1995), 14-73.

44 Wise, *Canadian Airmen,* 406.

45 Joe Warne, in Chadderton, *Hanging a Legend,* 172.

46 Bishop, *The Courage of the Early Morning,* 106.

47 McCaffery, *Billy Bishop,* 82.

48 This happened on April 25, 1917. *The Flying Career of William Avery Bishop* at <http://raven.cc.ukans. edu/~kansite/ ww_one/comment/bishop.html>, 2.

49 William Fry, in McCaffery, *Billy Bishop,* 83-85

50 McCaffery, *Billy Bishop,* 147.

51 Ibid., 148.

52 Baker, *"Billy" Bishop,* 53.

53 At the request of the squadron mechanics, Bishop would overfly Filescamp and fire a red flare from his Very pistol for every enemy aircraft he had vanquished in a sortie. It was yet another attempt to foster unit esprit de corps.

54 William Molesworth, in Scott, *Sixty Squadron RAF,* 62.

55 McCaffery, *Billy Bishop,* 91-94 .

56 Actually, Bishop's recollection was faulty in this case. He would correctly have been referring to the four additional losses incurred *two* days later, on April 16. Franks, Guest, and Bailey, *Bloody April,* 49.

57 McCaffery, *Billy Bishop,* 95.

58 Ibid., 100.

59 Ibid., 101.

60 Ibid., 69.

61 "As his letters from home reveal, he was also driven by an intense urge to win recognition. His personal and family correspondence contains many accounts of his victories, as well as references to his 'score,' his decorations, and the number of victories registered by RFC and French rivals." Wise, *Canadian Airmen,* 406.

62 Chadderton, *Hanging a Legend,* 211.

63 Arthur Bishop, letter to author, November 1, 1999.

64 In another letter home to his fiancée, Bishop wrote: "They have killed my dear friend, Richthofen and his scarlet gangsters. They are going to pay for this Margaret." McCaffery, *Billy Bishop,* 113. Although it has been fiercely debated over the years, Lothar von Richtohofen, Manfred's younger brother, has been credited with Ball's death.

[65] *William Avery "Billy" Bishop*, 5.

[66] H.A. Jones, *The War in the Air* (Oxford: Clarendon Press, 1932), 3: 378.

[67] Bishop, *The Courage of the Early Morning*, 149.

[68] After a meticulous examination of the fragmentary German records that are available, Dan McCaffery has been able to assign most likely specific details, including crew names, to Bishop's May 27, claim. This verification is important because it is one of the most contentious of all his victory claims. They were Vizefeldwebel Fritz Johanntges and Oberleutnant Gerd von Boedern (both killed in action), from FFA A256, in a Rumpler two-seater. McCaffery, *Billy Bishop*, 214.

[69] Ibid., 122.

[70] Ibid.

[71] Bishop File, Directorate of History and Heritage, NDHQ Ottawa.

[72] H.A. Jones, *The War in the Air* (Oxford: Clarendon Press, 1934), 4: 129.

[73] Philip Markham, "The Early Morning of 2 June 1917," *Over the Front* 10, 3 (1995): 240.

[74] McCaffery, *Billy Bishop*, 123.

[75] W.M. Fry, *Air of Battle* (London: William Kimber, 1974), 135.

[76] Markham, "The Early Morning," 242.

[77] A.A. Nicod, "Reunion Memories," *Popular Flying*, December 1934; Chadderton, *Hanging a Legend*, 322.

[78] In fact, it was the example for many airfield raids thereafter repeated. Most immediately, during the Battle of Messines, Trenchard's orders to 9 (HQ) Wing, June 7, included mention of specific low-flying raids on the airfields of Bisseghem and Marcke, near Courtrai, events that had not been undertaken prior to Bishop's action. Jones, *The War in the Air*, 4: 130.

[79] Fry, *Air of Battle*, 136.

[80] AIR1/1555/204/79/75, Markham, "The Early Morning," 245.

[81] Christopher Shores, Norman Franks, and Russell Guest, *Above the Trenches: A Complete Record of the Fighter Aces and the Units of the British Empire Air Forces, 1915-1920* (London: Grub Street, 1990), 77.

[82] Fry, *Air of Battle*, 137.

[83] McCaffery, *Billy Bishop*, 134.

[84] A. Roy Brown, ibid.

[85] Letter to Margaret in Bishop File, Directorate of History and Heritage.

[86] Letter to father, after he had been hit in the fuel tank by ground fire, crash landed with the aircraft on fire, and narrowly escaped with his life. Bishop File.

[87] Bishop to his friend George Stirrett, McCaffery, *Billy Bishop*, 149.

[88] However, at least two of the claims were witnessed by Allied aircrew. Ibid., 214.

[89] Arch Whitehouse, *The Years of the Sky Kings* (London: MacDonald, 1959), 184.

[90] On the day in question, April 30, 1917, Manfred von Richthofen did not even fly. He was too busy preparing for an extended leave from the front, which would commence the following day. H.J. Nowarra and Kimbrough S. Brown, *Von Richthofen and the Flying Circus* (Letchworth: Harleyford, 1958), 56.

[91] In a newspaper interview given to the Toronto *Globe and Mail* dated September 12, 1956, Bishop stated: "It is so terrible that I cannot read it today. It turns my stomach. It was headline stuff, whoop do doop, red-hot, hurray-for-our-side stuff. Yet the public loved it."

[92] Chadderton, in McCaffery, *Billy Bishop*, 132.

[93] McCaffery, *Billy Bishop*, 164.

[94] Ibid., 208.

[95] Richard Townshend Bickers, *The First Great Air War* (London: Hodder & Stoughton, 1988), 245.

[96] A term which, according to Arthur Bishop, his father deplored throughout the rest of his lifetime when it was applied to his preferred style of air combat. Arthur Bishop, interview with author, November 5, 1999.

[97] Shores, Franks, and Guest, *Above the Trenches*, 77.

[98] *The Flying Career of William Avery Bishop*, 4.

[99] On his last day of combat, notoriously unreliable German records claimed no losses in battle. Ironically, it fell to one of Bishop's later detractors, Welsh ace Ira T. Jones, to vindicate the Canadian after a fashion, though there were also Allied aircrew witnesses involved. In his 1954 book *Tiger Squadron*, Jones wrote: "On June 19, 1918, Major (later Colonel) Billy Bishop VC, DSO, MC, DFC, who was commanding 85 Squadron, shot down five Huns before breakfast, and Captain Cobby DSO, MC, DFC, Number 1 Australian Squadron, shot down one Hun after tea. These were the only victories claimed that day by the Royal Air Force. In reply to our query, the German Air Ministry said [after the war] that they had lost neither pilots nor aircraft on June 19th. I know for a fact that this statement was a lie. Captain Cobby's victim was lying, riddled with bullets, in my hangar at Clamarais North aerodrome, near Saint Omer, on the evening in question." McCaffery, *Billy Bishop*, 207. This testimony by Jones also further calls into question the reliability of German records.

[100] Norman Harris, *The Knights of the Air* (Toronto: Macmillan, 1958), 129.

[101] A classic exercise in this respect is to compare the unvarnished facts contained in his April 30, 1917, combat report with

his fanciful recollection of the same events, in a *Popular Flying* article entitled "Chivalry in the Air," and dated October 1934. Chadderton, *Hanging a Legend,* 260. Similar embellishments can be found in *Winged Victory*, 137-48.

[102] Wayne D. Ralph, *Barker, VC* (London: Grub Street, 1997), 171-72.

[103] Brereton Greenhous, "The Sad Case of Billy Bishop, VC," *Canadian Historical Review* 69, 2 (1989).

[104] Fry, *Air of Battle,* 136.

[105] McCaffery, *Billy Bishop,* 132-35.

[106] Markham's technical analysis of Nieuport 17 endurance as reference makes fascinating reading. He has been careful to use the correct fuel consumption and fuel specific gravity figures for a band of different altitudes flown in a reasonable combat profile. Markham's careful analysis made perfect sense and was completely logical to this writer, as an experienced fighter pilot. Markham, "The Early Morning," 257.

[107] Bishop, *Winged Warfare*, in Chadderton, *Hanging a Legend*, 252.

[108] Chadderton, *Hanging a Legend,* 35.

[109] Specified in Grid Caldwell's supplementary report to Wing HQ dated June 30, in Markham, "The Early Morning," 246.

[110] A.A. Nicod, "Reunion Memories," in *Popular Flying*, January 1936.

[111] Bishop, *The Courage of the Early Morning*, 103.

[112] Alan Morris, *The Balloonatics* (London: Jarrolds, 1970), 54.

[113] Bickers, *The First Great Air War,* 197.

[114] Bernard Fitzsimons, ed., *Weapons and Warfare* (New York: Columbia House, 1978), 19: 2037.

[115] Fry, *Air of Battle,* 135.

[116] Chadderton, *Hanging a Legend,* 164.

[117] Bishop, *The Courage of the Early Morning,* 193.

[118] Chadderton, *Hanging a Legend,* 189. It is interesting to note that, although Bishop was in some doubt as to the exact location of his raid, "either Esnes or Awoignt" are the exact words that appear in the "locality" section of his combat report for that day.

[119] Stewart K. Taylor, ibid. Historians Norman Franks, Frank Bailey, Russell Guest, and Rick Duiven have also independently corroborated Jasta 20's transfer and move north to the Flanders front under the 4th German Army during the time frame specified by Taylor. As an aside, the unit appears to have had a lacklustre performance record overall, and apparently lacked inspirational leadership and the esprit de corps demonstrated by other Jastas. For example, no distinctive unit markings or paint schemes were applied to its aircraft until mid-1918, when its Fokker DVIIs were given white vertical stabilizers and rudders. In the eight months from its formation in November 1916 until July 12, 1917, after it had transferred to the 4th German Army, it had still claimed a total of only twelve aerial victories, including a meagre three claims for the entire month of Bloody April. Norman Franks, Frank Bailey, and Rick Duiven, *The Jasta War Chronology* (London: Grub Street, 1998). While Jasta 20 scored at least sixty-four victories during its two years of wartime existence, it also suffered forty casualties, including nineteen pilots killed, eleven wounded, four killed in flying accidents, and three more injured and recorded as such. Also of passing note, although no more specifics are available, including the date of occurrence, is that three of its pilots were at some time "wounded in a bomb raid on the airfield." Norman Franks, Frank Bailey, and Russell Guest, *Above the Lines* (London: Grub Street, 1993), 38. By comparison, Jasta 21, under the charismatic leadership of Oberleutnant Eduard Ritter von Schleich (35 victories) and Oberleutnant Oskar von Boenigk (26 victories), both Ordre pour le Mérite winners who eventually became generals in the Luftwaffe, ended the war with at least 148 victories, for a loss of eight pilots killed, six wounded, and one taken prisoner. Its aircraft sported distinctively striped elevators as well as a black-and-white striped fuselage band aft of the cockpit.

[120] Specific documents relating to the support unit have not been unearthed, and they may be part of the legion of lost German documents.

[121] Markham, "The Early Morning," 245. Markham, as a secondary source, also confirms that there was a German aerodrome just to the north of Esnes village, in addition to the 1918 aerodrome to the south. Ibid., 256. Jasta 20 was only one of many German scout units that relocated north into 4th Army territory in Flanders over the period. Between May 17, 1917, and July 1, 1917, 4th Army's complement of Jastas swelled from four to fourteen attached units, and the majority of them came from Armies south of that 6th Army portion of the front over which Bishop was operating. This movement renders the establishment of a temporary staging base in the Esnes area during the period all the more logical. Franks, Bailey, and Duiven, *The Jasta War Chronology,* 55, 63, 73, and 285.

[122] By the same token, Bishop may have seen, or thought he saw, Albatros DIIs on the ground at Esnes, as Jasta 20's total specific equipment inventory for the period has not been uncovered. The DII had still been present in strength at the front during Bloody April. In March, still significantly less than half of the 315 Albatros then at the front were the newer DIII models. Richard P. Hallion, *Rise of the Fighter Aircraft, 1914-1918* (Annapolis: Nautical & Aviation Publishing, 1984), 68. In fact, it was not until the summer and autumn of 1917, when the newer DIIIs became available almost exclusively, that the Bavarian Military Administration squadrons were given second-hand DIs and DIIs to replace the heterogeneous collection of aircraft types that they had been flying to that point. Also, Bishop had been away from the front for much

of May, a month when many of the earlier DIIs were replaced with the newer DIIIs. This absence may have predisposed him to identify the earlier type. At any rate, it is not difficult to imagine Bishop incorrectly identifying the subvariant under the circumstances, if that in fact was the case. Thomas R. Funderburk, *The Fighters* (New York: Grosset & Dunlap, 1965), 93, 149.

123 Stewart K. Taylor, in Chadderton, *Hanging a Legend,* 189. Also, American historian Ed Ferko testified to the Canadian Senate on November 28, 1985, that most Jagdstaffeln Kriegstagebuchs (Fighter Squadron War Diaries) did not survive the two wars.

124 Ibid., 171.

125 Ibid., 203.

126 H.J. Nowarra and Kimbrough S. Brown, V*on Richthofen and the Flying Circus* (Letchworth: Harleyford, 1958), 64.

127 Taylor and Bauer testimony, in Chadderton, *Hanging a Legend,* 24, 189, 203.

128 Norman Franks, Frank Bailey, and Rick Duiven, *The Jasta Pilots* (London: Grub Street, 1996). Heising later became a Luftwaffe Generalmajor during the Second World War. <http://www.enteract.com/~alowe/bishop9.html>.

129 Voss was appointed temporary Jastaführer of Jasta 20 on May 20, 1917, following the death of Hauptmann Hünerbein. He remained in temporary command until June 28, when he was given command of Jasta 29, then rapidly Jasta 14 and Jasta 10. Peter Kilduff, *Richthofen: Beyond the Legend of the Red Baron* (New York: John Wiley, 1994), 141.

130 In point of fact, the German denial, read carefully, is not categorical. It also contains a date error (marked *): "*Nachrichtenblatt der Luftstreitkräfte, Nr. 37,* 8 November 1917, *Seite 379*: Captain Bishop, according to *'Guerre Aerienne'* (La guerre Aerienne Illustre) of 4 October 1917, is the foremost English combat pilot, having achieved 40 victories in the air. *'Guerre Aerienne'* also reveals that Captain Bishop is the English flyer who, on 7 June,* at 10-1000m altitude over a German aerodrome, claims to have shot down four aircraft … This feat was widely acclaimed in the English press. Bishop was awarded the Victoria Cross. In reality the fact is that only two German aircraft were lost along the entire English Front." Markham, "The Early Morning," 251; see also 243-56.

131 "Here again was a case exemplifying such outstanding daring and success that without the bare official facts to prove it the story would have been incredible." *The Times: History of the War* (London: The Times, 1918), 15: 221.

132 Arch Whitehouse, *The Years of the Sky Kings* (New York: Doubleday, 1959), 191. Whitehouse was a Great War scout pilot.

133 A. Roy Brown, "Bishop of the Eagle Eye," in *Liberty*, September 27, 1930. Brown, a distinguished Canadian scout pilot, was initially credited with shooting down Manfred von Richthofen in April 1918.

134 Colonel George Drew, "Billy Bishop (Air Fighter," *Popular Flying*, March 1936.

135 Arch Whitehouse, *Decisive Air Battles of the First World War* (New York: Duell, Sloan & Pearce, 1963), 344.

136 Stephen Longstreet, *The Canvas Falcons* (Cooper, 1995), 29.

137 Townsend, *Cross & Cockade* 16, 3 (1985): 188.

138 McCaffery, *Billy Bishop,* 204.

139 Markham, *The Early Morning,* 255.

140 McCaffery, *Billy Bishop,* 205. In correspondence with this writer in 1998, McCaffery regretted that he had not pressed Stirrett for more details about the capture of these particular German airmen, especially the date of the occurrence and the capturing units. "At that time there was no controversy about Bishop's record so I didn't think to ask *who* exactly captured them." Dan McCaffery, letter to author, July 30, 1998.

141 McCaffery, letter to author, July 17, 1998.

142 This induction occurred in Berlin in 1928. George Drew, in Chadderton, *Hanging a Legend,* 16.

143 Chadderton, *Hanging a Legend,* 189.

144 McCaffery, *Billy Bishop,* 213-17.

145 Nowarra and Brown, *Von Richthofen and the Flying Circus,* 61, and later Peter Kilduff, *Richthofen: Beyond the Legend of the Red Baron* (New York: John Wiley, 1994), 91.

146 McCaffery, *Billy Bishop,* 137.

147 Jack Scott was fully justified under the RFC claiming rules of the day. The enemy aircraft had been removed from the combat arena as threats. Ibid., 136 .

148 Chadderton, *Hanging a Legend,* 214. Joe Warne, in the official 60 Squadron History, has itemized seven such claims from Bishop's tenure at 60 Squadron alone. Other sources cite four specific unconfirmed claims from 60 Squadron service, and one more from his short tour with 85 Squadron. At any rate, there are a number of them. Warne, "60 Squadron: Part Four," *Cross and Cockade* 11, 4 (1980): 177, and <

149 Shores, Franks, and Guest, *Above the Trenches,* 60.

150 Ibid., 269. Ironically, McCudden was Bishop's choice to succeed him as Commanding Officer of 85 Squadron in 1918. In a rare display of rebellion, the squadron rejected McCudden's appointment, perhaps fearing more indifferent leadership from another warrior known to prefer solo hunting. Instead, it demanded (and received) the more team-oriented Irish ace Edward Mannock. Christopher Cole, *McCudden, VC* (London: William Kimber, 1967), 188. Ball, another great "lone wolf," also had his share of detractors. Shortly after the war, a British historian published a book in which he suggested that Ball had stretched the truth in some of his claims. Ball's father, Sir Albert Ball, Lord Mayor of Nottingham, was enraged and

threatened legal action. There was also an immediate and violent public reaction. Chadderton, *Hanging a Legend*, 63.

151 Ibid., 272. In fairness to McElroy, he, like so many others, may be the victim of aviation historians who have arbitrarily assigned to someone else victories that were rightfully his, thereby frequently closing the door on name accreditations. Dan McCaffery, among others, believes this process has been commonly employed, and not just with respect to Bishop's claims. McCaffery, letter to author, July 30, 1998.

152 Shores, Franks, and Guest, *Above the Trenches*, 69, 95, 217.

153 Philip Markham, in Ralph Barker, *The Royal Flying Corps in France* (London: Constable, 1995), 97.

154 Jones was a distinguished ace in his own right, with thirty-seven accepted claims and a string of decorations, including the DSO, MC, DFC (Bar), and the MM. Shores, Franks, and Guest, *Above the Trenches*, 216.

155 Mannock was unquestionably an exceptional warrior and mentor. Worshipped by his men, he was known occasionally to accredit victories he scored himself to his underlings, to further their self-confidence in combat. While these were exceedingly selfless gestures, there is still no empirical evidence to suggest that they resulted in Mannock's bettering of Bishop's total of accepted claims. Shores, Franks, and Guest, *Above the Trenches*, 255. Also, Mannock's lower score relative to Bishop's has already been publicly acknowledged in a British tribute to James McCudden, VC. Cole, *McCudden, VC*, 197.

156 Chadderton, *Hanging a Legend*, 192.

CHAPTER FIVE: *PER ARDUA AD ASTRA*, 1918

1 Donald R. MacLaren, *Chamber's Journal*, 7th Series, Vol. 9, No. 438, April 19, 1919, 305.

2 Desmond Morton and J.L. Granatstein, *Marching to Armageddon: Canadians and the Great War, 1914-1919* (Toronto: Lester & Orpen Dennys, 1989), 177.

3 Allan D. English, *The Cream of the Crop* (Montreal and Kingston: McGill-Queen's University Press, 1996), 20.

4 Kenneth Guthrie, interview with RCAF Memorial Museum, Trenton, July 1989.

5 S.F. Wise, *Canadian Airmen and the First World War: The Official History of the Royal Canadian Air Force*, Vol. 1(Toronto: University of Toronto Press, 1980), 117.

6 Christopher Shores, Norman Franks, and Russell Guest, *Above the Trenches: A Complete Record of the Air Aces and Units of the British Empire Air Forces, 1915-1920* (London: Grub Street, 1990), 22.

7 Canada, Department of National Defence, Howsam DHist Biog File, Creagen Collection.

8 The award was bestowed on February 25, but not gazetted until April 22. F.E. Brown DHist Biog File, Creagen Collection.

9 Dodds received recognition for only two of his three claims of January 9. However, his three victories of March 8 endured. Shores, Franks, and Guest, *Above the Trenches*, 141.

10 R.V. Dodds DHist Biog File, Creagen Collection.

11 Shores, Franks, and Guest, *Above the Trenches*, 24.

12 150 Squadron Air Combat Report, June 1, 1918, Air1/2353/225/4/105/pt. 1.

13 H. Brooke Bell, War Experiences of H.Brooke Bell, M.C., Q.C., p. 6, from Creagen Collection.

14 Ibid., 10.

15 Barker DHist Biog Files, Creagen Collection, from *Toronto Telegram*, April 1920.

16 Wayne D. Ralph, *Barker, VC* (London: Grub Street, 1997), 139.

17 Barker Files, Creagen Collection, new addition received August 18, 1999.

18 Ralph, *Barker, VC*, 138.

19 Stanley Stanger, letter to Mr. J.N. Harris, February 27, 1957, from Creagen Collection.

20 McEwen DHist Biog File, Creagen Collection.

21 Ibid.

22 Ibid.

23 H. Brooke Bell, from Creagen Collection.

24 MacLaren, in *Chamber's Journal*, 305.

25 Shores, Franks, and Guest, *Above the Trenches*, 23.

26 McLeod DHist Biog File, Creagen Collection.

27 Ibid.

28 Raymond Collishaw, letter to R.V. Dodds, June 1962, Creagen Collection.

29 V.M. Yeates, *Winged Victory* (London: Jonathan Cape, 1934), 119.

30 Military Cross citation, awarded to Lieutenant William James Arthur Duncan, July 26, 1918, Duncan DHist Biog Files, Creagen Collection.

31 Bar to DFC citiation, awarded to Captain William Henry Hubbard, Hubbard DHist Biog File, Creagen Collection.

32 H.A.S. Molyneux, June 24, 1962, Creagen Collection.

33 Henry J. Burden War Diary, Creagen Collection.

34 MacLaren, in *Chamber's Journal*, 306.

[35] Citation to DFC, August 11, 1918, W.S. Stephenson DHist Biog File, Creagen Collection.

[36] Henry J. Burden War Diary, Creagen Collection.

[37] Ibid.

[38] Ibid.

[39] Norman Franks, Frank Bailey, and Russell Guest, *Bloody April … Black September* (London: Grub Street, 1995), 246.

[40] Ibid.

[41] MacLaren, in *Chamber's Journal*, 307.

[42] Shores, Franks, and Guest, *Above the Trenches,* 25.

[43] Bill Gunston, *The Encyclopedia of the World's Combat Aircraft* (London: Hamlyn, 1976), 180.

[44] T.Watson DHist Biog File, Creagen Collection.

[45] Con Farrell, letter to W/C R.V. Manning, RCAF Air Historian, June 22, 1962, Creagen Collection.

[46] Citation to DFC awarded August 22, 1918, Farrell DHist Biog File, Creagen Collection.

[47] Citation to DFC awarded August 25, 1918, Thomson DHist Biog File, Creagen Collection.

[48] Ralph, *Barker, VC,* 157.

[49] Wise, *Canadian Airmen,* 567-68.

[50] Ralph, *Barker, VC,* 162.

[51] Initial press reports credited Barker with downing between six and ten enemy aircraft in this epic battle. In fact, he was officially credited with four enemy aircraft destroyed during this engagement, including the two-seater, and the citation to his VC reflects these official scores. Shores, Franks, and Guest, *Above the Trenches,* 63.

[52] Morton and Granatstein, *Marching to Armageddon,* 233.

CHAPTER SIX: ARTHUR ROY BROWN AND MANFRED VON RICHTHOFEN

[1] Others included Lloyd Breadner, Sterne Tighe Edwards, and Murray Galbraith.

[2] A. Roy Brown File, Directorate of History and Heritage, NDHQ Ottawa (Notes made by F/O H.A. Halliday, RCAF Air Historical Section, 1962).

[3] Letter from Mrs. Edith Hirsh to Brown's mother, July 31, 1916, courtesy of Alan Bennett, August 19, 1999.

[4] H.J. Nowarra and Kimbrough S. Brown, *Von Richthofen and the Flying Circus* (Letchworth: Harleyford, 1958), 112.

[5] Alan Bennett, interview with author, February 22, 1999.

[6.] *Arthur Roy Brown: World War I Fighter Ace,* at <http://www.accessweb.com/users/mconstab/brown.htm>.

[7] Norman Franks and Alan Bennett, *The Red Baron's Last Flight* (London: Grub Street, 1997), 27.

[8] Ibid., 28.

[9] W.R. May, "Winged Adventures: Encounters with Richthofen," November 3, 1937, from von Richthofen DHist Biog File, Creagen Collection.

[10] Franks and Bennett, *The Red Baron's Last Flight,* 35, 45. It was also witnessed by several ground observers.

[11] Captain A.R. Brown, Army Form W.3348, *Combats in the Air*, April 21, 1918.

[12] Franks and Bennett, *The Red Baron's Last Flight*, 111.

[13] Ibid. 10.

[14] Plaque accompanying the seat for many years in the private museum of the Royal Canadian Military Institute, Toronto, Ontario. In a preceding sentence, Brown states that von Richthofen was felled by a shot through the heart.

[15] Consultation with Canadian Forces Air Navigation School, February 19, 1999.

[16] Franks and Bennett, *The Red Baron's Last Flight,* 45.

[17] Ibid., 68.

[18] In fact, the 25 miles-per-hour winds out of the east, totally contrary to the prevailing westerly winds in the area, may well have lulled von Richthofen into thinking he was still further east than he actually was. Also, he was not particularly familiar with this geographic area, especially from a low-level perspective.

[19] Idiomatically, this translates to "It's over," or "It's finished." Franks and Bennett, *The Red Baron's Last Flight,* 61.

[20] As an internal postmortem was never conducted on von Richthofen, it is impossible to say with certainty that the fatal round pierced his heart.

[21] Results of the second (and official) postmortem. Franks and Bennett, *The Red Baron's Last Flight,* 91.

[22] Ibid.

[23] The presence of this single bullet hole, which would align with von Richthofen's wounds if the shot were fired from the beam on an extended wingline position, was testified to by witnesses Captain R. Ross, Lieutenant W.J. Warneford, and 1AM A.A. Boxall-Chapman. Ibid., 120.

[24] Ibid., 103. Franks and Bennett have also pointed out another critical and frequently overlooked fact. During the initial cleanup of von Richthofen's body, in preparation for the first postmortem, Corporal Edward McCarthy, a medical orderly, discovered a spent .303 bullet inside von Richthofen's clothing and next to his body. The round, now lost, was also apparently

marked in a manner coincidental with having first struck a hard object, such as a spinal column. The presence of a spent round next to the body lends further ballistic credence to its having been fired from long range. Ibid., 82 Further, Bennett has mentioned that a long-misplaced sketch by Sergeant Popkin was located in Australia in November 1998. This sketch appears to place the Baron's flight path, when Popkin fired at him for the second time, as being approximately 200 yards further south of where it previously had been thought to be. That would have placed Popkin's firing range on the second shooting occurrence at approximately 600-650 yards, versus 800-850 yards as previously suggested. Alan Bennett, interview with author, February 22, 1999.

[25] Letter from Lieutenant. M.S. Taylor, dated France, April 26, 1918, to Oliver Hezzlewood, from A.R. Brown DHist Biog File, Creagen Collection.

[26] Alan Bennett, letter to author, October 8, 1999.

[27] Franks and Bennett, *The Red Baron's Last Flight,* 129.

[28] As late as 1993, Philip Markham wrote an in-depth article for *Over the Front* which was flawed from the outset by acceptance of the right-hand attack theory.

[29] A.R. Brown, at <http://www.accessweb.com/users/mconstab/brown.htm>, 5.

EPILOGUE

[1] *The Canadian Encyclopedia* (Edmonton: Hurtig, 1988), 1067.

[2] Letter of condolence to Mrs. Edwards, November 24, 1918, Canada, Department of National Defence, Edwards DHist Biog File, Creagen Collection.

[3] S.F. Wise, *Canadian Airmen and the First World War: The Official History of the Royal Canadian Air Force,* Vol. 1 (Toronto: University of Toronto Press, 1980), 611.

[4] Letter to Mrs. R. Lindsay, Camrose, Alberta, February 22, 1919, courtesy of Mr. Colin Pomfret, December 2, 1998.

[5] Kenneth Guthrie, interview with RCAF Memorial Museum, Trenton, July 1989.

[6] Raymond Collishaw, from Collishaw DHist Biog File, Creagen Collection.

[7] Barker DHist Biog File, Creagen Collection.

[8] Wayne D. Ralph, *Barker, VC* (London: Grub Street, 1997), 271-72.

[9] Reader's Digest, *The Canadians at War, 1939-1945* (Westmount: The Reader's Digest Association of Canada, 1986), 285.

[10] At the time of writing (autumn 1999), Henry J.R. Botterell of Ottawa was the only known surviving Canadian scout pilot from the Great War. Alert and mobile at 102 years young, Botterell was one of fourteen Canadian Great War veterans to be made a Chevalier de la Legion d'Honneur by France in November 1998. He flew 150 combat missions between May 14 and November 9, 1918. Mike Minnich, "Canada's Lone Eagle," *Airforce* 22, 4 (1998-99): 6.

APPENDIX C: A NOTE ON SOURCES

[1] Philip Markham, "The Early Morning of 2 June 1917," *Over the Front* 10, 3 (1995): 240.

[2] Norman Franks and Alan Bennett, *The Red Baron's Last Flight* (London: Grub Street, 1997), 133.

[3] Dan McCaffery, letter to author, July 24, 1998.

[4] *Over the Front* 11, 2 (1996): 189.

[5] Ibid.,12, 1 (1997): 95.

[6] Norman Franks, Russell Guest, and Frank Bailey, *Bloody April ... Black September* (London: Grub Street, 1995), 199.

[7] A.E. Ferko , in J. Clifford Chadderton, *Hanging a Legend: The NFB's Shameful Attempt to Discredit Billy Bishop, VC* (Ottawa: The War Amputations of Canada, 1986), 171.

[8] Ibid., 41.

[9] Ibid., 178.

[10] Franks, Guest, and Bailey, *Bloody April,* 4.

[11] Stewart K. Taylor, in Chadderton, *Hanging a Legend,* 166.

[12] Ibid.

[13] Ibid., 167.

[14] Ibid., 203.

[15] Ibid., 25.

[16] Alan Bennett, interview with author, February 22, 1999.

INDEX

PHOTO CREDITS

167   NA photo AH-489
168   NA photo AH-491
171   NA photo AH-494

Epilogue

176   DND photo PCN3865
178   NA photo PA6011
179   DND photo RE17474
180   Courtesy of Lowell Butters
181   DND photo RE68-5450
183   NAM photo 26306

MAPS CREDIT

The maps on pages 6, 7 and 56 are reproduced courtesy of the Department of National Defence – Directorate of History and Heritage.